MW01014093

CASTING ONWARD

CASTING ONWARD

Fishing Adventures in Search of America's Native Gamefish

STEVE RAMIREZ

Illustrations by Bob White

Foreword by Chris Wood

Guilford, Connecticut

An imprint of Globe Pequot, the trade division of
The Rowman & Littlefield Publishing Group, Inc.
4501 Forbes Blvd., Ste. 200
Lanham, MD 20706
www.rowman.com

Distributed by NATIONAL BOOK NETWORK

British Library Cataloguing in Publication Information available

Library of Congress Cataloging-in-Publication Data

Names: Ramirez, Steve, 1961- author.
Title: Casting onward : fishing adventures in search of America's native gamefish /
    Steve Ramirez ; illustrations by Bob White ; foreword by Chris Wood.
Description: Guilford, Connecticut : Lyons Press, [2022] | Includes
    bibliographical references and index. | Summary: "In writing Casting
    Onward, author Steve Ramirez traveled thousands of miles by plane, motor
    vehicle, boat, and foot. The focus is the author's experience fishing
    for native fish within their original habitats, and telling the story in
    part through the eyes of the people who have lived alongside, and come
    to love, these waters and fish. It is a story of fishing and friendship
    - a story of humanity's impact on nature, and nature's impact on
    humanity"-- Provided by publisher.
Identifiers: LCCN 2021054073 (print) | LCCN 2021054074 (ebook) | ISBN
    9781493062294 (hardcover) | ISBN 9781493062300 (epub)
Subjects: LCSH: Fishing--United States. | Native
    fishes--Conservation--United States.
Classification: LCC SH463 .R35 2022 (print) | LCC SH463 (ebook) | DDC
    799.10973--dc23/eng/20211117
LC record available at https://lccn.loc.gov/2021054073
LC ebook record available at https://lccn.loc.gov/2021054074

♾™ The paper used in this publication meets the minimum requirements of American National
Standard for Information Sciences—Permanence of Paper for Printed Library Materials, ANSI/
NISO Z39.48-1992.

To Alice . . . my wife, best friend, ardent supporter, and, most importantly, the mother of our amazing daughter Megan. When so much of what I thought I knew to be true became fiction, and I found myself at a point in life where the only sane thing to do is "turn the wheel" and travel in a new direction, she wrote these words to me, and in doing so, gave me permission to follow my life's true path:

You have a gift of seeing clearly what others can't see and comprehending what it all means and what it can be. I believe that the mission of your tomorrow is to do what you have not had the time to do until now. Use your freedom to read, learn, and write. Fighters fight and writers write.

We have traveled together for almost forty years, through hardship and fortune. We have raised a wonderful child together and watched her become an adult who adds much-needed light to this world. And we have grown older together with as much grace, courage, and love as we could muster. I am forever grateful.

There are times when the world is rearranging itself, and at times like that, the right words can change the world.
—ORSON SCOTT CARD, ENDER'S GAME

Contents

CONTENTS

FOREWORD

Steve Ramirez is one of those people that make deep connections quickly. When he decided to leave his professional life in academia and instead adventure across America in search of native fish in their home-waters, he also found new friendships with kindred spirits all across the nation. After spending a career as a US Marine, Texas Master Peace Officer, homeland security professional, and college professor, he decided to "turn the wheel" and go in a new direction. That's when he became a Texas Master Naturalist, outdoor and nature writer, and began to pursue his passion, which distilled to its essence is to live authentically, love sincerely, and, happily for us readers, fish.

In Steve's words, "Life is not a dress rehearsal. This is it. There's no going back, and we can only go forward so far before we run out of runway. I'm determined to surround myself with kind, brave, intelligent people and clean, wild, natural landscapes. I intend to follow Henry David's [Thoreau] path and suck out the marrow of every bone that life tosses my way."

Casting Onward is simultaneously about nature, native fish restoration, and natural history with a smattering of "how-to." But to say this book is about native fish or even conservation would be like saying fishing is about catching fish.

As I write this, I think of the two hours I spent on the Potomac early this morning. Two days ago, fishing alone, I caught ten striped bass. Yesterday, again alone, four. Today I took a friend along, and we marveled at the osprey's fishing and the cormorant's persistence. We watched the early morning fog burn off with the rising sun. We talked about our families and friends. We saw goslings drift by with their parents ("watch out for the gar!"). It was one of the best days I had on the river this season.

And we caught no fish.

At the beginning of the Atomic Age, William Faulkner accepted the Nobel Prize for Literature, and said:

> Our tragedy today is a general and universal physical fear so long sustained by now that we can even bear it. There are no longer problems of the spirit. There is only the question: When will I be blown up? Because of this, the young man or woman writing today has forgotten the problems of the human heart in conflict with itself which alone can make good writing because only that is worth writing about, worth the agony and the sweat.

I have no reason to believe that Steve has ever read Faulkner's speech. But the path he has chosen is all about better understanding the human heart in conflict with itself. After a childhood and professional career marked by the worst of human nature, and in a gentle and self-deprecating manner, Steve challenges us to focus on the human heart in conflict with itself—what Faulkner calls the "problems of the spirit."

Steve makes a strong case that the problems of the spirit extend to our lands and waters, too. Many freshwater fish have declined by 75 percent or more in the past fifty years. Three of America's twenty-eight native trout species are extinct. More than half of the native trout that remain occupy less than 25 percent of their historical habitat. The situation is worse for migratory fish. More than one hundred stocks of Pacific salmon and steelhead are extinct. Twenty-eight species of Pacific salmon are listed for protection under the Endangered Species Act. Atlantic salmon on the East Coast hold by the slenderest of threads from extinction.

When fishing for smallmouth bass with the renowned painter, Bob White, Steve writes, "Native brook trout and their cold-water streams are worth saving. The St. Croix and the American Northwoods are worth saving. . . . I propose a new restorative justice ethic for how we choose to treat each other and the Earth. It is within our ability to hold ourselves accountable and find redemption in creating healing where hurt has been caused."

Trout and salmon are the ultimate indicators of the health of our lands and waters. Gravity works cheap and it never takes a day off. Everything we do on the land is ultimately affected by the quality of our lands and waters. As Steve says, "Native fish are the perfect indicator of the health of an eco-system, and I don't mean just the water, but also the entire riparian habitat, watershed, and evermore increasingly the Earth. Their absence reflects our folly, and their preservation and persistence reflect our greater selves."

In his journey across America, Steve recounts the decision of the White Mountain Apache Tribe in the Southwest to ban fishing on their tribal lands in 1955 to keep the Apache trout from becoming extinct. He talks about the resilience of the Gila trout and the heroic efforts of volunteers and state and federal agencies to recover them in the aftermath of a devastating fire. He writes of the extensive work that Trout Unlimited and other organizations have done to care for and recover greenback and westslope cutthroat trout in the West and native brook trout in Appalachia.

Over the years, people have asked me, "Why do you fish? You are trying to save these fish and their rivers, so why fish for them?" I have given many answers, but Steve perfectly captures the sentiment of a con-servation-minded angler when he says, "I almost feel a little guilty for catching [brook trout]. Still, we save only what we love, and we love only what we know. By meeting these wild natives where they live, I have a greater appreciation of their amazing beauty and resilience. I have a stake in their survival."

Like many anglers, Steve's bond with wild and native fish is a lot deeper than, for example, with the hatchery-sustained Lahontan cutthroat trout at Pyramid Lake. The Pyramid Lake fish are huge but cannot naturally repro-duce because of irrigation withdrawals and other conservation challenges. Setting up a stepladder and casting to cruising twenty-pound fish sounds like a blast until you realize they were reared in concrete tanks and then released from white buckets or the back end of a hatchery truck.

Imagine, on the other hand, if we could develop creative and collabora-tive solutions to remove unneeded dams, fix habitat, allow irrigators to get their water, and leave enough water for Lahontans to migrate to Pyramid

Lake from the Truckee River. Now that would be cool. That is conservation! That is the path Steve gently suggests we follow.

Steve has dedicated himself to spending the rest of his life with people who fish—more important, the people who fish and give back to the lands and waters that give anglers so much joy. While fishing for Colorado River cutthroat, Steve observes, "Relationships are like dry-fly fishing for wary native fish in their native homewaters. You have to pay attention, stay focused, drift without drag, and above all, care enough to keep casting forward. Fishing and friendships require patience, understanding, and a genuine respect for each other. My dad taught me to be an ethical angler and hunter, and I taught my daughter the same lessons. Is there any greater gift we can give each other?"

Too many people think that conservation is about preserving land, or protecting wildlife and fish or water. No. Conservation is about people, and helping people better understand the connections to the lands and waters that sustain them, their families, and our great nation.

Steve writes, "This book is about more than fish, it's about people. It's about how we find our tribe and cherish them every day. It's about friendship and pulling together for some common good. It's about living a life worth living."

In truth, I prefer to fish alone than with friends, but one of the best parts of Steve's writing is the celebration of the people who make his fishing for native fish possible.

Ted Williams is an award-winning conservation writer and a maniac fisher who loves to chase down striped bass and bluefish in the waters of his native New England. Writing about his time fishing with Ted, Steve says:

This time with my friend was meaningful because the water was clean, the air was fresh, the seals were swimming with the fish, squid, sharks, and whales. It was meaningful because birds flew overhead as the sun shone clearly across the water and the land. This adventure was an adventure because all around us was the power and beauty of nature, the only home we will ever know. I want the generations ahead of me to know a natural world full of native wildlife and plants, that causes them to feel as grateful as Ted and I felt on this single day at sea. This is why it all matters to an angler like me. How about you?

Steve's question, "How about you?" is important. Fifty million people in America fish, seven million fly-fish. After the 2020–2021 pandemic, we will see those numbers swell. Significantly. Our ability to convert existing anglers and new ones into conservation advocates will likely help determine how good our fishing is in the future and, much more important, how rich, or poor, the legacy we leave for our children.

More than seventy years ago, William Faulkner closed his Nobel acceptance speech by saying the writer must leave "no room in his workshop for anything but the old verities and truths of the heart, the old universal truths lacking which any story is ephemeral and doomed—love and honor and pity and pride and compassion and sacrifice."

Casting Onward is a rebuke of the ephemeral, and a celebration of the role we can all play to help care for and recover our native species and the lands and waters on which they depend. This work is a tribute to love, honor, empathy, resilience, compassion, and sacrifice—all of which define the attributes of conservation.

Most important, the work Steve celebrates is fun! Get your hands dirty. Meet your neighbors. Learn more about your local streams. Become a better angler. Join Trout Unlimited. Hell, become a better citizen by helping care for and recover the lands and waters that sustain us all. Steve writes:

I have spent most of my life hiking and hunting and fishing alone. When I was a boy, I sometimes had my dad beside me. . . . Then I became a man, and I sometimes had my daughter beside me, casting our lines into Texas Hill Country rivers. . . . But then my dad grew old and passed away, and my daughter grew up and moved away, and once again, I walked and fished alone. . . . But then something truly life-changing began to happen. . . . I've met the best friends of my lifetime while writing this book, traveling the nation, and seeking out native fish and new waters. I have been able to write of these magnificent wild, native fish and the places they call home, through the eyes of the people who call those waters . . . "homewaters." It has been a great adventure, and I am forever grateful.

Fishing books, especially fly fishing–focused books, lend themselves to self-refection. Most are quickly forgotten. Some change our lives.

The River Why, by David James Duncan, so profoundly influenced me that I named a beloved dog after the protagonist, Gus. *A Fly-Fisherman's Blue Ridge*, by Chris Camuto, and *Holy Ghost Creek*, by Frank Weissbarth, are two of the finest fishing books I have ever read—mostly because they are not really about fishing.

Casting Onward sits in the pantheon of these books. It is a book about fishing, but on a much more important level, it is about us, our relationship with one another, and our relationship with the lands and waters that sustain the planet.

—CHRIS WOOD, PRESIDENT/CEO, TROUT UNLIMITED

PROLOGUE

*Dreaming the future can create the future. We stand at the threshold
of a singular opportunity in the human experiment: to reimagine how
to live on Earth in ways that honor the web of life, each other, and
future generations.*

—KENNY AUSUBEL, DREAMING THE FUTURE

THIS IS A STORY ABOUT REIMAGINING HOW NATURE AND HUMANITY CAN
live together, from this moment onward. Everything is created twice: first in
our imaginations and then in our realities. Once we can imagine and envision the way the world "should be" and "can be," we can act on that vision,
like raindrops on limestone, drop by drop, building a canyon and filling a
sea. Nothing is as powerful as an idea whose time has come.

In my first book, *Casting Forward*, I wrote of my love for my Texas Hill
Country homeland and homewaters, and of my determination to find the
best in human nature within myself and others. I wrote of my concerns for
my homeland, community, and world, and of my hopeful optimism about
the resilience of nature and humanity. I wrote of the healing and teaching
powers of nature and the need for all of humanity to reconnect with our
one and only true home.

Casting Onward is a continuation and expansion of my first work.
When I set out to write this book, my original plan was to travel across
North America, connecting with and learning about these native gamefish
within their historical range and natural habitat. I planned to learn about
them and their watersheds and what that could teach me about the state
of our nation's environment, both human and non-human. And I decided
that I would tell these stories through the eyes of the people who live

within the watersheds where each native fish originates, and currently clings to existence.

I could never have known that this adventure would become so much more than I had ever imagined. In these all-too-often seemingly hopeless times, I found an abundance of reasons for hope. I began to notice that this global community of people who love and respect nature—not from an armchair but from a riverbank or mountain trail—are some of the best human beings I could ever dream of befriending or being befriended by. In an all-too-often heartless human world, I found bastions of kindness, generosity, humility, resilience, empathy, determination, courage, selflessness, and love. On the edges of oceans and rivers, I found hope strung like beads through generations of outdoorsmen and woman who personify the best of humanity. And then there was the fish and the fishing . . . moments and memories I will never forget and that I am sharing here in these pages with you, my readers and my friends.

It doesn't matter if you're an angler, hunter, hiker, naturalist, birder, rockhound, mountain climber, scuba diver, or just someone who enjoys a walk in the park. If you pay attention, you can see that things are changing rapidly, and not for the better. As an angler and a Master Naturalist, I know that, like songbirds and salamanders, native fish are bellwethers of environmental health. Even if you do not currently feel a passion for the seemingly cerebral concepts of environmental and social justice, and even if you do not fish, this is your book. We need nature; nature doesn't need us.

So much has happened since the writing of *Casting Forward*. Our environment, both human and global, has come under threat more than I could have ever imagined. Since the time of my first book, it has become ever more obvious that humanity is heading headlong toward the Sixth Extinction, with massive climate change and mass immigration, public health, and safety challenges, and yet, I am still hopeful. After all, we are almost all of the problem, and therefore we are almost all of the solution. It's up to us.

The key to everything that harms our quality of life and the lives of our progeny boils down to environmental and societal health. The presence or absence of native fish is one way to read our report card. Any dysfunctional mob can destroy things; it takes a healthy society to fix things. At this moment in time, we've worked ourselves into a solid D grade. We've got a long way to go and a short time to get there. I hope you will join me on this adventure across America the Beautiful. As long as we keep *Casting Onward* together, we can make America the world leader in the new age as we move from the Anthropocene, the age of humanity, to the Naturaecene, the age of nature.

First Cast—Longnose Gar

Lower Potomac River, Fletcher's Cove

Whether we or our politicians know it or not, Nature is party to all our deals and decisions, and she has more votes, a longer memory, and a sterner sense of justice than we do.

—WENDELL BERRY

WHEN I DECIDED TO LEAVE MY JOB, I WENT FISHING AND NEVER LOOKED BACK.

I went fishing in part because I knew that the rivers and the hills could teach me the truths I once knew and had forgotten. I went fishing because I knew that rising trout and singing warblers have wisdom, and because for the first time in my life, I knew all the things that I never wanted to do again, and all the places I never wanted to be, and all the people I never wanted to be around. I knew that life was too damn precious and fleeting for meaningless meetings and malignant greetings. I knew that from this moment on, I wanted to be free, feral, authentic . . . even revolutionary in my pursuit of a life worth living. I went fishing because it causes me to feel alive, and because the life that I was walking away from was draining my soul and killing my passion, little by little, irrevocably.

In his beautiful book of essays titled *Bright Rivers*, Nick Lyons told of a time when he was "where the game for the big green is played." He spoke of meetings that lasted hours and of a tightness in his chest. He wrote, "I have been a juggler, flinging my several lives high and carelessly into the air, never catching them, barely feeling one as it touches my hand." And finally, he declared that "I do not want the qualities of my soul unlocked only by this tense, cold, gray, noisy, gaudy, grabby place." This is what I was walking away from, and after thirty years of working toward it, I knew with great certainty that I no longer wanted that life.

Understanding something with great clarity is a gift that cannot be taken lightly. Rejecting the aspects of modern society that feel wrong also means seeking the elements of earth, water, sky, and humanity that feel right. So I decided to let go of friends who really weren't friends. To separate myself from the dark, dramatic, and negative, and invest my time and energy in the people and places of value. I decided to turn this cold, distant, inauthentic, anti-empathetic e-world on its head, and seek out my one true tribe of human beings who share my love for nature and the best of human nature. I decided to surround myself only with those people, places, and things that add value to my life, and to whom my life might add value.

No person and no thing can have any power over us unless we choose to surrender it to them. Life is a beautiful and brief gift. We must live it, fully. We must choose to keep casting forward. I wouldn't fish in dark, dirty waters; why would I choose to live in them? My first cast of this journey was where the waters of the Potomac River arrive at our nation's capital. Why not begin my journey where the problems and the solutions of my homeland converge? At every crossing, we have the power to choose.

—◦—

Looking out the window of the airplane I could see the world changing as I moved from west to east. Open wilderness and wild canyons became farmers' fields in multiple shades of green, and I began to see the proliferation of rooftops and roadways and had the stark realization that in most of the eastern United States, the hand of humankind has been busy rearranging things, turning streams into canals, prairies into corn fields, and ponds into reservoirs. In many places I noticed that the only woodlands were the thin riparian borders of each river or stream. We can do better, I thought. We can reverse a lot of this, with just a little bit of vision and willpower, and a whole lot of action. We can turn this gray into green. We can rebuild a beautiful world to live in. We must.

As my plane descended into Washington, DC, I was pleased that we were following the southern bank of the Potomac River. After all, I had traveled all this distance from Texas to spend some time with my dear friend Chris Wood on his homewaters at Fletcher's Cove on the Potomac River. Our plan: to fish for gar fish with rope flies. It was a good plan full of uncertainty. I love plans that are only "plannish." Like in life, anything can happen.

There is something special for me when a plane en route to Ronald Reagan Airport comes in for a landing. Passengers on the right fuselage get a view of the Pentagon, but I was on the left and watched as we floated over history, past the White House, to the National Mall, with the Capitol Building, Washington Monument, and Jefferson Memorial; the last thing I saw before landing was the Lincoln Memorial. It just seemed right. It seemed poignant.

The plan was that as soon as I got off the plane and into my rental car, I would meet Chris at Fletcher's Cove so that we could get in some afternoon fishing before heading to his home for dinner with his family. Chris assumed that I was a twenty-first-century man and tried to give me GPS coordinates. I said, "Chris . . . I have a map." There was a long pause and then I heard Chris say, "Steve, nobody uses a map anymore." Hilarity ensued with me driving in circles on the Virginia side of the river before finding the bridge to the DC side. Finally, miraculously, I arrived at Fletcher's Cove with Chris smiling ear to ear as we disassembled his bike and stored it in the back of the car.

Fletcher's Cove, often called Fletcher's Boathouse, has been there in its current state since the 1850s. This little cove along the mighty Potomac River has witnessed the American Civil War and every moment of American history from then until now. It is a place where US senators can seek solitude and find their constituents casting lines from the shoreline.

Presidents and paupers alike drink and depend on these same ancient waters. The Potomac is the "Nation's River." It reflects us.

As part of the Chesapeake and Ohio Canal National Historical Park, Fletcher's Cove is known for its white perch runs in March, American shad and herring shortly after, and striped bass (locally called "rockfish") in late spring. But we were here for something else. We came for the hot sticky weather of June, weather that is locally referred to as "gar weather."

One of the great traditions of Fletcher's is the use of its iconic wooden rowboats. Each boat is painted light gray inside the hull, slate gray on the bottom, and red on the sides, with the words "Fletchers D.C." painted in white on the bow. There was a feeling of tradition to the creaking, grinding, banging sound of the oarlocks as Chris expertly rowed us out to the downstream edge of the cove. Night herons rested in the trees along the shore as great blue herons angled where the river met the forest. It was clear and sunny, and the river had a slight choppiness due to the breeze; the water was brown, and the fish were invisible. It was a bit cool—not gar weather. Nothing was rising to the surface.

We were using Sage seven-weight rods that Chris had brought, along with the white, nylon rope flies that he tied himself. They remained fluffy and soft for exactly one cast and then became water-soaked weights for the remainder of the day. I had to get used to the resounding "clunk" feel of the big soggy flies reaching their end state on the back cast, and although Chris was getting distance on his double hauls, my fly seemed more reticent and tended to keep much closer to the boat. Perhaps I had a shy fly.

After a while we began to see and hear splashes on the water's surface, which may have been indicative of gar fish rising to gulp air, but we didn't see any gar beneath those splashes, so it was impossible to tell what caused them. On one cast Chris felt a pull on his line, but it could have been anything, since these waters are also full of rockfish, catfish, and other fish, and our rope flies did not have hooks. The idea is that although gar fish are hard to hook due to their bony jaws and a myriad of teeth, they can strike a rope fly and get their teeth tangled in the rope. Chris has been successful at this on numerous occasions, and I was hoping to have my shot over the next two days. I've been fishing in gar water all my life, and I have never caught gar on rope, lure, bait, or dynamite.

The longnose gar fish is an ancient species, and fossil records show that its ancestors may have been swimming the Earth's waters for some one hundred million years. They are naturally found from the East Coast of North America west into Kansas, Texas, and even parts of New Mexico. Gar fish are apex predators, eating other fish and prey of opportunity, living up to twenty years on average, and attaining a size of six feet in length and up to fifty pounds in weight. Gar fish also have a superpower in that they can "breathe" in both air and water, thus allowing them to live in low-oxygen aquatic environments.

Still, gar fish have been declining in much of their range due to habitat loss, dams, riverine construction, and, most of all, indiscriminate overfishing. In some places in America "sportsmen" seem to think it is acceptable to kill as many gar fish as possible and leave them dead on the riverbanks to rot in the sun—it isn't. For me, these highly evolved yet ancient fish are as special as they are an important part of the ecosystems where they naturally occur. I think gar are beautiful in their complexly simplistic nature as voracious predators and tenacious survivors. There's nothing trashy about this fish.

It was a perfectly beautiful evening of fishing, even if the catching was not immediately forthcoming. We'd see a gulping splash and cast in its direction, to no avail, and then see another and cast in the new direction, always hopeful . . . an angler's constant state of being. I guess that's one of the things that make fishing so healthy for our spirits; it keeps us hopeful.

Methodically we kept casting until the light grew more dim and the promise of dinner at Chris's house grew more promising. It was a stunningly beautiful evening, which was part of the problem, of course. Gar like the weather to be tough, hot, humid, skeeter-infested, T-shirt-clinging-to-your-sweat-soaked-body weather, and instead we had lovely blue skies and cool breezes. Day one done; we were skunked but it didn't stink. It was perfect, almost.

When we arrived at Chris's home, his wife Betsy and their three sons, Wylie, Casey, and Henry Trace, had not arrived yet, so Chris and I enjoyed some backyard time with glasses of wine in hand. Parker, the old and gentle hound dog, made his best show of barking at me from the couch before begrudgingly accepting my hand patting his head, and from that moment on, I was deemed part of the family or at least tolerable. I tried to imagine Parker as a pup. Then I tried to imagine me as a pup. Both seemed hard to imagine.

For those of you who aren't yet fortunate enough to know Chris Wood, he is among other things the president and CEO of Trout Unlimited, an organization that I am proud to be a Life Member of and that impresses me more with each passing year. Chris is also a dedicated family man with a wonderful family. All three boys are the kind of young men that any father and mother would be proud of, and Betsy is brilliant, bold, and able to create the best Moroccan lamb dish I have ever experienced. We enjoyed an evening of music and conversation, and when Chris and the boys retired to the basement for some video games together, Betsy and I swapped stories about living in Africa. As it turned out, we both lived in West Africa in our younger years, me in the Marine Corps, she in the Peace Corps. Life is ironic as hell.

Fly fishing, bird hunting, or any such outdoor activity is about far more than the kill or the catch. It's about the times shared around the campfire or kitchen table. It's about the laughter and the friendship that binds those moments into memories. It's about the places and the people who understand how to live close to the bone. Nature teaches, heals, inspires, and bonds us; it reminds us that we are all of the same feral tribe.

A steady rain fell throughout the night and began to let up slightly as we arrived at Fletcher's Cove the second day. We arrived at first light because Chris had a meeting on Capitol Hill later that day with a US senator about the efforts to save and revive the wild salmon populations of Idaho. We only had a half day of fishing time and wanted to make the best of it. Chris asked me if the rain was going to be a problem and I laughed and said, "I'm a Marine . . . I'm amphibious." So we bailed the rainwater out of the old wooden boat and rowed down to the south end of the cove. At this point there was only a light cool drizzle coming down. It was refreshing.

One of the great pleasures of Fletcher's Cove is the wonderful people who call it home. On the way from Chris's house to the cove, Chris picked up coffee and breakfast sandwiches for everyone that he knew would be present when we arrived. Dan Ward was behind the counter, and I came to know him as the resident historian. Dan has worked at Fletcher's for fifty years. Alex Binstead, a dedicated angler who runs Fletcher's, also has ties to this little cove that included learning to walk his first steps as a toddler while visiting at the cove with his family. And I met Mike Bailey and Gordon Leish, who I learned are considered a close match for the title of best angler on the river.

Dan opened a cooler and showed me a northern snakehead fish that he had caught and was going to happily consume later that day. I love nature in almost all its forms, but to me the snakehead is a dangerous-looking creature with its almost eel-like body, oversized head, and massive mouth full of teeth. Native to China, Russia, and the Korean Peninsula, the snakehead most likely found its way into these waters via aquarium dumping or live fish market releases. It is a voracious predator of other fish, amphibians, and freshwater crustaceans and is likely to outcompete and prey on native fish.

We talked about the impact of invasive snakeheads and blue and flathead catfish as the rain drizzled down on the lot of us, anglers one and all. The thing that impressed me most is that in a city as dysfunctional as Washington, DC, the people I met at Fletcher's Cove seem to personify the essence of community, bound together by their affection and gratitude for this place on the river and each other. How cool is that?

Everyone at the cove treated me kindly and made no mention of my Texan accent or the fact that I had traveled all this way to catch gar fish with rope flies in miserable weather so that I could struggle to untangle their teeth and immediately release them as if nothing had ever happened. If any of them found my plans to be strange, they didn't mention it. Well, all except one; we'll call her "Linda." It became quickly apparent to me that Linda is a practical angler, and I suspect that she eats what she catches and that she catches a lot of fish. There's nothing wrong with that as long as the fish you're killing aren't dying out.

I will never forget my one and only audience with Linda. She was colorful, and being an artist of sorts, I appreciate color. She walked up slowly, even painfully, and leaned on the railing in front of the little tackle shop. She wore a camouflage jacket, well-worn jeans, and an old floppy hat, and her eyes squinted at me as she sized up the stranger in their midst. She had a lit cigarette bobbing up and down from the edge of her lips, and I suspect she could burn that thing to the nub with a single drag. She spoke quickly, often without removing that glowing death-tube, and when she turned her gaze toward me, her eyes narrowed and she said, "So what's your story?"

I told her of my quest, traveling and fly-fishing around the country for native fish in their original waters and of how I use only barbless hooks and carefully land and release each fish. After I had explained my presence there, I said, "So . . . what do you think of what I'm doing?" She looked at me hard and said, "I don't like it. I don't like it one bit. Makes no sense!" I smiled. Candor, it's so refreshing.

Things were looking up. Just before we left the dock we looked out and saw a long series of gulping splashes. We looked at each other and smiled; this was going to be a good morning. It was a bit too cool to be gar weather and the rain had changed the character of the river, but still, there were gulps everywhere. How could we miss?

We brought eight-weight rods this time to help toss those waterlogged rope flies, and indeed Chris's flies gained some extra distance, but for some reason I seemed to get another shy fly that did its best to stay closer to the boat. But we were both getting the flies out there to the many splashes we were seeing. Sometimes there were so many splashes to chase that I'd drop my back cast in and take a couple strips of the line, then forward cast and get the other side of the boat. There was a feeling of hope in the air as we both flung our mop-head flies back and forth into the murky waters. That's when the sky opened and the rain came down, and we pulled up our raincoat hoods and hunkered down for some serious fishing.

I love fishing in the rain. I love the way the world seems to be washed clean, and how the river jumps at every impacting raindrop. I love the fresh fragrance in the air and the soothing sound of wild water running home toward the sea. It's humbling to think that every drop of water on Earth today has always been here. Humans have been such an insignificant part of the Earth's story, until our misbehavior made us seem significant. As the murky waters of the lower Potomac reflect us as a nation and a people, so does the falling acidic rain give an image of our deeds and misdeeds. We can restore these waters, those raindrops, and ourselves. I still have hope.

With the rain came a change in the river. The air cooled, the current picked up, and in short order we noticed that the hopeful splashes and gulps had given way to a serene silence. The river rolled by us. We moved from section to section of the cove and kept casting with that sort of optimism that only anglers and slot-machine addicts have. It is an article of faith that the next cast will be the one that connects us to our quarry, so we cast through the rain and the sun and the day and night, and it remains a mystery what actually triggers the fish to bite, or the angler to snip off the fly and call it a day.

———

Chris and I stopped back by the house so we could get cleaned up and change clothes, and then we drove to the headquarters of Trout Unlimited. Nobody at TU has an office; everyone has a cubicle. The only difference between the cubicle of the CEO and the rest of the staff is that his cubicle is at the end of the long line of cubicles, and therefore he has a wall on one side. The only other unique aspect to the CEO's cubicle is that it contains the front third of a red and gray wooden jon boat with white lettering across its bow that reads, "Fletcher D.C." That's it. The people who operate and love the cove gifted the boat's bow to Chris out of respect and affection for the man and his work. This pleases me.

Leadership sets the tone, and I can tell you that there are many reasons that Chris and I are friends, but one is that I respect his dedication to family, friends, and the mission of making this world and its cold-water habitats a little better than we've left them thus far. I share those priorities.

While Chris went to Capitol Hill to meet with the senator and fight for dam removals, clean water, and the restoration of wild native salmon in Idaho, I took the metro to the National Mall and walked in the rain and drizzle from the White House to the Capitol, to the Washington Monument, past all the memorials for our many wars and the Americans who died fighting them, along the Reflecting Pool, and to the steps of the Lincoln Memorial.

Behind the Lincoln Memorial, the Potomac River rolled toward the sea. I knew that it was full of rockfish, American eels, and American shad, and somewhere, I still had faith, there were gar fish. Some four hundred miles to the east in Highland County, Virginia, and Seneca Rocks, West Virginia, the headwaters of the Potomac run clear and clean over freestone stream beds, and wild, native brook trout are making a comeback in these waters where once they were in jeopardy from the effects of humanity's choices. This river once teemed with fish and wildlife. The fish included bass, muskellunge, pike, and ultimately brook trout in the upper waters, and the aforementioned gamefish of the lower waters at Fletcher's Cove.

When Europeans first arrived in the watershed, they found the now-extinct eastern strains of bison, elk, wolves, and cougars. A combination of overhunting, overfishing, and habitat fragmentation and degradation including mining and agricultural waste, urban sewage, and runoff led to the moment when the algal blooms of the 1960s caused then-president Lyndon Johnson to declare the river a "national disgrace." There is hope for this river and others due to the 1972 Clean Water Act and the dedication of organizations like TU, The Nature Conservancy, the Potomac River Conservancy, and others. I envision a day when the waters of this great American river reflect a new nation and a new time. I see these waters running clean and free and supporting healthy populations of fish and other wildlife. It's not a dream, it's a goal.

—◦—

We never caught or even saw a gar fish during my two days on the Potomac in Fletcher's Cove. I could tell Chris was concerned that I had flown from Texas and caught no fish, but it was a wonderful fishing trip. I had the chance to fish from a wooden rowboat with a dear friend, in the sunlight and in rain showers. In the end, we decided to challenge each other to be the first one to catch the next gar on a rope fly, either Chris on the Potomac or me on the Llano.

When I returned home to my beloved Texas Hill Country, I decided it was time to go fishing again. It just seemed like the right thing to do, as if I was reassuring my homewaters that I hadn't cheated on them . . . not really. As I packed up my gear, I looked at the rope fly that Chris had given me the day prior and decided not to bring it. I was going to the Guadalupe River, not the Llano, and I almost never saw gar fish in the Guadalupe.

It was a beautiful morning at my favorite and secret spot along the river. I worked my way downstream from the bridge whose belly was heavy with the mud nests of cave swallows. They darted above me as I cast, swung, and stripped my streamer under familiar cutbanks and across clear, deep pools. I caught and released Guadalupe and largemouth bass, yellow bellied and green sunfish, and even a Rio Grande cichlid.

By the time I reached the last pool before the riffles turn into a small waterfall, I'd had enough catching and releasing. I reeled in my line, snipped off the one fly that had caught all those fish, and just stood there in the clear, clean water—and that's when it happened. Something brushed my leg. I checked for snakes but instead found two beautifully colored gar fish swimming just three feet away, looking up at me. The thing is, they just floated there, looking at me for a moment, and when they finally swam leisurely away, I'm quite sure they were grinning at me. Cheeky bastards.

CHAPTER TWO

Striped Bass and Bluefish
North Atlantic, Cape Cod

*We have reached a time in the life of the planet, and humanity's
demands upon it, when every fisherman will have to be a riverkeeper,
a steward of marine shallows, a watchman on the high seas.*
—THOMAS MCGUANE, THE LONG SILENCE

I GUESS I FINALLY FELL ASLEEP AROUND 11:00 P.M. AND WOKE AT 2:00 A.M.
We were on the road to the boat ramp on Cape Cod by 2:30 a.m., pulling
my friend Ted Williams's green and white boat, *The Assignment* behind us
through the foggy New England night. There was a "Sleepy Hollow" feel
to some of the darkened backroads, but as tired as I was, the morning felt
like an adventure, and it was.

We arrived at the docks just before dawn. It was July, but just cold
enough in the early morning half-light and ocean breeze to cause this
Texan to wear a coat and zip it up all the way. I was awake now, sort of. Ted
wore green rubber boots, brown trousers, and a well-worn long-sleeve shirt
with suspenders to hold everything in place. I wore water shoes that were
too open, hiking trousers that were too thin, a raincoat that was just barely

enough to keep me from shivering, and a Hill Country Outfitters hat that I was determined to hold on to at all costs.

I asked Ted if I could help with the boat and he nicely declined, saying, "I appreciate it, but I'm usually fishing by myself, and I need to be able to do this by myself . . . it's good for me." He has that smooth, able way about him that shows he's done this more times than he cares to count. At one point I think I tied a bowline to the dock, but that was the extent of my contribution.

I donned my self-inflating emergency vest, which Ted told me he always insists everyone on his boat wear. We motored out of the small inlet and out to sea, rounding the bend of a sliver of beach as the sun rose from the eastern horizon. I sat on the bow of *The Assignment* until we began to pick up speed, moving across the sea toward a choppy rip, a place where the incoming or outgoing tide collides with the transition of deeper to shallower water. Baitfish and squid get caught up and accumulate along these rips, and the striped bass and bluefish seem to know this, so we anglers try to know what they know. In nature, everything is eating everything. That is the true circle of life.

The basic process for fishing for stripers and blues off the coast of Cape Cod is much the same as fishing for Guadalupe bass in the Texas Hill Country, only bigger. We were using RIO 400-grain, sinking, shooting-head line, and one-piece Loomis nine-weight rods. Having the right equipment and the right person by my side really made a difference. I easily fell into the pattern of sling-swing-strip, sling-swing-strip, sling-swing-strip-strike!

Ted gave me first shot on the rip, and after a few tries I hooked into a nice bluefish that fought with authority and caused my arms to feel the first fabulous fight of the morning. There were many more to come. When we got the bluefish to the boat I was overjoyed. It was the first bluefish I had ever caught. I loved him. Just as I was reaching for my camera, I noticed the skill and speed with which Ted slipped out the hook and slid my first bluefish back into the ocean.

I was dumbstruck until I managed to say, "I was hoping to take a photo of that."

"There will be more," replied Ted. In that moment I was reminded of what a tourist I am in these waters—and each new place I visit. But in truth, I'm not a tourist as much as a wide-eyed post-middle-aged boy who is discovering so many things for the first time. That is the magic of this adventure. It's not the fish, it's the fishing. It's spending time on the ocean with someone who has become a part of this seascape and it a part of him. It's trying to see their homewaters through their eyes.

Ted repositioned *The Assignment* and in short order we were back along the edge of the rip, Ted casting off the bow and me off the stern. We both started catching fish, and this time I managed to catch the first striped bass of my life. Recalling the fate of the first bluefish, I grabbed hold of the moderately sized striper and said, "Maybe we can take a photo of this one?"

Ted looked at me with the eyes of a man who knows how to fish like a man and was wondering why I would stop fishing to take a picture of a fish. There was kindness in his voice when he said, "There will be bigger ones." I dropped my first striper back into the ocean. I grew determined to fish like a man, too.

Pound for pound I think the bluefish fight harder than the stripers, especially at the surface. They both pull hard and seem to dig down deep, bending both rod and angler toward the sea. Bluefish add a vicious flourish to the fight once you bring them to the surface. Those teeth aren't false advertising; these fish are warriors. At the end of each battle, I had to shake out the pumped-up feel of my arms, then pick up the line and cast again. Sling-swing-strip, sling-swing-strip, sling-swing-strip-strike!

We both were catching fish, but Ted caught at least two fish to my one. At one point, out of pure kindness, he said, "Let's switch," and I moved to the bow and he to the stern. We began casting and catching again until at last the catching died down, as it often does in fishing, as if someone had flipped a switch that turned off the bite. I shook out my arms to get the blood flowing again as Ted pointed us toward the next rip and called out, "Hold on!"

It didn't matter where I stood in the boat; Ted still outcaught me two or three to one, just as I would expect. It wasn't the place we stood that changed the outcome; it was the skill of the angler standing there. Still, I was catching enough striped bass to fulfill my every daydream, and we had only just begun. This, my friends, is a life well lived.

———

One of the things I love about fishing is that it forces you to connect and participate in nature. It's not for the faint of heart. It's not some animated virtual world with singing bluebirds and dancing starfish. Angling, hunting, hiking, and even arrowhead hunting requires you to pay attention, live in the moment, and become part of the ecosystem.

When not moving from rip to rip, we followed the various seabirds that were searching for the same squid and baitfish that the stripers and blues were hunting. By paying attention to nature's cues, we became an integral part of the whole. Sometimes this took the form of following flocks of herring, black-backed, and laughing gulls, or the delicate yet deadly common terns that swept down from the sky picking up pieces of squid that had been slashed by blues and stripers. In one case I watched as one of these tiny birds lifted an entire squid from the water, carrying its still living quarry toward the beach. Sometimes nature's cues came in the form of the nature of the water itself, or the pudgy porpoising bodies of seals, or the swirl of sharks that were hunting the seals that hunted the fish that hunted the squid. Nature is a constant fight for survival punctuated by moments of beauty and elegance.

As an angler, and I suspect in life, too, Ted is relentless. He is all business, focus, and determination. We'd sling and swing and cast and catch until the catching died down, and then Ted would notice the seabirds massing in another place and he'd call out, "Hold your cast and hold on!" He'd power up the 200 Yamaha and we'd bounce across the ocean toward the next likely spot, where we'd cast and catch until my arms ached. There were no breaks, just solid hard-core fishing.

Did I mention how little sleep I'd had? At one point I grabbed a granola bar and an iced coffee drink, and held the mouth of the open bottle against my own open mouth so that the glorious elixir would bounce into my sleepy maw with every drop of the bow as we crossed the ocean chop. It worked beautifully. I felt refreshed.

Ted slid *The Assignment* into the next line along a rip or under the next flock of seabirds and we'd repeat the casting and catching. Occasionally, one of us would catch a striper that was larger than most, and Ted would measure it against a ruled line on the gunnel of the boat. I don't know how many fish we caught, but to me, it was more than I could have dreamed of, and I was overjoyed. Ted, on the other hand, said that he "wanted to get me into bigger fish." Did I mention that my arms already ached from the fish we did catch?

The action seemed to be moving closer and closer to the shore, and we were quite close to a pod of gray seals resting on the beach. According to the National Park Service, Cape Cod National Seashore is visited by about four million people each year. The greater Boston area reports a population of nearly five million people, each person generating waste that goes into the air, land, and sea. Making nature accessible and protecting it from all the access is going to be an ongoing battle for our nation and the world. As I looked toward the seashore at those wild, native seals, and out at the sea to those wild, native fish, and up into the sky at those wild, native birds, I was surer than ever that this is a battle we must win. And it is winnable. After all, we are only fighting with ourselves.

Ted pulled *The Assignment* into position quite close to shore where the seabirds were uproarious, crashing into the ocean and picking up squid, as the striped bass and bluefish continued to pound the little cephalopods from below. We were using squid-like flies, and I was getting, but missing, a lot of strikes on the surface. Occasionally one or both of us would bring a fish to the boat, and we could see squid flashing iridescently just below the surface as if they were taking some joy in their tormentors' predicament. At other times squid that were fleeing the gamefish would leap completely out of the water only to be beset by terns and seagulls. It was a bad day to be calamari.

As we continued to sling, swing, and catch, I noticed that one of the seals had become curious. He repeatedly popped his head up, watching us bring fish to the boat, then watching us unhook and release them as fast as we had caught them. The expression on his little seal face was something between amusement and bewilderment. I half expected him to shout, "Hey! Why do you keep throwing your food away?" I understood his confusion.

There are two kinds of seals regularly found off the coast of Cape Cod. They are the smaller harbor seals that range up to five feet long and three hundred pounds, and the much larger gray seals that can reach eight feet long and eight hundred pounds. Possible, but rarely seen, are the hooded, ringed, and harp seals. Several decades ago, these were all but wiped out across New England, with the spotting of a single seal being rare by the 1960s. With the advent of the 1972 Marine Mammal Protection Act, seals began to resurge into the area, with harbor seals like my curious friend now giving birth to pups not much farther to the north on some lonely islands off the coast of New Hampshire and Maine. This one good piece of legislation has managed to bring New England's seal population from the brink of extinction up to around thirty thousand gray seals and over seventy thousand harbor seals, according to the NOAA Fisheries Division.

From time to time I'd see the swirling of fins that appeared to be sharks, most likely hunting the seals. The population of sharks, including great white sharks, has been on the rise off the coast of Cape Cod, with the Atlantic White Shark Conservancy reporting more than 160 confirmed sightings in 2019, as of the end of summer. Other species may include blue sharks, thresher sharks, mako sharks, and the occasional tiger shark during the warmer months. The sharks, like the seals, bluefish, striped bass, squid, common terns, and whales, all belong here. They are all part of the experience of these North Atlantic waters, and although I would loathe to fall overboard, I would not have it any other way. And this brings me to the story of Bobby.

Once the bite had died down, Ted and I spent a few moments just scanning the distant waters, looking for any new flocks of shorebirds to follow, trying to squeeze the last drop of adventure from our day. That's when I mentioned the coldness of the water and the proliferation of seals and sharks, and how much I was making sure to follow his directions and hold on as we crossed each choppy expanse of ocean. Ted pointed to my life vest and said, "That's why I make us wear these."

Bobby was a gentleman in his eighties who Ted volunteered to take fishing as a gesture of appreciation for all the support he had given wild-life conservation organizations such as Trout Unlimited and The Nature

Conservancy. Before they set out, Ted had given him the same safety talk that I received; part of that discussion is about holding on to the crossbar behind the driver while the boat is in motion. They went bouncing across the sea just as Ted and I had, moving toward and then across the rip and its waves and swells that bunch up the baitfish and call up the gamefish.

As the story goes, at one point they were crossing a bit of choppy ocean on their way to the next fishing spot when Ted called back, "How ya doing back there, Bobby?" There was no reply. When Ted cut the engine and looked back, there was no one else in the boat. Bobby was bobbing in the ocean close by. It all ended well, with the tough octogenarian changing into dry clothes and declaring it a good day. The moral to the story is, listen to the captain and hold on—adventure can get bumpy.

The Cape Cod National Seashore is a beautiful land and seascape that needs to be protected. Like all things in nature, it is connected to everything else around it. Just to the north is Boston Harbor, which was once known as the dirtiest harbor in America. There, the sewage, and runoff from forty-three municipalities must be contained, treated, and released. According to the Massachusetts Water Resource Authority, $3.8 billion was spent to reverse the damage caused by the sewage of five million people, along with $850 million to control runoff and storm sewer overflow and an additional $30 million to conduct oceanographic monitoring of pollution in the sur-rounding waters.

Legislation such as the Clean Water Act of 1972 has enabled places like Boston to greatly improve conditions through education, innovation, and enforcement of environmental laws. It's important for us to stay the course. There is still much to be done. The environment is improving, but it could all be undone with the stroke of a politician's pen.

I grew up as an independent-minded outdoorsman with a healthy sus-picion of big government, and I have not lost that suspicion after thirty years of working within the system. But I have also learned that, sadly, human nature being what it is, businesses, billionaires, and big-oil are not going to control themselves any more than big-government, big-trade, or big-mobs of uniformed people acting on knee-jerk emotions. We need well-considered, science-based, and far-reaching ways to change the way we treat the Earth and each other. What does this have to do with fishing? Everything.

The striped bass and bluefish Ted and I were catching are on a comeback from the brink of disaster, but they are still in danger of reversal. They are controlled and doled out by a mass of agencies with conflicting interests—interests that have little to nothing to do with the conservation of gamefish and their forage fish, or their habitats. For example, the US Department of Commerce plays a big role in deciding the fate of these fish, and you might note that commerce has nothing to do with conservation. The USDC operates the National Marine Fisheries Service, which manages bluefish and is focused on resource extraction, not protection.

The fox is protecting the hen house when it comes to our nation's oceanic fish. Organizations divvy up influence over "catch limits" and "by-catch," with each one acting as a special interest for the industry of fish extraction. To name a few, there is the New England Fisheries Management Council, Mid-Atlantic Fisheries Management Council, and the Atlantic States Marine Fisheries Commission, which manages striped bass. The worst may be the International Commission for the Conservation of Atlantic Tunas, which Ted has described as a "sorry congregation of fishmongers and politicians"; and the Recreational Fishing Alliance, which is representing the commercial "catch-and-kill" charter boat industry, not the conservation of native gamefish or their forage fish.

Why does this matter to an angler like me? This time with my friend was meaningful because the water was clean, the air was fresh, and the seals were swimming with the fish, squid, sharks, and whales. It was meaningful because birds flew overhead as the sun shone clearly across the water and the land. It was an adventure because all around us was the power and beauty of nature, the only home we will ever know. I want the generations ahead of me to know a natural world full of native wildlife and plants that causes them to feel as grateful as Ted and I felt on this single day at sea. This is why it all matters to an angler like me. How about you?

There is good news, and we can create more. There are organizations such as Pew Charitable Trusts, Oceana, Atlantic White Shark Conservancy,

The Nature Conservancy, Billfish Foundation, Sea Turtle Conservancy, Island Conservation, and Stripers Forever, which are working to make a positive difference in the restoration and conservation of our oceanic fish and their habitats. As ethical anglers and hunters who love our oceans, rivers, lakes, and watersheds, we can and must band together and take a lead in saving the natural creatures and places we have come to love.

This is not a partisan issue, it's a moral imperative. An ocean is not a toilet, it's a natural wonder. A fish is not a resource, it's a living thing of intrinsic value. How we treat the Earth's air, land, and sea reflects who we have become, or who we choose to be.

We grew quiet as the day was ending, the inlet grew closer, and the afternoon grew dimmer. Then Ted said, "I don't want to even think of a time when I can no longer do this." It was a beautiful moment, and I found myself drinking up every sight and sound and feeling.

Just then two young women rounded the bend, kayaking out of Cape Cod inlet. One of them called out to us, "Catch anything?"

Ted and I replied simultaneously. "Lots!" I said, clearly thrilled with the day we'd shared. "A few," replied Ted with the perspective of a man who knows these waters, these fish, and the value of understatement. I have a lot to learn.

The drive back to Ted's house was thoughtful. We listened to Ted's amazingly eclectic soundtrack of classic country, bluegrass, big band, jazz, and show tunes. It was luxurious to drink an iced coffee and think of the warm shower and cold gin and tonics ahead of us. I knew that Ted's wonderful wife Donna was making pizza, my favorite food, and that his pup, Governor Benning Wentworth, would be thrilled at our arrival (Ted's arrival). The thought of this, plus a warm shower, brought a smile.

"I can't thank you enough for the day," I said.

Ted smiled, just with the corners of his eyes. "You don't have to thank me; it takes nothing to get me to go fishing." Then after a pause he said, "Nobody fishes with me anymore."

I was surprised and asked, "Why?"

"They're not serious," he said. "Nobody wants to get up at two in the morning."

I thought about what Ted had said and wondered if I was a serious fisherman. We listened to the music for a while, and I began to review the day's adventures. For the most part, I fish the same way I play guitar, casually. Still, when it's part of the adventure, I can do as writer John Gierach once described as "bearing down and fishing." Mostly though, I had to admit to myself that I'm a take-it-easy fly fisherman.

I felt fortunate indeed to be in the company of a genuinely great fisherman, who is also my friend. I'd love to fish with Ted again. I'd happily get up at two in the morning to relive this day. I don't know if I can qualify as a serious angler, but I feel certain that I am a fortunate one.

Ted's words caused me to think of my dad, who loved and lived for the ocean. I recalled the day he finally sold his boat, *The Triton*. I had grown up and moved away, just as Ted's kids and my daughter had done. It is the way of things. When I asked my dad why he sold *The Triton*, he said, "I'm getting too old, Steve. I can't do it by myself anymore." That was a sad day for me. I felt like I had let my dad down by moving away. There's so much I understand now that I didn't understand then. I guess that also is the way of things.

On the way back to the house I asked Ted, "What do you love most about this?"

Ted, being a man of few words, replied succinctly. "Everything," he said. "I love everything."

I thought about that for a moment, and I smiled. "Me too," I said. I love everything about it . . . just like my dad, and Ted.

———

I first read Henry David Thoreau's *Walden* as a young US Marine who dreamed of a small cabin in the woods. The words and meaning contained within that book spoke to me back then when I was overseas and so far from home, and they still do. Even with all my world travels, I had not visited New England before this fishing trip with Ted, and I knew that I had to add an extra day to visit the small lake where Henry David fished and penned within those immortal pages, "Time is but the stream I go fishing in."

I won't fish or hike with just anybody. For me, being in nature is a sacred, spiritual experience, deserving of my respect and undivided attention. When I wade in a river, casting into the morning breeze, I do so with reverence. When I walk in a canyon, wood, or along some empty beach, I do so awake, in tune, and connected. You can't do that with just anyone. A perfect walk in the woods is as intimate as an embrace, as memorable as a smile that comes from the soul and through the eyes of someone you love deeply. That is why I choose to walk and wade with true friends who, like me, love nature—or I choose to walk in solitude.

Maggie Serva has been one of my dearest friends. She sat beside me the day my father died, and we listened to some of his favorite music: Sinatra, Bennett, Armstrong. We've hiked together and fished together and spoken of life and death and life's big questions, most of which have the same answer, "Who knows?" We've shared thoughts about honeybees and cypress trees and the way olives taste when they are at their best. A little over a year before this trip, Maggie moved to Boston from her home in the Texas hills not far from my own. I knew who I wanted to walk with at Walden Pond. She agreed.

It was a cloudy, wet morning when we arrived at Walden Pond. It had been raining all night, and the trees were deep green and the pond was clear, and either by random fortune or universal design it turned out to be the 202nd birthday of the man who once wrote, "A lake is the landscape's most beautiful and expressive feature. It is Earth's eye; looking into which the beholder measures the depth of his own nature." ·

Each day of the year, the Massachusetts State Parks department posts a copy of the journal entry that Thoreau made on that same day, sometime before his death in 1862. To our amazement, today it spoke of the need to walk with someone who resonates with you and the place and path, or to walk alone in solitude and peace. We smiled.

The trail around Walden Pond was well groomed, but narrow. It was wooded to one side and provided picture-frame views of the lake on the other. Along the way we avoided poison ivy and counted chipmunks and squirrels, and I noticed a few people taking what I guessed to be their daily morning swim in the lake. I wished in that moment that I had brought two float tubes and two fly rods so Maggie and I could fish the morning away in Henry David's lake. A blue jay called out and I smiled. I hadn't heard one in a while.

We walked until we reached the site of the original cabin where my literary friend sat and slept and read and wrote. There was a small cove at the cabin site, and I imagined him spending his days in and around that cove whenever he wasn't fishing, or hiking, or hoeing his bean fields. Visitors had created an impromptu shrine of stone cairns next to the cabin site, and Maggie and I added our stones to the mix. Some of the visitors had written messages on the stones, most of them in dull black ink with sharp meaningful prose, but one was written in gold glitter, and it read, "Hot 2017!" I'm not sure what Henry David would have thought of that.

Walking back, I found myself daydreaming of a morning or evening spent floating across the lake, casting my line to native pickerel and perch. They are still in there, just as they were in the 1800s. It amused me to think that I might catch the progeny of Henry David's "ones that got away." If I ever come back to Boston, I will fish this lake.

Visiting the replica of Thoreau's cabin, I was struck by its elegant simplicity and how at home I felt within its four walls. Except for the lack of a bathroom and running water, and the need of a table to replace his tiny desk, it felt like a place where I could live my life happily without want for much more. (It needed a porch too.) But standing there with my dear friend, I thought of how words can travel. I thought of how much his words have touched my life, and how much I want my words to touch the lives of others in some positive and meaningful manner. I thought of his love for this land and the sea, and the irony that the website for the Cape Code National Seashore has a quote from Thoreau across its masthead. It reads, "A man may stand there and put all America behind him."

I don't want to do that. I don't want you to do that either. The waters and landscapes of this great nation are its legacy far more than any building, road, technology, or ideology. I want us all to love these wild places enough to restore and preserve them for future generations. I want this country to lead the way in demonstrating how a great nation respects and treats each other and the Earth.

As I stood on the bow of *The Assignment* casting to wild, native fish in a sea teeming with life, all I could see was America's brighter future. In that future we tell the story of our flirtation with unlimited extraction and waste, and we end that perilous story with the happy tale of how we turned it all around, together.

If I could live another life, I'd come back in a hundred years and take a kid fishing off the coast of Cape Cod. I'd watch the magic in their eyes at the strike of a bluefish, the dive of a tern, the dance of a Wilson's storm petrel, the sea-cutting dorsal of a great white shark, the inquisitive eyes of a harbor seal. If I could live again, I'd want that kid to look at me as we rounded the corner into the inlet and ask, "What do you love most about this place?"

"Everything," I'd reply. "Absolutely, everything—wild, native, and free."

CHAPTER THREE

Northern Pike, Smallmouth Bass, and Muskellunge
St. Croix National Wild and Scenic River

Sharing the day on the water with a good friend, fish or no fish, is more memorable than the number of fish I land.
—BOB WHITE, THE CLASSIC SPORTING ART OF BOB WHITE

BOB WHITE IS AN OUTDOOR ARTIST AND WRITER WHOSE WORK I HAVE enjoyed, admired, and appreciated for many years before we ever met and became friends. He and his wife Lisa and their family, daughters Tommy and Jaime, son Jake, and dogs Frisbee and Quill, are the kind of family that give me hope. As a writer I am expected to find just the right word to express everything, but I'm not sure which word I'd use about our friendship; for now, I'll choose grateful.

When I arrived, Quill and Frisbee became so excited that they knocked me off the back porch and almost to the ground. It's not that they had any special feelings about my arrival, although I'm sure they're always happy to see Bob and Lisa come home from a trip, or Tommy from school. No, they were simply happy to see the new human, and although I did have fun feeding them tortilla chips from the table later that evening, I felt bad that I wasn't more fun for them to be around. Perhaps I've forgotten how to play. I need to fix that. I guess I need to find my inner puppy. Thinking back, I can't recall which of the pups liked their chips "neat" and which liked salsa.

The "White House" is not a house, it's a home. There is a difference. The two-story wood-sided structure is painted in a perfect shade of yellow, with white trim and a red wooden door leading from the back deck to the kitchen. (The same color combination I would have chosen.) On the porch is a grill, a table with a beautiful wooden frame that Bob built and a large slab of thick, clear glass as the top, and chairs featuring Lisa's bright and cheerful flame-red cushions. (It's important that I mention the cushions.) A carved Alaskan-looking fish hangs from the porch wall, and vintage-style tin lamps containing candles illuminate the scene. An old-fashioned brass hurricane lamp is the centerpiece of the table, with Lisa's potted herbs framing the edges of the porch. Mississippi Delta blues music filled the air, augmenting the red wine, homemade cider, delicious steaks, and crisp fresh salad. It was the perfect setting for friends to enjoy the evening before the float. The best part of any adventure is often the anticipation.

I know what you're thinking . . . what do playful dogs and perfect dinners have to do with fly fishing and the outdoors? Everything, my friend. Everything. You see, I don't write fishing stories. I write living stories. I write about the things that make life worth living. I write about the joy of being truly alive. These are the things that truly matter; all the rest is morning mist and evening light—fleeting.

⁓

When we arrived at the river and Bob handed me the "bug jacket" and said, "You might want to wear this while you wait by the boat . . . there may be some mosquitoes," I really didn't take it all that seriously. We were dropping Bob's drift boat in at Nelson's Landing so that we could float the St. Croix over the next five to seven hours, pulling out at Soderbeck Landing at the end of the day. Bob and Lisa drove the truck and trailer down to the pullout while I awaited their return to our launch point. They do this all the time, but I was new to this neck of the woods, watershed, and wilderness. I had a lot to learn, including that the mosquitoes were no joke. I put on the bug jacket and watched the river drift by through a mesh facemask as hordes of the bloodthirsty bugs circled around my head. That jacket was a lifesaver. (Thanks Bob.)

We launched from the Wisconsin side of the river, with Brant Piner State Natural Area along the east bank and Chengwatana State Forest to the west bank. Bob decided to take us down the river by way of the Kettle River Slough, toward the Kettle River and back onto the St. Croix. It was a perfect choice on a perfect day.

The St. Croix River became one of the nation's first Wild and Scenic Rivers with the signing of the National Wild and Scenic Rivers Act of 1968. Eight rivers were included in the original act, and, thankfully, many more have followed. The National Park Service describes the St. Croix as having "flowing, shifting, dynamic, changing water levels" with "shifting sand bottoms and banks." Part of what I love most about wild rivers, streams, and creeks is their ever-changing nature. I have no love affair with canals.

On either side of the river are vast northern forests that once contained native elk and bison, and still contain black bears, beavers, coyotes, bobcats, and gray wolves. The forests themselves hold a mix of conifers and deciduous trees that give the feeling of both rural America and American wilderness. Within the river itself lives a vast variety of fish including the smallmouth bass and pike we were targeting, and the muskellunge that we held out a slim but real hope of connecting with and bringing to the boat.

When Bob and Lisa returned, we launched the drift boat. Once on the river the mosquitoes vanished, and I was able to forgo the mesh jacket. With Bob on the sticks, we floated down Kettle Slough, Lisa and I casting our eight-weight lines and heavy streamers toward the bank in that familiar rhythm that made me feel at home. It took no time at all for us to get into the action. With each bend in the river, we found new areas of rocky bottom or submerged blowdown, and both Lisa and I were connecting with nice-sized smallies with some degree of regularity.

I brought my first smallmouth to the boat, and Lisa lifted hers. They were both nice and colorful, but neither one was a lunker. No matter, I prefer color to weight anyway, but something weird kept happening to both of us. Cast after cast we were connecting with smallies. I knew this couldn't last, but it was exciting while it did, and some of the fish were big, by my standards. But here's the thing. All the big ones got away. One time after another either Lisa or I would hook up with a heavy fish, and it would bear down and fight for a moment or two before shaking its angry head and throwing the hook. We were catching them, but the big ones continued to shake free. And then it happened, I hooked my first northern pike.

When I saw the strike, I could barely believe my eyes. It was vicious, brutal, primal, magnificent. It was everything I had dreamed of when I boarded the plane in Texas and pointed myself north. I came to fish for smallies, but deep down inside, this Texan harbored a desire to fight, land, and free a toothy pike or musky. It pulled hard and away, and the eight-weight bent like a divining rod over an aquifer. Bob got off the sticks just long enough to expertly swing the landing net toward my fish, but I blew it. The first pike of my life had been taking lessons from those big old bass. He was gone. I think I heard him laugh.

Things like that can take your breath away. You find yourself standing there with a slack line wondering what the hell happened. In a flash, your mind relives the vast expanse of time that ten seconds can become, and you wonder, "What did I do wrong?" But in the end, you count yourself lucky. You laugh and call it a "long-distance release." You say, "Oh well, it's better for the fish." I try to be noble like that. Still, under all that nobility I was thinking, "I'm going to come back here and get you next time . . . just you wait!" I cast again.

Eventually the action slowed, and Lisa and I continued to cast method-ically, each cast hopeful. Bob maneuvered us time and time again into good-looking coves and rocky-bottomed strips where we would make some good casts, and I'd make a few bad ones. After one or two notably crappy casts, Bob said in the slow, wise tone of a veteran Alaskan guide, "You know Steve . . . sometimes you can catch your best fish of the day with your worst cast." We both smiled. I knew I was getting plenty of chances to catch my best fish of the day. I was getting used to the heavy streamers, but mostly, I was letting myself get too excited and rushing it.

"Slow down and wait for that back cast," I told myself.

"Nice cast," Bob said, ever the gentleman.

"Nice duck," I replied. "You know, Bob, I just might get my best fish on my worst cast."

"Right as rain, Steve, right as rain." We both smiled.

We continued down the slough with the current running nicely downstream, sometimes smooth and sometimes choppy. The entire float we had planned that day was about eight miles long, with stretches of Class I and II rapids. I have to admit that I love going through the rapids as much as I love the fishing. I was watching Bob as he maneuvered us through each bumpy stretch, working the oars backward and forward as needed to control the craft, holding us almost suspended over the fastest water and then guiding the bow of the boat over each rush of water as if it were the easiest thing on Earth to do—when it's not. It's such a joy watching someone who knows what they're doing.

Rounding a bend in the river, we came to a cove with some fallen trees submerged so as to create a large backwater. Bob dropped the anchor and indicated it might be a good spot for a musky. He finally got his chance to do a little fishing. Grabbing a twelve-weight rod that was rigged with a fly that seemed to consist of an entire chicken's worth of feathers, he swung it out with authority along the length of the log. Swing, cast, strip, strip. Swing, cast, strip, strip.

When he reached the point of the cove, something big and dark and ominous looking made a rush toward the fly, or perhaps away from it, I'm not sure. Being a Texan used to catching twelve-inch Guadalupe bass, it appeared like a Russian submarine was rising from the river bottom. Whatever it was, it never bit, and it never came back. Muck'n Fuskies!

❦

The muskellunge, or musky, is a large, solitary, stealthy predator that can reach seventy pounds in weight and can move through the water at up to thirty miles per hour. Its mouth is filled with razor-sharp teeth, and its eyes contain a look of malice, or perhaps just constant hunger, I'm not sure. According to the US Fish and Wildlife Service, muskies are native to the

St. Lawrence, Great Lakes, Hudson Bay, and Mississippi River drainages. They live in every habitat, from clear lakes, rivers, and creeks to backwater pools. They are wolfish and mystical and are sometimes called "the fish of a thousand casts." I did not cast that many times on this trip. I want to come back in autumn and have another go at these river monsters. It seems like a spiritual imperative.

Water, especially moving water, is one of the most magical things I know. We set anchor on the edge of a nice current, with some small rapids just above and below us. We enjoyed a lunch together that tasted like everything does when you're on an adventure—magnificent.

With our off-shore lunch complete, Bob took a couple more casts into that musky-looking cove, but there wasn't a ripple beyond the one caused by Bob stripping that half-a-chicken fly though the water. We pulled up anchor, Bob took to the oars, Lisa and I switched positions, bow for stern, and down the river we went. The water looked dark yet clear, and the banks were pristinely green. This place has the feeling of wilderness. I love that feeling. We all need to experience more of that, not less.

The St. Croix Wild and Scenic Riverway is a warm-water system draining out of the Great Lakes and into the Mississippi River drainage. Prehistoric humans have occupied this area for at least ten thousand years, and it was once the homeland of the Ojibwe and Dakota Tribes of Native Americans. Burial mounds, campsites, rock quarries, stone tool chipping stations, and village sites attest to the importance of this river for both wildlife and humans. The St. Croix and Brule Rivers were both once important transportation routes for the fur trade, and only after the Treaty of 1837 was the area opened to Euro-American settlement. As we drifted down the river, I was left with the same feeling I've had before during my wilderness travels. I found myself wishing I could have known it before humans of my complexion had arrived. I wish I could have seen it before "we" arrived.

These boreal forests and northern prairie lands were once a wilderness that could have rivaled Africa's Serengeti for diversity and plentitude of wildlife. Before the arrival of European-Americans, this landscape included the prairie and eastern elk, bison, caribou, moose, white-tailed deer, and between three thousand and five thousand gray wolves in Wisconsin, with at least that many across Minnesota. Unregulated hunting and habitat loss led to the extirpation of both species of elk, bison, caribou, and wolves from Wisconsin, while a remnant population of gray wolves remained in northern Minnesota.

With the changing conservation ethic of the 1960s and 1970s, and the passing of the Endangered Species Act in 1973, the gray wolf was able to repopulate and flourish in these Northwoods, with an estimated population today of just under 2,500 in Minnesota and just under 1,000 in northern Wisconsin and Michigan's Upper Peninsula. As we drifted down this beautiful river with its dark green forest edges, I found myself dreaming of nights where the stars were bright and the snow fell softly, and the sound of wilderness filled my ears; the sound of wild wolves calling to each other . . . calling out into the darkness and singing, "I'm still here. I am still here."

It doesn't matter to me if I am imagining wild gray wolves of the forest or wild, wolfish muskellunge of the rivers, we need these places and these creatures of our nightmares and dreams. We need these beings to cause our hearts to beat a little bit quicker and set our imaginations on fire with the images of our ancestors. We need wild landscapes and rivers where we too can call out to that feral part of our own souls, "I am here . . . I am still here."

~~~~

We continued down the Kettle River Slough around several large, wooded islands near the confluence with the Kettle River. Bob positioned us again and again over beautiful stretches of rocky river bottom, and with each approach Lisa and I would pick up numerous strikes and several landings on brightly colored smallies. From time to time, we'd anchor in a backwater notch in the river's edge, and Bob would swing that big twelve-weight for all it was worth toward the dark waters, submerged tree trunks, and other musky-looking spots. I don't know how many casts he took at each location, but I kept hoping they were accumulating with those from his past floats and that I would be looking in the right direction after he reached his 999th cast. I really wanted to see him catch one of those lovely monsters.

At the Kettle River, Bob paddled us a short way up that tributary so Lisa and I could take some shots at likely spots along both banks. I cast up- and downstream of a protruding rock, and on the downstream cast I saw what looked like an underwater lightning strike that ended in a powerful pull from the fish I wanted most to catch on a fly, northern pike. This one made it to the boat, and after an obligatory grip-and-grin shot and Bob noticing that my fish seemed to have the scars of an encounter with Mr. Musky, we returned him to the river. This was turning out to be a perfect day. I could not have wished for more.

We rejoined the St. Croix, although the slough itself was such big water for me that I would not have known the difference had Bob and Lisa not pointed it out. We came to a section of rapids, and for a while I just sat there in the stern of the boat watching as Bob expertly maneuvered through each section of churning water and around each bend of this magnificently beautiful river. Just before we arrived at our pullout spot of Soderbeck Landing, just below where the Snake River joins the St. Croix, I reeled in and watched as Lisa made the last few casts in the quickly fading light of evening. It was a moment in time that I will never forget. Watching my two friends laughing and smiling as Bob cheered Lisa on, and they both traded good-natured jabs, was simply a wonderful ending to our beautiful day on the river. The fishing was wonderful, the catching was great, but the sharing of this river and these times with my friends was the best thing. It always is.

                    ━ ━

I slept well that night, the windows open to the backyard that contains Bob's studio, Lisa's office, some deer and squirrels, and a stream that tumbles into town. Although the brook trout in the Marine in St. Croix Millstream are not the original, native, genetic strain that once lived in the St. Croix watershed, efforts are under way to repopulate "heritage" brook trout in Minnesota and northeastern Iowa. Earlier on the evening of our float, we walked into town past the lovely little Marine in St. Croix General Store and over to a little pub that the little brook trout stream ran under and through. The pub was full of wonderful people, delicious food, cold local beer, and great conversation. I forgot my reading glasses and had to wear Lisa's so that I could order, but it all worked out nicely. It would be easy for anyone to fall in love with Minnesota.

The St. Croix is a warm-water environment, but it has a number of cold-water systems that drain into it, and these delicate streams, like the one behind Bob's house, are the only areas where native brook trout can survive. They are each a sensitive and vital environment that has been damaged by farming, logging, fire suppression, erosion, development, and climate change. The overpopulation of beavers and their dam-building activities cause reduced tree shade and slower water flows. All of these challenges lead to rising temperatures and lower water quality. That's a lot for a little stream and little fish to endure.

There is good news. Cooperative efforts by the National Park Service, Minnesota and Wisconsin Departments of Natural Resources, Great Lakes Indian Fish and Wildlife Service, and national organizations such as Trout Unlimited and The Nature Conservancy are making a positive impact. Organizations like the Minnesota Conservation Corps are working to restore native plants and remove harmful invasive species. Conservation easements are being established to protect delicate riparian habitats, and old buildings are being removed to restore the wild and scenic feel of the river.

These forest streams, along with a few in northeastern Iowa, are the westernmost homewaters for native brookies. Brook trout require cold, clean water; shade; and, ideally, the lack of foreign brown and rainbow trout to compete with for food, spawning, and winter holdover areas. In other words, all they require is what nature gave them, and we humans have taken away.

Before I chose to focus all my professional energies toward a life of learning, teaching, writing, and living in the outdoor world, I served for thirty-five years in a world of homeland security and criminal justice. I became a strong advocate for restorative justice, where the focus is placed on healing the injuries caused by humans, including healing the humans who commit the injuries, whenever possible. Restorative justice centers on two separate but equal lines that form the crosshairs of the idea. First, that we are all accountable for our behaviors and actions, individually and collectively. Second, that we need to have a path to redemption for those willing to do the work of repairing the harm they have caused.

Native brook trout and their cold-water streams are worth saving. The St. Croix and the American Northwoods are worth saving. Gray wolves and black bears are worth saving. I propose a new restorative justice ethic for how we choose to treat each other and the Earth. It is within our ability to hold ourselves accountable and find redemption in creating healing where hurt has been caused.

As I write this, I am sitting outside on a beautiful day in my beloved Texas Hill Country. I love this place, just as Bob and Lisa love the Northwoods of Minnesota. One of the greatest joys of this journey has been the opportunity to see each beautiful landscape, seascape, and homewater through the eyes of the people who call it home. As I write this I think back to an evening when Bob and I first walked to the brookie stream behind his house, and then up to his second-floor studio where he paints his magic and Lisa does hers by running the business end of the art. For me, there was a feeling of the sacred in that room. Bunches of brushes and canvases surround the easel that is placed directly below an overhead skylight window. I fell silent as Bob showed me the original painting that was to become the jacket cover for John Gierach's newest book, *Dumb Luck and the Kindness of Strangers*. That painting is based on a trip that Bob, John, and Mike Dvorak shared in Minnesota's Driftless Area, a part of Wisconsin, northeastern Iowa and northern Illinois that was not flattened by glaciers. This used to be native brook trout country. I hope we can protect it so that, perhaps one day, it will be again. For me, that is redemption.

Not far from the wild and scenic St. Croix with its green forest and quick clean water and singing wolves, there are dangers looming. The first is called the Polymet/Northmet mine and the second is the Twin Metals mine. Polymet is owned by a Swiss company and Twin Metals is owned by Antofagasta Company of Chile. Both mines have the potential to pollute the water and landscape from Lake Superior to the Boundary Waters Wilderness.

Everywhere I go it's the same old story of extraction, destruction, exploitation, and abandonment. Foreign companies promise short-term jobs to rural areas, and then they ruin what made the areas worth loving and living in. Yes, we do need copper, nickel, platinum, and cobalt to make pipes, wires, stainless steel, and batteries. But there is a better way than burning the Earth's candle at both ends. We don't have to do it this way. We are better than this, I hope. We can seek redemption from our throwaway lifestyle. We can repair the harm and restore wild places for future generations of hopefully wiser humans.

—⁓—

On my last morning in Minnesota, I sat down to breakfast in the front room of Bob and Lisa's lovely home. I love breakfast; it may be my favorite meal. I reveled in the flavor of the warm, black coffee, the sweetness of the egg yolks, the crunch of the toasted bread, and the crisp, smoky flavor of the bacon. We chatted about the previous day's fishing and what a beautiful day we shared. I soaked up the ambience of the room with Bob's original artworks adorning the walls and Tommy's violins hanging nearby. The dogs rested peacefully in the living room; even Quill seemed to be enjoying the morning calm.

When Lisa went to the kitchen, Bob and I sat there talking about life and love and art, and the love of all three. It was a morning that stands among the best of my long life. It was magic—like Bob's paintings, which transport me instantly toward a memory I once shared, or one that I wish I had and still hope to create. There is always hope.

Remember that, my friends. We create our own hope. We can be the architects of a better future for ourselves, each other, and this beautiful world. We don't need to be the victims of the future we're currently drifting toward. It's okay if we've made mistakes as long as we keep casting forward, learning and leading, trying again and again to mend for a better drift. It's okay if we've fallen down and short, as long as we learn, get up, and cast our efforts in a better direction. After all, a wise man once told me, "Sometimes we can catch our best fish with our worst cast."

CHAPTER FOUR

Brook Trout
Allegheny National Forest, Pennsylvania

Have you ever noticed how often anglers tend to share their good fortune? I have seen this happen many times among perfect strangers who simply meet on a stream.
—A. J. McClane, The Song of the Angler

STANDING AT MY FATHER'S GRAVE, I FELT SORROWFUL, BUT NOT FOR THE reasons you might expect. My dad had died three years earlier, but for reasons of my own I did not go to his burial in his home state of Pennsylvania. Instead, I chose to remember him by hiking in Mystic Canyon of my Texas Hill Country home, the last wild place he and I had walked together. I did not want to remember my father as he was in the end, but rather as a strong young man who used a whippy, yellow fiberglass fly rod to dap and precision cast to small, wild, native brook trout in his Allegheny Mountains homewaters.

Standing next to his plaque in the memorial garden where he was buried next to his mother, brother, and two sisters, I felt sad because for the first time I was seeing that the place he chose to be buried was a humble plot of grass that overlooked old houses and congested roadways. It was the kind of place that nobody would visit or even slow down to notice. There were no trees or birds or anything that he would have loved, only a weedy plot of grass overlooking suburban Pittsburgh. At that moment I realized I had done the right thing by going hiking on the day my dad was lowered into the earth. I knelt down and touched the brass memorial plague that read, "Stephen J. Ramirez, SSGT, US Air Force, Korea, 1931–2016," and I said, "I love you dad . . . I'm going fishing."

Charles Cantella and I first met over social media as we both swam through the contents and commentary of a world of outdoorsmen and women. He had written a book titled *A Touch of Grayling* and had sent me a copy, which caused me to smile and chuckle as I read his self-deprecating tales of fly fishing and life. This led to phone chats and plans to fish together when I made the trip up to Penn's Woods to visit my dad's grave. I had shared with Charles my desire to find a little native brook trout creek in the Allegheny National Forest not far from where my dad was a young man dapping for brookies in his heyday. Charles said that he had a perfect place in mind, and so we hatched a plan and made it happen.

It was cold and raining on the morning that we met—not the kind of rain that pounded down on you, but rather a steady drizzle that made everything feel damp and primordial, as if a dinosaur might lift its head from behind any moss-covered pile of rocks. We drove through the misty morning gloom, sipping coffee and chatting as if we'd known each other forever. This is the power of finding your tribe. Thin blue lines on topographical maps, cold mountain streams, rolling blue oceans, glassy clear flats, and rushing canyon creeks—all attract similar souls. When you follow the same feral calling, you find others who speak your language. It gives you hope and makes the world seem a little less hollow. Many kindred spirits stand in knee-deep water while casting a line or walking behind a good bird dog. We are not alone in our love of solitude and kinship.

We arrived at the little creek, which was so deeply hidden in the forest, I would never have known it was there. Charles had found it while scouting for our trip and had since fished it both alone and with his daughter, Anna. We had discussed the condition of the creek as it tumbles toward the mighty Allegheny River. It is as fragile as the diminutive brookies that call it home. We both decided that it would be best if I not mention it by its given name, so I suggested we call it "Anna's Creek." Charles smiled. That settled it, Anna's Creek it is!

Charles was wearing blue jeans, a dark blue and black long-sleeve shirt, and a bright yellow cap with his Pennsylvania fishing license prominently attached. He smoked a classic-looking pipe that gave off a pleasant aroma like only pipe tobacco can. It fit him perfectly and I'm glad he brought it.

I, on the other hand, was in full camouflage earth-tone stealth mode right down to my brown digital camouflage Buff that hid everything but my predator eyes. Charles smiled as he donned the yellow hat and said, "It's deer season. . . . I don't want to be mistaken for a buck!" A moment later came the distinctive crack of a rifle shot in the near distance. Suddenly, my small-stream stealth didn't seem so smart. We hiked on.

Anna's Creek is a typical freestone stream that tumbles over boulders and slabs of slate beneath a canopy of hemlock trees, and along a forest floor of ferns and multicolored mushrooms. It's not very fertile, so the trout are hungry and not selective. We each tied on a small soft-hackled nymph and began prospecting downstream through the forest. It didn't take long for me to spot a few six-inch brookies meandering in the little plunge pools that were dispersed along the creek every ten to twenty yards. As I mentioned, these fish are not selective, but they are skittish. The water is clear, thin, fast, and the little trout are used to looking up.

As much as I love casting on an open river and wading across an expanse of saltwater sand flats, I also enjoy the stealth and delicacy of fishing small streams for eight-inch native fish. It's as much hunting as it is fishing, and I spend as much time observing a fish and planning my approach as I do in the act of fishing. Sometimes I find myself sneaking up behind a tree and carefully dapping my line over the creek's stony edges. Sometimes

I'm making sure to have the mountain laurel at my back so that I might blend in as I approach a bit of pocket water. And other times I stalk down an embankment and slowly turn a corner so as to place a quick, short cast into a pool that is otherwise inaccessible. It all puts you in the moment and forces you to slow down and connect to the landscape, the water, and the fish. When I'm doing this, there are no worries, no plans beyond the next cast, and nothing but the feeling that I am a lucky man doing exactly what I want to do, where I want to do it.

Charles was being the perfect homewater host as he puffed his pipe and allowed me the first, second, and third try at presenting my fly to a jumpy little trout. More often than not the brookies saw me before I could do anything about it. I'd slip around a tree trunk or patch of rhododendron only to see a bright, wild fish swimming under a rocky ledge or root. But as the gradient began to increase and the nature of the creek went from a gentle flow to a series of little waterfalls and plunge pools, I was able to dap my fly in just the right spot, and out from under a ledge came a bright little brookie that soon danced on the end of my line.

These are small fish living in a tough environment. Could you imagine if your whole world were a bubble of air between a jumble of rocks, and you had to keep hoping that the fresh air blowing in equaled the amount going out? Could you imagine watching that bubble increase and decrease as if the sky were falling? And if this weren't enough, you'd have to constantly be on the lookout for something to eat and for anything that may want to eat you. When I think about this, I almost feel a little guilty for catching them. Still, we save only what we love, and we love only what we know. By meeting these wild natives where they live, I have a greater appreciation of their amazing beauty and resilience. I have a stake in their survival.

It didn't take long for Charles and me to begin leapfrogging along the stream from pool to pool and pocket water to pocket water, picking up a fish here and there and missing or spooking at least as many as we caught. I was switching back and forth from dapping and bow and arrow casting a size 16 Adams dry fly and the same size nymph, and I was having luck with both, but the best thing I had was this black fuzzy thing that Charles gave me. Wherever I travel I almost always find that the locals have some nondescript imitation of nothing you've ever seen in nature that triggers strikes like a chunk of beef heart in a piranha pool. The black fuzzy thing was seemingly irresistible.

The day prior, I had been fishing for brook trout in West Virginia with my buddy Dustin Wichterman of Trout Unlimited. All the trout we caught there were in full spawning colors. Had I dropped one in the autumn leaves that line the stream, I might have lost it as it would have blended in so well. I had been concerned with causing any stress to spawning fish, but Dustin, who is a fisheries biologist, assured me that the transition was in its earliest stages and our activities would not negatively impact the fish. These Pennsylvanian fish were not yet in color, but they were pretty, nonetheless. Whenever I see a brookie in spawning color, I wonder how Van Gogh might paint it. I wish he had.

At times we had to cross back and forth on the stream because the terrain would become dangerously steep on one side or the other. We climbed up a rise over some blowdown and through the wet, green, magically fern-laden landscape until we were looking down on the little stream from the cliff's edge. I could see a nice-sized waterfall and deepish pool just at the base of the cliff, so I decided to make my way down the other side of the rise to the water's edge, just downstream of the cliff face. It was going to be a tricky cast. Too far to bow and arrow and not even a good spot for a roll cast, so I gathered up my courage like a golfer planning a putt and sent my back cast between the waiting arms of the overhanging hemlock trees and then forward toward the falls.

The first cast landed nicely, if a little too far out into the middle of the pool. But it gave me confidence, which can be a good thing if you don't go overboard. I cast again, watching my leader flick inches from the waiting tree branches and then land gently at the head of the pool, exactly where I wanted it. I glanced up toward the embankment to see if Charles had seen that amazingly perfect cast (it was pure luck), but he was hanging back so as to not disturb my concentration. That's when a little brookie chose to strike. I attempted to set the hook as if I were fishing for tuna, and that sent my delicate little line into the waiting arms of a particularly tall tree. It was okay for Charles to come down now and he knew it, as the sound of the air deflating my lungs indicated. I don't think I cursed. So much for the "perfect cast."

I recently thought that it might be fun to take note of the dendrology of the trees I've caught across the country. In my native Texas Hill Country, I've caught cypress along the Guadalupe, box elder on the San Marcos, sycamore on the Sabinal, and mesquite on the Llano. I hooked a bunch of willow in New Mexico's Gila Wilderness, a spruce tree in Arizona's White Mountains, a red mangrove in Florida, and a sugar maple in West Virginia. I didn't catch any trees in Minnesota, but I did manage to connect with my friend Lisa White, who was casting from the stern while I cast from the bow, but that doesn't count since she's not a tree. (I have never forgiven myself for snagging her lovely pink casting shirt.)

I'm in love with trees. When I left the Marines in 1985, I studied forestry at Penn State, Mont Alto. I loved being out in these transitional Mid-Atlantic woodlands where trees of the Northeast mingle with those of the American South. But I remember getting into discussions with the professor about forestry practices like clear-cutting and monoculture replanting. Nature demands diversity, and it punishes us when we try to override those demands. I guess a better way to put that is that we cause everything to run amok when we start playing around with the natural equilibrium of an ecosystem. Monoculture of anything opens it up to unchecked infestation and decimation from insects and pathogens. I remember the professor's face growing red when I said a crop of trees isn't a forest and board-feet isn't a good measurement of success. I left forestry school after a year; I don't think they missed me.

The Allegheny National Forest became an addition to our public lands after the signing of the Weeks Act in 1911 that authorized the Secretary of Agriculture to "buy land in eastern states for the establishment of National Forests." It's important to note that these forests fall under the control of the Department of Agriculture, which indicates that the government views them as a crop, growing trees as if they were corn, soybeans, or hogs. When you see the forest only for the trees that can be used to make wood or paper, it's not a forest anymore, really. I have more faith in us than this; we can do better. We can choose to have forests filled with a variety of native trees, shrubs, forbs, grasses, and fungi and still be able to build houses and bind books. As a naturalist and outdoorsman, I know everything is connected. I'd rather walk in a living forest than a tree plantation. I'd rather fish in a living stream, not a drainage ditch. How about you?

Our original plan was to work our way down Anna's Creek until it met up with the Allegheny River, but as we fished our way downstream, we became increasingly aware that this was probably not going to happen. It wasn't the rain or even the gunfire that dissuaded us . . . although the sounds of rifle shots were frequent enough to make us wonder if the Whisky Rebellion had started up again. I wasn't exactly wishing I were wearing a bright yellow hat, but I was glad that we were following a stream through a hollow between the hills. But rain and rifle shots weren't the reason we decided not to keep going; it was simply that we had already had such a perfect morning and turning around felt right.

We stopped at a pretty little spot to have the lunch we were carrying in our packs—nothing fancy, sandwiches, chips, and bottled water, but it tasted wonderful as food almost always does when you are outdoors. While we were eating, we chatted about the woods around us, the reasons Charles loved this place he calls home, and the stories my dad used to tell me of fly fishing for brook trout with his buddy Charlie, just like I was doing with my buddy Charles. (Charles does not like being called Charlie.)

After a few more gunshots rang out from the forest above us, I began to reminisce of my dad's tales of deer hunting up here. He used to tell me of snow-covered conifers and a buck stepping out from behind one just as he lifted his Savage Model 99 and fired. He was proud of that buck even though it was a youngish fork-horn that no modern Texan would shoot, unless it was to cull it. But back then the hunting pressure in western Pennsylvania was so high that deer rarely made it to a truly mature age. Things are getting better. Pennsylvania has been improving its deer herd management and working to change perspectives about stewardship. This is a good thing.

Deer hunting is such a part of life in my dad's home state that it's hard to believe that by 1900 deer, wolves, eastern cougars, and eastern elk had all been extirpated from western Pennsylvania. White-tailed deer were eventually imported from other states to repopulate these woods, and young trees were planted to replenish the forests that had vanished in steam-powered sawmills. Now the second-growth forests are filling in where they can, and the deer herd is growing in size and health. Some Rocky Mountain elk have been placed into north-central Pennsylvania as they have in Kentucky, Tennessee, and North Carolina, but they are not the same native elk that lived here in the time of the Algonquian or Cherokee. We can plant new trees, but it's hard as hell to turn a parking lot into a forest, and shopping malls almost never become wetlands again. Some things we can't undo. I don't want wild brook trout to become one of those things. How could we live with that?

—◦—

As my friend Bob White might say, "Fish were caught." I think the biggest brookie we connected with was eight inches long, although I saw a couple that might have gone ten. Had we made it farther downstream I suspect a twelve-inch trout wasn't out of the question, but I did not come here to catch big fish. I came here to experience the same small-stream fishing my dad loved when he was a young man escaping the poverty of his steel mill hometown along the banks of what was back then a polluted Allegheny River. Things are getting better now. A large section of the Allegheny is now designated as an American Wild and Scenic River and as part of the Pennsylvania Water Trail System.

Once we decided to turn around and begin working our way back upstream, I made a few halfhearted attempts to connect with the "big ones," those few eight- to ten-inch fish that had evaded me, but they continued to evade me. In time I decided to snip off my fly and just enjoy walking along the stream and through the wet, dripping forest that protects it. I came here to fish, but in truth I could have had just as much fun walking along Anna's Creek simply spotting brook trout. Perhaps I could count each brookie I spot as a "long-distance catch and release."

These waters and forests will never be pristine again, as they might have been in the time of the arrival of early Americans. Yet even the Native

Americans altered the landscape. It's what we humans do. I doubt there is anywhere left on Earth that is untouched by humanity. I am reminded of being in the middle of the Skeleton Coast Desert of Namibia and saddened by all the tire treads that scarred the ancient lichen fields. And then there was the time I was hiking cross-country in a mountain wilderness area, and I stopped to admire the vast expanse of seemingly endless and roadless forest. Just as I thought to myself, "I bet I am the first human to ever stand here," I noticed something shiny on the forest floor. It was a gum wrapper.

Yet I am hopeful, and "hope" is a call to action. And I am grateful that I am still able to find places like Anna's Creek where the water runs clean and the wild, native fish defy all logic by remaining as they were in the time of the Shawnee, Monongahela, Lenni-Lenape, and my father. Driving through Pittsburgh and across the Allegheny landscape, I can reimagine what is possible, and it is a beautiful and hopeful image. I can imagine the three rivers running through this great American city, with clean water filled with native fish and attracting wildlife to the river's edge. I can imagine the greening of cityscapes, tree-lined streets, parklands, urban and rooftop gardens, recirculating, tumbling waterworks that cool the city, and roads that reflect and reject the heat. And I can hear the laughter of inner-city children escaping into the arms of nature, just like my dad once did. I envision a time when no child grows up without picking and eating a fresh tomato or apple from a community garden, and no person grows old in a landscape without native natural things around them. Nature and nurture are two sides of the same coin.

As Charles and I walked back upstream, I found myself burning the images of these sodden woodlands into my mind. I knew that I'd never see this place again, except in my memories. Each time I spotted a small brook trout holding in the current of a tiny pool of mountain water, I felt privileged just to be there. And I thought of my dad and his buddy Charlie, and how they would place two Rolling Rock beers in the stream at the point where they knew the day would end so that they could return to them, ice cold from the same water where the brook trout lived, and celebrate being alive. I thought about that and wished I had thought of it before Charles and I arrived.

Traditions like that hold meaning. They bind moments and memories and remind us of the real circles of life. The brook trout that Charlie and my dad once caught are the ancestors of the fish I was catching. And my dad still lives on through me; in fact, I see him every time I look at my own hands or hear myself laugh. They are his hands and that is his laugh. Life lives on, even after we are gone.

My dad used to always say that it is every generation's duty to leave the world a little better off than they found it. I never really saw that happening. I used to tell him that the only thing that's changed about humanity is the technology we use to destroy things. I'd say, "Dad, we've just moved from rocks to rockets." But he remained hopeful that we'd choose to make better choices. And the truth is, I think, that it is all about choice and planning ahead for the outcome we wish.

Perhaps there was a bigger lesson hidden within those two beers chilling in a mountain stream. As I thought of this, Charles and I were just making it back to the twisting country road where the car was parked. We had enjoyed a wonderful, wet day together on a beautiful little creek. If only we had thought of the cold Rolling Rock beers. Maybe next time. In my mind's eye, I can almost see my dad . . . smiling. After all, there's always hope that we will make better choices.

CHAPTER FIVE

Guadalupe Bass
Llano River, Texas

*I have never yet caught a fish on a first cast, nor have I ever made a
first cast without thinking I would catch a fish.*
—Ellington White, Striped Bass and Southern Solitude

WE COULD NOT HAVE ASKED FOR A MORE BEAUTIFUL MORNING. THE RIVER
was rolling over rocks and roots, clear and sunlit, as we stepped into my
friend Kevin Hutchison's bright blue boat. Kevin pushed off and got behind
the sticks, a place where he is at his best. I, on the other hand, can best
serve us by sitting quietly in the front and simply letting Kevin move us
over riffles and rapids, from pool to pool, all the while cracking jokes and
telling stories that had me missing shots because I couldn't stop laughing. It
was a good start to a wonderful day on one of my favorite rivers on Earth.

The Llano River is a tributary of the Colorado River that winds through
about one hundred miles of the Llano Uplift and Edwards Plateau in the
Texas Hill Country. The river originates in the springs of the far western
Edwards Plateau where two tributaries, the North and South Llano, rise

from the otherwise arid limestone earth and stretch across canyons and hills. These tributaries merge just east of the town of Junction, Texas, to form the mainstream of the Llano River. The river meanders from Junction to Mason and on toward the towns of Llano and Kingsland where it empties into the Colorado River and begins its journey toward the Gulf of Mexico. Most of the river cuts through the Llano Uplift, which consists of a geologic dome of Precambrian pink granite igneous rock surrounded by the limestone of the prehistoric sea that once covered much of Texas.

The Llano is home to the endemic Guadalupe bass, as well as northern largemouth bass, various sunfish, gar fish, and Rio Grande cichlid. On this float I was destined to connect with largemouth, native green- and non-native yellow-bellied sunfish, bluegills, and hard-fighting Rio Grandes, but my main objective in these hills is always the state fish of Texas, the Guadalupe bass.

Guadalupe bass are found only in the Texas Hill Country and are native to the Llano, Guadalupe, Colorado, Brazos, and San Antonio river basins. Guadalupe bass have been caught in excess of 3 pounds, with the record thus far being 3.71 pounds. Most fish will be in the pound to 2-pound range, with a good day of catching ranging from five to fifteen Guadalupes in addition to largemouth bass and the various sunfish you may land.

The size of this fish belies the size of the fight in this fish. You might think of Guadalupes as "Texas trout" with attitude. As my friend Kevin Hutchison said, "Trout fishing is ballet . . . this is a street fight." Guadalupe bass prefer moving water and are adept at using the current to their advantage, fighting hard, and demonstrating plenty of head-shaking acrobatics. Add to this the fact these fish will use submerged structure to tangle and break the line, and the angler finds their hands full in a heartbeat.

I've been fishing these waters for several decades, but I don't know anyone who knows them better than Kevin, and his book, *Fly Fishing the Texas Hill Country*, is as good a reference for these waters as I have seen. Five- to eight-weight rods with floating line are appropriate. As for technique, this is a place for a simple straight-line retrieve, keeping your rod tip down, touching the water, and retrieving your streamer, subsurface fly, jig, or surface popper directly back toward you. Slack is not your friend.

Casting a weighted white streamer as close to the bank as possible, allowing it to sink just a little, then retrieving in short strips, I received strikes at every point in the process. Often the bite came as soon as the fly hit the water. Just as often it came anywhere along the jerking journey of the fly from the bank to the boat. Sometimes the strike came in the form of a wide-open bucket-mouthed assassin rising up from a deep, dark pool. On the Llano, action happens all around you.

I switched from the weighted streamer to an olive-colored woolly bugger with plenty of flash. Kevin worked us around each twist and turn and over the rocky riffles as I cast alternately toward each bank. I was catching a lot of pretty native green sunfish, bluegills, and the biggest cichlid I've ever caught. I love those fish almost as much as I love Guadalupe bass.

In one deep pool next to some massive boulders, I saw a shadow materialize and a three-and-a-half-pound largemouth bass engulfed my streamer and put a serious bend in my five-weight rod. He treated me to all the acrobatics and fighting style for which that species is known. Largemouth bass in the Llano can range between three and nine pounds, with larger fish possible. But by far my favorite part of fishing the Llano and other rivers of the Texas Hill Country is when I'm catching and releasing Guadalupe bass. If you want to target Guads, focus on areas with moving current, undercut banks, stones, and organic structure.

As we drifted past the plethora of woody debris lining the riverbanks, I continued to slap my streamer up under the embankment. Time and again my casts were greeted by vicious strikes from Guadalupe bass that always seem convinced they are a force to be reckoned with. They jump and dive and shake their angry heads, and they remain incensed even once you have them in hand. But the reason I love them more than any fish in these hills is because they are beautiful, wild, and native. In short, they belong here, and they can be found and caught only in the rivers and streams of the Texas Hill Country. Still, their future is not assured. We almost lost the state fish of Texas.

During a recent visit to the Heart of the Hills Fisheries Science Center in Mountain Home, Texas, I had the opportunity to see firsthand the work of dedicated Texas Parks and Wildlife Department (TPWD) biologists Paul Fleming, Nate Smith, and Preston Bean. These fisheries biologists and others like them are working hard to reverse the downward trajectory of Guadalupe bass. TPWD is utilizing a "watershed-scale and ecosystem-based" approach to saving this important gamefish and its native waters.

The primary threat to the continued survival of Guadalupe bass has been hybridization and competition with non-native smallmouth bass. Regretfully, "bucket biology," both professional and amateur, has been practiced for decades across the globe. Bass from the United States can now be found on every continent except Antarctica. Smallmouth bass stocking by the TPWD began in 1958 and became intensive in 1974, "with the intention of improving angling opportunities in Texas rivers." In a recent conversation TPWD biologist Nate Smith shared, "By the 1980s we began to understand the threat to the endemic Guadalupe bass that was posed by the introduction of non-native smallmouth bass, and in the early 1990s TPWD began active restoration efforts via the establishment of genetically pure broodstock, scientifically based stockings of fry and fingerlings, and removal of invasive smallmouth bass."

According to TPWD Guadalupe bass biologist Preston Bean, "Our evaluation of stocking of Guadalupe bass fingerlings shows that the genetic influence of smallmouth bass in the Llano River has been reduced to meet our targets for restored populations. The success of the stocking coupled with the watershed and riparian restoration projects that we've implemented with landowners will ensure that an outstanding Guadalupe bass fishery persists in the Llano. There are no smallmouth bass (non-hybrids that could create new hybrids) remaining in the Llano."

One challenge with wildlife conservation and human outdoor recreation in Texas is that most of the land here is privately owned. The designated "navigable waterways," of which the Llano River is one, are public property within the waterway up to the high-water line. In a recent conversation with TPWD fisheries biologist Paul Fleming, he said, "Most of the landowners along the Llano River and across the Texas Hill Country want to take care of the river and its health as it passes through their ranches and are working with Texas Parks and Wildlife and other agencies to protect riparian and riverine habitats in Texas rivers." State initiatives such as the Landowner Incentive Program, Aquatic Vegetation and Invasive Species Management Program, and the Riparian and Spring Management Programs are helping to educate and incentivize landowners and anglers to help protect these rivers and their native fish. This is good news for all of us who love angling and the outdoors.

By the time we drifted down the river to our pullout point, I had long since lost count of how many fish I had caught. There was a multitude of sunfish, bright and beautiful in my hand, along with some nice-sized northern largemouth bass, which rose from the deep like sea monsters engulfing deer hair flies rather than Norse ships and sailors. But the most beautiful sight to my eyes was of the Guadalupe bass that jumped and danced on the water and came to my hand, looking as native as the pecan trees and as natural as the limestone banks they grew along.

I no longer see myself as a "sportsman" as much as a participant in nature and a respectful and responsible resident of the bioregional community of the Texas Hill Country. This is my home and I love it. If every angler begins to think in terms of homewaters, home-watersheds, and bioregions, we will all do our part to restore, preserve, and perpetuate the kind of outdoor experiences our great-grandfathers once knew. If we don't, we won't. We save what we love; we love what we know. Drifting down the Llano River is an experience that's worth knowing and loving, and the Guadalupe bass is a gamefish that's well worth saving.

Chapter Six

Apache Trout
White Mountains, Arizona

Some people talk to animals. Not many listen though.
That's the problem.

—*A.A. Milne*, Winnie-the-Pooh

Driving the four and a half hours from Phoenix to the White Mountains was an adventure. The vast changes in landscape and ecosystems are astounding. Tonto National Forest is a steadily elevating expanse of saguaro cacti that reach for the sun like alien totems. I find them to be both starkly beautiful and eerie. In time, distance, and ever-increasing elevation, the saguaro forest becomes a landscape of juniper and pinyon pine, and higher up these also give way to the largest continuous forest of ponderosa pine and then, ultimately, spruce and fir trees. All of this change and diversity is experienced in a single four-hour drive.

When I arrived in Greer, Arizona, it was dark, raining, and cold. I checked into my cabin and met the owner at the time, Linda. We had been corresponding about my journey, about the fairly recent passing of my father, and how it was my intention that this trip act in part as a commemoration of my father's life. I had timed this trip to coincide with the one-year anniversary of his passing. I wanted a celebration, not a mourning. That's what he would have wanted too.

Life can be ironic and tragic, but it is also always a beautiful, magical gift. Linda had just lost her husband of many years to a sudden and unexpected heart attack. Bob was the same age as me and had lived the same active, healthy outdoor life. It was obvious to me that, like my father, he had caused so much joy and love during his lifetime. It was obvious that his life, like my father's life, was one where he shared the joy, magic, and poetry of the landscape and homewaters he loved with those people he loved.

Author Terry Pratchett once wrote, "Nobody is truly dead until the ripples they cause in the world die away." That evening I met Linda and Bob's daughter, Lori. We spoke of our fathers and their love of wild trout streams and high-mountain trails. We spoke of the love and gifts they gave us. It was a moment I will never forget.

In the morning the rain had been chased away by sunshine and birdsong. I met my new lifelong friend, Cinda Howard, and I fell deeply in love with her fishing companion, a sweet dog with a childlike spirit named Jules. For me, dogs and people are semi-domesticated creatures, and like Papa Hemingway, I can only love them one at a time. Every now and then I am fortunate enough to meet a person or a pup with a deep heart and playful soul. Cinda and Jules were a perfect match. I could not have dreamed of better partners for my first adventure in Arizona's beautiful White Mountains.

The Apache Wilderness is wild and stunningly beautiful. It's a historical landscape that has been touched—often painfully—by humanity, and yet has managed to hold onto much of its wild spirit. Vast forests of ponderosa pines give way to aspen trees and ultimately fir and spruce as the elevation increases and the oxygen in the air decreases. Elk, deer, mountain lions, black bears, and Mexican wolves run freely through its forests and meadows. The reason I have flown from my home in Texas to Arizona, and then drove for hours from the Sonoran Desert to the southernmost Rocky Mountains, was not to see any of these great creatures of the subalpine and high-desert wilderness. I had traveled all this way to find and connect with a diminutive native of these high-mountain streams. I was searching for Apache trout.

I am a Texan, through and through. But my father spent his early years carrying a little yellow glass fly rod through the ancient mountains of the Allegheny. There he lost himself and found himself fishing for small, colorful brookies in fast freestone streams. And, now I felt as if I was panning for gold with a slightly less whippy yellow glass rod than my father had. I love catch and release fly fishing for wild, native fish. I live for those moments when I am connected to another beating heart, and then for that moment when I set that heart free. Each fish that I connect with and then set free is a kindred spirit.

The secret stream (the location of which will follow me to my grave) was narrow, twisting, and simply lovely. It was high enough up the mountain to keep the water cold and clean enough for these imperiled natives, although I worry that as global temperatures rise, no amount of conservation will save them. In a recent conversation with Arizona Game and Fish biologist Zach Beard, I asked him about this concern, and he replied that he was choosing to remain optimistic that they would be able to find enough cold-water, spring-fed, high-elevation streams within the Mount Baldy watershed to keep the Apache trout from going extinct in its home range. I will choose to remain optimistic, too, but not unrealistic; things are touch and go for this beautiful native fish.

Apache trout are the state fish of Arizona and one of Arizona's two native trout species. The other Arizona native, the Gila trout, is native to the Gila and Verde watersheds. Apache trout are beautiful, with bright yellow-golden bodies and fine spotting across the tail, dorsal fin, and back. In all the world, they are only found in the White Mountains of Arizona in high-elevation streams such as the Black and Little Colorado Rivers, upper Silver Creek, and various tiny waters spilling out of the White Mountain Apache Nation. In fact, these trout would be extinct today if it were not for the actions of the White Mountain Apache Tribe, who banned all fishing on reservation land in 1955 in an effort to save the last few Apache trout.

After a bit of hiking and prospecting, Cinda brought me to a bend in the tiny stream and gave me some guidance as to imitation and presentation that I would not have figured out organically. I was drifting a dry-fly-and-dropper combination around each bend and undercut bank when I received and missed my first strike. At least I knew they were there and willing. Now I simply needed to learn how to be more ready and able.

This is a place for short, artful casts, where back casts must be thread between the waiting arms of spruce trees. This is a stream where Apache warriors once sipped the clear cold water, where Mexican wolves still lap and bright yellow trout still leap. This is an ancient place that needs to be protected and preserved from the unintended consequences of human invention. We do not burn our museums into smoke, so why do we so casually allow our wild places to evaporate? Perhaps our greatest legacy as a species is not what we build, but rather, what we save.

Cinda pointed to a bend in the stream that created a deep cutbank pool. I drifted my fly through the current and into the hole and received an instant strike, and my first wild Apache trout came to my hand. Neither I nor Jules could contain our glee. Jules quickly taught me how I was expected to release a trout. As soon as I'd hook up, she would wait as tense as a pointer on a pheasant until I brought it to hand. Then, and only then, she had to inspect the fish and sniff its tail, and with a joyful look of "you finally caught one!" she allowed me to return each brilliant little trout home. If every person on Earth could have the same heart and soul as that little dog, we'd be so much better off. My dad would have loved her.

We worked our way upstream, crossing back and forth as we did, to get the best opportunities at the best water. I missed as many strikes as I connected with, including a "big" fish that might have gone ten inches in length. That was the only strike I had on the dry fly, and I think I was just surprised by the whole thing, as up until then the dry was acting exclusively as an indicator for the small hare's ear nymph that I was using as the dropper. Most of the Apache trout I was catching were in the six- to eight-inch range. One time I overpowered the hook set when the dry fly submerged, and I wound up with a three-inch trout airborne, gratefully landing in my hand rather than in a spruce tree.

Catching large native fish is a good sign because it tells me that they are surviving to maturity in these waters and growing well past the size and age they were when placed here by Arizona Game and Fish via the Silver

Creek Hatchery. Catching tiny native trout makes me happy because it tells me that fish are being born in the little creek—wild, natural, and free. Native fish are the perfect indicator of the health of an ecosystem, and I don't mean just the water, but also the entire riparian habitat, watershed, and evermore increasingly the Earth. Their absence reflects our folly, and their preservation and persistence reflect our greater selves.

We worked our way along this pretty little stream as it meandered between spruce and aspen trees. Jules seemed torn between wanting to watch us fish and chasing ground squirrels. She kept reminding me of the importance of childlike exuberance in life. Watching her as she watched me was as much fun as the fishing.

Cinda and I kept a wary eye on Jules whenever she'd wander forward, because one of the charms of these forests is that they contain bears, mountain lions, and Mexican wolves. In fact, her playful, carefree nature and propensity to take the lead has gotten her in trouble a few times. Once she received a "dry bite" from a black rattler, and another time she was chased downstream by a rather large and angry black bear that wasn't amused by Jules and her big brave spirit. I suspect she was initially trying to protect Cinda from the bear but soon found herself with a bruin on her butt. Jules is sweet, and we now know that she can outrun a bear.

I hooked up with a few more fish, each one a bright replica of the other, all between six and eight inches in length. We watched as a few dark clouds began to appear above the treetops. Then a couple of big raindrops fell, before the clouds passed and the sun reappeared. It wasn't the rain we were watching for, but the lightning that comes with the thunder. Did you know that lighting can release as much as one gigajoule of energy? I don't actually know what that means, but it sounds like something I want to avoid.

After the clouds drifted past, we decided we had found a good place for lunch, and we broke out the sandwiches and chips while sitting on some rocks near a bend in the stream. Even though we were in a wilderness area, we could plainly see that these rocks had been arranged by human hands who had camped in this site fairly recently. It was a perfect place within a small clearing in the trees, next to a meadow covered in blue, purple, and white wildflowers.

While we were enjoying our lunch together, we also enjoyed a chat about our lives, our loves, and our families. We swapped recent photos of our kids—my daughter, Megan, and her daughter, Codi, and son, Shade. We talked about fishing and fish and the changes we've witnessed in our homewaters, and what it all might mean. We discussed how the Apache trout have been retreating farther up-elevation each year as the waters of these mountain streams continue to warm, and I wondered aloud if there is anything we can do that will save them in their native land.

At 11,409 feet in elevation, the mountain we were standing on was the highest in the White Mountains. We were fishing at around 10,000 feet in elevation. There isn't all that much more mountain left for these fish to count on. To my mind, an Apache trout that can only be saved in a hatchery or by transplanting it to some high-mountain lake in Colorado isn't an Apache trout anymore. It is a relic.

It was July, monsoon season in Arizona. The wolves I hoped to see never came, but the thunderclouds I expected to see did. The air grew cooler, and the rumble of coming rainstorms was a proper signal to send us walking back down the mountain, beside the stream. And then I said farewell to a place I now carry in my heart. Had I caught only a single Apache trout, my day would have been complete. Instead, thanks to Cinda and Jules, I caught and released seven bright little fish in all, and I missed as many as I caught. Cinda said we'd had a good day of catching and I believe her. I felt lucky.

Beyond my fascination with Apache trout, I am drawn to this area because the White Mountains of Arizona, and the Gila and Aldo Leopold Wildernesses in New Mexico, are some of the best bets for the rewilding of Mexican wolves, Mexican black bears, ocelots, and even jaguars. On numerous occasions, the northern jaguar has been documented crossing the border into Arizona. Just as much as native trout are a wonderful indicator species for watershed health, native apex predators are a key to a healthy environment for both animals and plants. As controversial and emotionally charged as this topic has become, it doesn't need to be either.

Wolves that are traditionally native to the part of North America we now refer to as the "Lower 48" include the gray wolf, Mexican gray wolf, and red wolf. The red wolf (*Canis rufus*), which used to range from the coastal plains of Texas to the eastern forests, was declared biologically extinct in the wild as of 1980. A small experimental population exists in the Alligator River National Wildlife Reserve in North Carolina, and about two hundred remaining red wolves survive in captivity across the United States. Still, the red wolf may never thrive in wild America again due to the expansion of humans and coyotes. Coyotes have learned to live and thrive in proximity with humans, and also to compete and hybridize with red wolves.

The gray wolf (*Canis lupus*) has been reintroduced in parts of the northern Rocky Mountains of Montana, Idaho, and Wyoming, and they are reported as recovering and naturally expanding into Oregon, Washington, northern California, and possibly northwestern Colorado. And the gray wolf population in the western Great Lakes region of Minnesota, Wisconsin, and northern Michigan seems to be expanding at a healthy rate. The fears of many of my fellow hunters are being countered by the reality that wolves and other predators are good for the health of elk and moose populations. The presence of natural predators is beneficial for the ecosystems where they and prey animals coexist. What does this have to do with fishing and healthy streams? Everything. Wolves keep elk herds moving in and out of riparian zones so that they cause less damage to the streamside vegetation and instream habitat. Nature is balanced. Apex predators are a part of that balance.

Mexican wolves (*Canis lupus baileyi*) are native to the mountain forests of northern Mexico and the American Southwest. They once ranged from Arizona to West Texas but are now confined to the Arizona White Mountains and three wilderness areas in New Mexico. In my past life, I served thirty years as a peace officer and homeland security specialist. I understand all too well the need to reinvent our immigration system and keep a watchful eye on our nation's borders. But I also understand that we need to protect the biodiversity that has no politics and clings to life on both sides of the imaginary line. These mountains and high deserts of southeastern Arizona and southwestern New Mexico are the only places where we can rewild the apex predators that once lived here. I believe that rewilding native species is a matter of ecological responsibility and national pride. There needs to be places where Americans know they have purposely regained and retained original species like Mexican wolves—and yes,

Apache and Gila trout. And as anglers and participants in nature, I believe we need a place where we are reminded to be vigilant, to travel together, and to watch the trail's edge and whatever might be just beyond your back cast. There is something primal and pivotal about navigating a wildscape that exists much as our ancestors once knew. Bears scare me, but I want them to be out there. I don't want to fish in the equivalent of a golf course pond. I don't want tame and contrived. I want to have the choice to go wild. Do you? Fishing is barely about fish . . . it's about connection.

On the walk back down the trail we crossed paths with two middle-aged men, who on seeing my fly rod asked, "Are there fish in that stream?" and "Any luck?"

I smiled and responded, "I'm lucky to be here on such a beautiful day!"

Cinda smiled and said, "Well, it's fishing." They smiled back knowingly.

I picked up a brightly colored stone and placed it in my pocket. This is my way of keeping this place and this moment with me always. I do this wherever I go. My writing desk is cluttered with stones, dried leaves, and seashells from around the world, each one attached to a memory. I don't know if I will ever go back to that high-mountain stream, but I definitely want to return. Cinda and I have talked of reconnecting here, spending a few days chasing Apache trout, and a few across the imaginary line in New Mexico, catching and releasing Gila trout. I can't imagine a more perfect life plan. I do know this: No matter if I make it back or not, I will do my part to help protect this unique wildland's memory and hopefully its potential future. What we did in this land to both the Apache Nation and the Apache trout reflects who we were. What we do in these southwestern mountains is ultimately a reflection of who we've become. Let's rewild America. It's the natural thing to do.

CHAPTER SEVEN

Gila Trout

Gila Wilderness Area, New Mexico

The idea of wilderness needs no defense; it only needs defenders.
—*EDWARD ABBEY*

I'VE WANTED TO GO TO SILVER CITY, NEW MEXICO, SINCE I WAS A BOY
reading of Billy the Kid and the outlaws and lawmen of the Old West. And
I've wanted to go to the Gila Wilderness since I was a young Marine and
read Aldo Leopold's *Sand County Almanac* for the first time. As a boy, it was
the childlike romanticizing of the western United States of the 1890s and
the clash between "cowboys and Indians" and "good guys" and "bad guys"
that ignited my imagination. As a young man, it was a landscape covered
in ponderosa and pinyon pine trees, and populated with deer, elk, bears,
and Mexican wolves that drew me. As I grew up, I learned that both the
Native Americans and Mexican wolves were getting a raw deal, but this
knowledge only served to fuel my desire to see this wild land, and fish its
improbable high-desert waters.

It took me about thirteen hours of driving across miles and miles of West Texas and southern New Mexico to reach Silver City and The Murray Hotel, which would serve as my base camp for a few days. The Murray is a restored 1938 Art Deco hotel that once was considered the ultimate in southwestern luxury and now is a restored relic of a boom era of mining, logging, and other extractive industries. Today, visitors are still a mix of mining and forest service contractors and outdoorsmen and women, all seeking something different from nature. As I pulled up, I noticed it was located on the corner of Texas Drive, which made me feel right at home.

Some people had told me that this hotel is haunted. I don't know about such things, but as I walked in, the sound of the Eagles singing "Hotel California" ran through my head. I walked up to the counter and, seeing no one, rang the bell. A woman with immovable hair came over, stared at me as if she were expecting me, and said, "Are you ready to check in?"

When I made my reservations online the website said, "Free Parking Available." I checked in and told the clerk that I was temporarily parked on the street in front of the hotel in the loading zone, and I inquired as to where the guest parking lot was located. She looked at me emotionlessly and said in a monotone, "You can park anywhere on the road."

"But your website indicated that the hotel has free on-site parking," I replied.

She stared at me eerily without blinking and after a long pause said, "Well . . . when you park on the street . . . it's free." Then she walked away, leaving me alone in the massive, empty lobby. I could almost see the images of people in 1930s garb mingling about to the tinny sound of a piano, each holding a martini and a cigarette. It was spooky.

My room was comfortable and clean and there was a *Star Trek* marathon on the television and no sign of ghosts, so I was content as I laid out my fishing gear on the couch and freshened up from my long day of driving. Taking the tiny elevator back down to the big, empty lobby, I walked out into the street in the middle of Silver City's Historic District. It's a neat little area with an old western-looking courthouse, a funky little coffee shop, a wonderful Mexican restaurant, and a brewery and distillery called Little

Toad Creek. Here too, the town seemed largely deserted on the outside, but once I walked inside the pub, the whole world came alive.

I sat down on a high stool at a table where I could watch the goings-on both inside and outside the window. I like to approach new places on the map the same way I approach new streams: I just observe and take it all in before making any choices. The walls were covered in flags of various nations from around the world, and on a sign near the bar I read the words, "Hippies Use Back Door." Music was playing and people were laughing and the whole scene seemed surreal, as if they all knew better than to be outside with the ghosts of dead miners and potential Chupacabra to consider. The aloneness I felt upon arrival began to drift away, and I started to feel at home in Silver City the moment she walked up and smiled.

Her name was Atziry Apodaca, and she was lovely, kind, and brave. She said that she was from Jalisco, Mexico, and that her name was Mayan, and asked where I was from and did not change her expression when I said that I hailed from Texas. I have traveled across four continents and many countries, and it saddens me to find that my country is becoming so cold, disjointed, and lacking in courage and empathy. I'm so used to being kind and open and Texan with people, only to have them look at me with suspicion as if to say, "What do you want from me?" I understand all too well that there are people with bad intentions, but we are becoming a people who expect the worst of each other, and this is a damn shame. You can't litigate relationships, understanding, acceptance, or kindness. You can't demand people's trust. Atziry made all the difference in my day, and she may never realize how much her warm smile and open heart began a fishing trip in the best way possible. I ordered the Baja fish tacos and Copper Ale. They were both glorious.

I slept well after having my Copper Ale with dinner and a glass of wine in my room while watching *Star Trek the Next Generation*, *Deep Space Nine*, and *Voyager*, and packing up my gear—rod, reel, flies, chest pack, hat, sunscreen . . . you know, the usual stuff. I knew it was all there, but it's fun to just mess with it and line it all up so that everything is ready to launch in the wee hours of the morning.

It was so nice to see my friend Cinda Howard and her amazing fishing pup Jules again. The last time we'd seen each other was about a year prior when I flew out to Arizona to fish with them for Apache trout in the White Mountains. Cinda is the real thing. She has more knowledge and skill as a fly fisher and guide than I could ever accumulate in what is left of my lifetime. And she is completely authentic, honest, and generous, without a smidge of pretense.

Whenever I meet some fly-fishing "rock star" who can cast a quarter mile and still manage a drag-free drift in the equivalent of a flushing toilet, and who says things like, "I only fish with paying clients and my fans," I'm not sure if I should laugh or feel sorry for them. They've missed the point. Cinda and Jules love fishing for fishing's sake . . . just like me. I have no interest in fishing with "fans." I want to fish with friends, or else in solitude.

It took about two hours of driving to reach Whitewater Canyon in the Mogollon Mountains, just north of the tiny town of Glenwood. This is a stunningly beautiful and wild country where the Rocky Mountains meet the Chihuahuan Desert. As we drove and gained elevation, we moved from one ecosystem to another, each with its own set of native plants and animals. At the lowest elevations, Chihuahuan Desert plants like cactus, yucca, and ocotillo dominate the landscape where pronghorn and mule deer browse. Just below six thousand feet the vegetation changes to pinyon and juniper, and just above that it transforms into one of the largest stands of ponderosa pine in America. At the very highest elevations, above nine thousand feet, spruce, fir, and aspen dominate. Elk, Coues deer, mountain lions, and some of the last remaining Mexican wolves populate these higher zones. If I ever chose to leave my beloved Texas Hill Country, southwestern New Mexico and the mountains of Arizona are some of the few places I'd consider. This is an outdoorsperson's paradise. Good thing I'm such a Texan.

Whitewater Canyon, often called the "Catwalk," is a place steeped in history. Chiricahua Apaches and Euro-American outlaws used this canyon to evade US Cavalry troops. Prior to that, not far from this canyon, the Mimbres people lived here and built cliff dwellings; some of which remain to this day. It is a magical place where massive boulders form the canyon's floor and ice-cold mountain water tumbles down from 10,895-foot Whitewater Baldy Peak, the highest in this range. Once populated with non-native brown and rainbow trout, it is now part of a concerted and thus far successful effort to bring back the native Gila trout from the brink of extinction.

We strung up our rods and approached the creek, quite shallow at first with small sections of pocket water. We were happy to see a nesting site dug into the soft gravel, our first indication that these fish are reproducing, or at least attempting to reproduce. Since it is such a small water, we planned to take turns leapfrogging from one pool to the next. It didn't take any time at all for Cinda to link up to a small, bright little Gila trout. It's amazing how wide a six-inch trout can make me smile.

Although the canyon is shaded by cottonwood and Arizona sycamore trees, it is open enough to manage a delicate cast in most places. As we moved up the canyon, the water seemed to move faster, the boulders grew larger, the falls became taller, and the plunge pools took on a lovely coppery color not unlike the microbrew I had the night prior. In each pool we'd connect with another small six- to eight-inch Gila, one after another. At one particularly pretty pool, Cinda's fly got slammed by a nice yellow-gold Gila that went at least twelve inches long and looked chunky in her hands. We were both thrilled to know the larger fish were here.

These fish are as beautiful as any I've ever seen. There is a lovely copper color to the gills, and their iridescent golden-yellow sides give way to a Milky Way–like cluster of profuse spots across the upper half of their body. Some of the larger fish have a faint salmon-pink-colored band along their body. In the water, they glow like living gold. I can't imagine what a sin it would be to lose them to humanity's foolishness and apathy.

We came to a deep pool between two rock faces where I felt sure a big one might be living. I made my best effort at a soft, precision cast over a boulder, a waterfall, and between the rock faces. The fly landed softly on the water and drifted without a hitch. That's when I saw something strike the surface, and I found a three-inch Gila trout at the end of my line. There were streamers in my fly box bigger than this tiny fish. But this was a good thing, because it was proof positive of wild reproduction. I gently returned him to the pool, feeling happy that he was home. I was also pleased with my delicate, on-target cast. But nature conspires to keep us humble; my next cast snagged a tree. That's more like me. All was right in the universe.

⌐◆⌐

Whitewater Canyon eventually meets with the Gila Wilderness, which was one of the first designated wilderness areas in the world, along with the nearby Aldo Leopold and Blue Range Wildernesses in 1924. Later, the Wilderness Act, signed by President Lyndon B. Johnson in 1964, created a legal definition to protect designated wilderness. Written by Howard Zahniser of The Wilderness Society, it reads, "A wilderness, in contrast with those areas where man and his own works dominate the landscape, is hereby recognized as an area where the earth and its community of life are untrammeled by man, where man himself is a visitor who does not remain." I am grateful that these places still exist, and I am certain they would not without federal legal protection.

To my mind, it is part of what makes this nation a great nation. We can't be great simply by what we can build, but rather by what we can save—from ourselves. Aldo Leopold was right when he wrote, "I am glad I shall never be young without wild country to be young in. Of what avail are forty freedoms without a blank spot on the map?" I don't want to live in a completely tame country. We need to keep our wild side alive.

This is rugged country. After I hooked that little tree clinging to a rock face, I was forced to stick my rod between my teeth and use both hands to scramble up the boulder and retrieve my line. Looking down into the pool, I could see that there wasn't a big hog of a fish in there. Once I climbed down, Cinda, Jules, and I waded through that pool and over a bit of slippery rock to move upstream.

As I was perched precariously above the pool, searching for handholds and trying my best to defy the Earth's pull, I realized that my passion for fishing for wild, native fish in wild places has led me to do many things I would otherwise consider precursors to insanity. Fourteen-hour road trips on two hours sleep, bushwhacking through rattlesnake country, outracing lightning storms on mountaintops, and now clinging to a rock face in wet water shoes with my four-weight glass rod in my teeth like a swashbuckler's dagger. Yep, life is good when we live it full throttle.

I didn't think the canyon could become any more beautiful, but I was wrong. We came into a section that contained one perfect plunge pool after another, with the sound of the rushing water adding to the sense of solitude and serenity. Above us, bolted to the canyon's wall, was the "Catwalk," a steel walkway once created to follow along a steel pipe that transported water to a gold and silver ore processing facility established in 1893. This area was mined from 1889 until as recently as 1942, and according to New Mexico state records, Billy the Kid's stepfather was a blacksmith in the little mining town of Whitewater that had sprung up at the base of the canyon. The original walkway was made of wooden planks, but after being washed away during flood events, it was replaced with steel. Had Cinda and I planned to hike here instead of fish, we could have continued past the Catwalk on a rugged trail that eventually leads to the edge of the Gila Wilderness. I intend to return and make that hike.

Cinda had already caught her biggest fish, which I would have guessed to be slightly over twelve inches long. It was my turn. We came to the first place along the way where we could both fish at the same time. Cinda offered me the lovely little pool beneath a waterfall. She decided to fish inside a cave that had a large opening on the downstream side and a small opening upstream, allowing the creek to flow through it. I began drifting my dry fly through the pool, and after a few tries a flash of gold rose from the depths and snatched it. I was thrilled, and in a few moments I held a brightly colored Gila trout in my hands. I'd guess it was slightly under twelve inches, but not by much.

I stopped fishing and decided to join Jules in watching our friend trying to catch a trout in a cave. Jules kept looking back at me as if to say, "What the hell is she doing in there?" Cinda was getting takes on her dry-fly drifts, but she kept hitting the cave ceiling as she attempted to set the hook. Again and again she'd drift the dry, get a strike, hit the cave roof on the hook set, and then laugh and say, "This is so cool!" Cinda is not one to be defeated, and with persistence she connected with and brought to hand a pretty little Gila. We were having a blast.

69

This is the kind of place that makes you wish to never leave, but evening was coming on and we still had to make it back to the truck and then drive to Silver City. I suggested we fish as far as we could, then snip off our flies and take the quick and easier way back along the Catwalk. By working our way up as we had, we ended up moving slowly, not only because we were fishing but also because the canyon floor is a rugged, rocky, and rigorous climb. It was worth every effort and any flirtation with the impact of gravity.

The walk back was almost as magical as the slow climb up. Squirrels crossed our path as bright yellow-orange tanagers flitted from tree to tree. Black-chinned hummingbirds buzzed by, while canyon wrens and mocking-birds competed for best musical score. I kept looking up at the high canyon walls hoping to get a glimpse of a bighorn sheep, elk, or mule deer, but all I saw were images in my mind's-eye of the ghosts of Apache warriors who were watching me watching them.

Sometimes I think that everything that ever happened in any place is always happening, just in a different dimension. This place was once an industrial site where mining and men took minerals and returned only waste. Now it is a national recreation site and a place to reclaim what was lost, including the Gila trout. How cool is that? In my conversations with New Mexico Game and Fish's Gila trout biologist Ryder Paggen, I learned of plans to extend the native-only Gila trout waters for several miles up the canyon. In time I may be able to return to Whitewater Canyon and hike it all the way to its headwaters, catching and releasing nothing but wild, native Gila trout for the entire distance.

Can you imagine a time where our children's children might look out at a wetland, prairie, woodland, or living desert and be able to say to their children, "All this was once a shopping mall?" I can. In fact, I dream of those days all the time. After all, every reality begins first as a dream. Hope is a call to action.

～～

The night of our glorious day at Whitewater Canyon, Cinda and I met up with Silver City native Jason Amaro. We chatted as we enjoyed an amazing meal at a little Mexican restaurant in the Historic District of Silver City.

After dinner we made plans to meet up early and make the drive to another Gila trout restoration stream named Willow Creek.

In the morning we met in front of my historic and possibly haunted hotel, loaded up into Jason's truck, and took off toward the town of Reserve, New Mexico, and ultimately, Willow Creek. The road up through the mountains was a mixture of pavement and dirt, passing through a ghost town that was being repopulated by people who obviously had more fear of living without nature than dying in the wilderness.

Ponderosa pines filled the canyons, and from time to time, entire mountainsides were covered in the burned matchstick-looking remnants of what was once a majestic forest before the three-hundred-thousand-acre Whitewater-Baldy Fire of 2012. Years of artificial fire suppression and the cumulative impact of climate change conspired to create the conditions for this massively destructive wildfire. The ash from that fire eliminated both Gila and invasive brown and rainbow trout from many of the streams in this area, and after evacuating Gila trout from several streams, the process of returning them began.

When we arrived at Willow Creek, Jason walked us down to a large, cement, dam-like barrier that has been constructed to keep invasive brown and rainbow trout from moving upstream where the Gila trout restoration would be taking place. Jason said that he wasn't going to fish, but just "hang out" while Cinda and I worked our way up the creek. We strung up, tied on a small dry fly, and began leapfrogging up the creek.

This was quite different water from the day prior. The creek was shallow, narrow, and lined with small willow trees, and the pools seemed much smaller to me. I wondered how these fish could overwinter and reproduce in such a sparse environment, and indeed the fish reflected the creek in their diminutive size. Cinda and I both had the feeling that if we could have gone into the creek closer to its headwaters, the fishing would have been better.

And there was something else about this place, something that I couldn't quite put my finger on, but it was the same eerie feeling I had in the hotel lobby. All around us were the skeletons of ponderosa pines, burned to death in the Whitewater-Baldy firestorm. Every now and then, I'd hear a sound like a person moaning in despair. And in those times when I was fishing alone, I had this feeling of being watched, as if something or someone was peering down on me from just beyond the willow thicket. Maybe it was Jason. Perhaps it was nothing. All I know is, when Cinda and I regrouped we compared notes and found that we were having the same experience. Creepy.

I've got to admit (and I'm not proud of this), but my heart wasn't into the fishing on Willow Creek as much as it had been the day before on Whitewater. I was too taken aback by the stark destruction of the fire and the knowledge that this place would not recover in my lifetime. In the end, Cinda caught about five small Gila trout, each one a beautiful little gem between six and eight inches long. And, like one of Jesus's apostles, I caught nothing. I received and missed a few strikes, but once an opportunity was missed, the pool was so clear and small that the gig was up. More than anything, I was thoughtful—about this place and our place within it, and about these wonderful golden fish and their future. I wondered about our future, too. Something deep down inside me feels certain that valuing and saving these fish, streams, and forests is the same thing as valuing and saving ourselves.

Evening was settling over the Mogollon Mountains as we drove south toward Silver City. The conversation became a mix of chatting about wild-life conservation and the need for more positive engagement by anglers and hunters. Jason's tales of high-mountain adventure sometimes left me wondering if he was serious or just pulling our leg.

At one point I mentioned the eerie feeling Cinda and I both experienced and the spine-tingling moaning sound we kept hearing, even though there was no wind and no trees.

"It was La Llorona," Jason said as he laughed.

"La Llorona?" I asked.

"Yes," he chuckled. "Some Mexican American families use old folk stories to make their kids behave and come home at night. La Llorona is the weeping woman. Legend says that she drowned her children in the river because she was jealous of the attention her husband gave them, and that she was denied entry into heaven until she recovered them, so she stalks along rivers at night moaning, '*Ay, Mis hijos!*' According to the story, when-ever she finds children wandering out at night and realizes they are not her own, she kidnaps them and drowns them in the river." Jason laughed again.

"That's a terrible story!" I said.

Jason laughed, "Yep, it's pretty jacked up!"

Cinda and I looked at each other, somewhere between speechless and aghast. I began to focus on the hillsides, hoping to see some elk and purge that awful story from my mind. That's when I thought about the strange sounds we heard and the feeling of being watched from behind the willows and I wondered . . . what the hell was that? All I know for sure is, if I ever return to fish Willow Creek, it won't be alone, and it won't be at night.

Before leaving Silver City, I went back to the Little Toad Creek Brewery and ordered another Copper Ale. The cheerful young server was not working that day, and although the service was swift and the beer and food delicious, it was not the same. People who sincerely acknowledge our existence and intrinsic value make all the difference in our life's journey, and we should strive to make the same difference in theirs. I enjoy my solitude, but kind interaction between fishing buddies or random strangers can improve any moment and memory. I sat there surrounded by people, yet alone with my thoughts, reliving the amazing few days I had spent casting to Gilas in deep, rocky canyons. I was already looking forward to the next time.

As I grow older, I am becoming obsessed with the idea of wilderness. I want to touch its edges, even if I can never penetrate its deepest center. Eco-modernist writer Emma Marris argues that the idea of saving nature in a pristine, pre-human state is an outdated dream, and in many ways I know she is right. We have touched everything from the Antarctic ice sheets to the Amazon rain forests, and from the Mariana Trench to the stratosphere. Even our moon contains human boot prints.

Still, I am convinced that the defining achievement of *Homo sapiens* will not be the way we've conquered the Earth and nature as much as the way we've chosen to save it. I do not want to live in a world without wild places. And I want to live long enough to be proud of humanity for finally living up to our species name, *Homo sapiens*—"wise man."

As a Marine, I always knew that my objective was not the violence I could create, but rather the violence and injustice I could negate. By putting myself between innocent people and those who would harm them for power and profit, I felt I was doing a noble act . . . even, an act of love. As I think about the wild landscapes of this great nation and the magic of a rising, wild, native Gila trout, I want to share that magic with others and recruit an army of Earth warriors. If this sounds crazy then I ask, how can anyone consider themselves an avid and responsible angler, hunter, hiker, kayaker, or human being for that matter, and not want to fight for this beautiful place we call home? And wildness matters; if it didn't, we'd all be happy hiking in a shopping mall, hunting in a petting zoo, and fishing in a hatchery pond.

I easily came to love this place of high mountains, rugged canyons, rushing waters, and golden-yellow trout. My life would have been less without seeing those native fish in these wild waters. It feels natural to me to acknowledge their existence and intrinsic value, and to try my best to make some positive contribution to their preservation and the protection of the wild places they call home. I guess I'm trying to do that now. Join me?

Chapter Eight

Rio Grande Cutthroat, Pecos Strain
Jack's Creek, New Mexico

Rio Grande Strain
Columbine Creek, New Mexico

The last word in ignorance is the man who says of an animal or plant:
"What good is it?"

—Aldo Leopold

Road trips, especially when traveling alone, can be a mixture of adventure and monotony. Adventure, because you are really "doing it!" You're passing through counties and states and taking notice of the changing landscapes and accents, counting off miles and milestones as you grow ever closer to your destination, which in this case was Santa Fe, New Mexico. Monotony, because when you're crossing miles and miles of West Texas cotton and oil fields, you can find yourself feeling positively giddy about a town with a coffee shop, or a rise on the horizon in the foreseeable distance.

For at least an hour in West Texas, all I could see were oil and natural gas pumps bobbing up and down like dozing dinosaurs spewing out their noxious fumes of methane. All I could think was, "What have we done to

75

this place?" I kept picturing it as it once was—short-grass prairie covered with antelope, bison, wolves, and the occasional Comanche hunting party. I was happy to be crossing into New Mexico where the oil fields ended and the prairie began. Just north of Roswell, I saw my first pronghorn. I felt better.

It took me fourteen hours of driving to reach Santa Fe, and though I was exhausted I was taken in by the beauty of the mountains and high-desert prairie and the adobe town that seemed to blend so naturally into the landscape. In the morning I'd be meeting up with my buddy Toner Mitchell, who among other things is the New Mexico Water and Habitat Program director for Trout Unlimited. Thus far, everyone I've met and befriended from TU has been an obvious member of my tribe, and Toner is no exception. We share the same passion for protecting wild watersheds and the native fish that call them home. I don't think there could be a better person to introduce me to the mountain streams of Santa Fe and Taos. This is the land where he was raised and the place he feels most at home, and it comes through in everything he says and does on its behalf.

In the morning, we met at a little café on the edge of Santa Fe with a great view of the mountains that were our destination. It was one of those places with a friendly local vibe, wonderful coffee, and delicious breakfast burritos, and if we weren't going fishing I could have stayed there all morning with a good book and a notepad, just daydreaming and looking out at the mountains. But we were going fishing, so I took everything to go and we started up the twisting roads into the Pecos River watershed where today's quarry lives.

The Rio Grande cutthroat trout is the southernmost subspecies of cutthroat trout, and it occurs throughout parts of southern Colorado and northern New Mexico. Originally found in the Rio Grande, Canadian, and Pecos River watersheds, it is now restricted to about 12 percent of its original range, according to the New Mexico Department of Fish and Game. It is the state fish of New Mexico and is recognized in two distinct strains, the Rio Grande and Pecos. Both fish are beautiful with brassy-colored sides, greenish-bronze backs, sparse spotting on the tail and across the upper back, and the namesake red-orange slash along the jawline and throat. The Pecos strain was the variety we'd be pursuing today, and it is distinguished in part by having less spotting on the back and almost no spotting beyond the dorsal fin.

Like many American native gamefish, the Rio Grande cutthroat has suffered from habitat degradation and loss, overfishing, competing for food and territory with non-native brook and brown trout, as well as competition and hybridization with non-native rainbow trout that have been dumped into their homewaters by the bucket biologists of the past and present. After decades of poor forestry practices and the quickly changing climate, drought and wildfire have added to this amazing fish's peril. Native trout live in high-mountain streams. They live in stunningly beautiful wilderness areas where wildfire threat is ever present and ever increasing. Native trout are a perfect indicator species to tell us how we are doing as stewards of water and watersheds.

Jack's Creek ranges from about eight thousand to ten thousand feet in elevation, spilling through the mountains toward the Pecos River. It is a small stream that you can step across in many places without getting wet. The water runs cold and clear over rocks and submerged blowdown, and the banks are lined with wild grasses, wildflowers, and spruce trees that seem to reach out every time you cast. Once we stepped off the road, the human world vanished. It was magical.

Bow and arrow casts and dapping are the order of the day here unless you are fishing for tree limbs and stinging nettle. Toner caught the first one, a bright little fish with that bloody slash and speckles along the last half of its back. We admired him for a moment and set him free. Now it was my turn. Toner was using a pretty little yellow glass three-weight, and I had my honey-colored glass four-weight. Except for their lovely color, they made perfect sense for this kind of fishing. I made a mental note to consider getting a small-creek glass rod that is green or some other earth tone, and that brings me to the next point. This is total camo-up, use the vegetation as a backdrop, slow stalk, stealth fishing. Don't expect to catch much if you come here wearing your bright blue bonefish shirt, stomping in the water like a Yeti. Patience is the order of the day. This is Zen time.

A pretty little waterfall caused by a blowdown log had created a nice plunge pool that was about six feet long from head to tail. I fired a bow and arrow cast to the head of the pool and got a strike almost immediately . . . but missed it. Toner was right, these fish are hungry, opportunistic feeders not at all particular about fly selection. Red and yellow Humpy dry flies worked well for Gilas in southern New Mexico, and I was about to find the same state of affairs with Rio Grandes in the north. I cast again, and this time hooked into my first Pecos strain Rio Grande. It was another six-inch, brightly colored fish, and frankly I was thrilled to see him in my hand and then swimming away, back into the little pool where I found him.

I was wearing water shoes and just wet wading in the ice-cold stream. This worked fine until a yellow jacket found its way from the tangle of wild grasses lining the bank into my shoe and decided to use the bottom of my foot for target practice. (Expletives may have been used.) The good news is that the brightly colored insect escaped from my shoe without a scratch, and I discovered that soaking my foot in Jack's Creek was a wonderful, natural anesthetic. Toner asked if I was "allergic" and I said, "Not so far!" He let me know that he kept an EpiPen in his daypack for such occasions. I soon learned that yellow jackets are not a threatened species in these woods.

Toner found a run that contained several nice Rio Grandes, and he actually had room for a short back cast where the spruce trees opened up into a small meadow. I hung back and watched as he sent one nice drift after another past these fish, only to have them ignore whatever he sent their way. The fishing had become a challenge, and I suspect the openness of that spot in the creek made these fish a bit spooky or picky, but Toner wasn't going to quit on them, so I made my way past him and found another pretty pool to work.

We leapfrogged each other from pool to pool, picking up another fish here and there, with Toner catching two for my one, just as I had expected. I was learning a lot just watching the way he approached each situation, strategically and thoughtfully, and I found him to be a kind and patient teacher. I was starting to get the hang of it as we moved upstream, using the vegetation behind me and staying in the shadows to disguise my presence. This kind of fishing always requires patience, stealth, and breathless attention to carefully setting the hook so as to catch a trout and not a tree. It was wonderful.

July was the start of the monsoon season, and every now and then I could see a dark cloud drift into view in an opening of the tree canopy, and the sound of thunder rumbling in the near distance caught my attention from time to time. We could hear the thunder but not see the lightning. I looked at Toner and said, "Whatcha think?" He looked up and then said, "We're still good." We fished onward.

I always find spruce forests to be both beautiful and formidable. My homewaters are the streams and rivers of the Texas Hill Country, which roll across the skyline in an open, western sort of way. There's a lot of blue sky and sunshine, even in the canyons. But I find the deep hollows of Appalachia and the dark spruce forests of the high Rocky Mountains to contain a lingering spookiness, as if something surprising and potentially threatening might be inside the shadows. Lions and bears come to mind, but no tigers. The vegetation was so thick in these areas that often Toner and I could not see each other, and I had the feeling of being completely alone in this beautiful new landscape. I imagined a bear around every corner, but none materialized.

Don't get me wrong, I love the idea and reality of hiking in country where large predators dwell. I have walked mountain trails in Europe that were crisscrossed with the tracks and traces of wolves and brown bears. I've walked through African thorn bush and mopane forest where the tracks of lions, leopards, and elephant were common. And I remember hiking in my home state of Texas, in the Chisos Mountains with my daughter Megan and her partner Nick, when Nick pointed out that there was something wonderful and primal about walking in a place that still had wild things that can eat you. I love wilderness that is as intact as we can manage in the days of the Anthropocene, but I also know to pay attention to the shadows. It's only natural.

One of the constants I have experienced in this journey has been the quality of the human beings I've met and befriended as I seek native fish in their native waters. Toner is knowledgeable, kind, and giving. We fished together naturally, in that way that allows both kinship and solitude. We were both catching these bright little fish with some regularity, and each one was like a gift.

Just before the thunderclouds loomed close enough to cause us to snip off our flies and begin walking back downstream, I found a lovely little pool under a spruce branch, across from a rocky, moss-covered outcrop and under a small waterfall. I love this sort of challenge. It's a puzzle that needs to be sorted out. There were all these obstacles, plus the swirling currents and a slash of sunshine hitting the water from an opening in the forest. I could see a nice Rio Grande holding in the water on the left bank of the pool, just along the foam line. It was too far away to dap and there was too much sunlight silhouetting my position on the bank. So the trick was to make a bow and arrow cast to the top of the pool, then get a perfect drift, without giving away my position or snagging a tree. No worries.

To tell the truth, I was shocked when my first cast hit the mark perfectly and drifted without a hitch directly in the feeding path of my objective. In fact, I was so shocked that when the strike came, I hesitated, then overcompensated but somehow managed to retrieve my fly before the spruce trees did. I cast, drifted, and missed two more strikes. Idiot! I decided to rest the pool for a moment and just watch the creek tumble, the bees bumble, and the shadows morph into the images of tiny-eyed bears with big teeth. Then I tried again. Nothing. And again—nothing.

I could still see that pretty little Rio Grande, holding steadily in the current. I hadn't put him down yet. He seemed hungry. I'm not sure about you, but I have that affliction where I tell myself, "Just one more cast." Then, if I make that cast and miss the fish, I pause, breathe, and say, "Okay, maybe just one more." (I'm the same way when hiking and come to a turn in the trail.) So I took another shot, and this time he rose, struck, and turned, just as I raised my little golden rod and found him dancing at the end of the line. Let me tell you, no seven-pound bonefish I've caught in the Caribbean ever gave me more of a thrill than this six-inch cutthroat did. He was stunning, and the only thing that felt better than catching him was the act of slipping the barbless hook from his lip and watching him return to the relative safety of his homewaters.

I wish everyone could find the joy that I find in a six-inch fish that looks like a miracle and lives in one of the most beautiful places on Earth. Many of my fishing colleagues become so fixated on how big a fish is or how hard it fights that I sometimes feel they forget what makes the act of fishing so special. I have caught a few big fish. I've caught stripers and bluefish, pike and bass, bonefish and barracuda, and a few big trout as well, but truly, I have never loved any of those fish more than my first Gila, Apache, or Rio Grande trout, even if those trout were only eight or ten inches long.

There is something noble about a creature that can make its living in a freezing cold pool of rushing water next to a rock or under a tree in the middle of the wilderness. The adventure is in finding them in their home-waters, catching them, and then releasing them, except in memory. I will always remember my first wild, native Gila, Apache, Rio Grande, or brook trout. Size didn't matter.

⟞ ⟝

The next morning, we got an early start because we were driving up to Taos and the Rio Grande watershed. One thing every angler should learn is to think of entire watersheds, rather than simply rivers and streams. Everything is connected. It's like a human body. You can't save the body if any of its systems are allowed to collapse. A strong heart will not save collapsed lungs, and inflated lungs cannot feed a failing heart. Everything is interdependent on everything else.

The drive up from Santa Fe to Taos is vast, grand, and unforgettable. I'm a breakfast guy and crave protein in the morning, so another coffee and burrito stop was in order. I'm a Texan who loves my Tex-Mex food, but I also love New Mexican styles of the same cross-border culinary magic and must confess to a green chili addiction. There are worse things.

With the Sangre de Cristo Mountains to the east and the high plains to our west, we drove and talked of trout and trout streams, and elk and elk hunters, and wolves and people, and the meaning of life itself. You know, the usual stuff. Toner pointed out the canyon near Taos where he caught his first trout, and we spoke of how the place has changed for better or worse.

We spoke of mining, logging, and the perils and promise of any area that is beautiful enough to be loved to death. And when he spoke of these mountains and rivers and streams, I could hear the same devotion in his voice that I hear in my own when speaking of my beloved Texas Hill Country. We are all of the same tribe, simply different villages.

Our destination was Columbine Creek, in the Columbine-Hondo Wilderness of Carson National Forest, not far from the mountain town of Questa. Columbine Creek is within the Rio Grande watershed and is one of the battlegrounds of Rio Grande cutthroat trout recovery. The battle includes the usual suspects of challenges to native fish, but in this case, competition from invasive European brown trout might be the most urgent threat. Browns are more aggressive fish and therefore have the ability to take over all the best water for feeding, spawning, and holding over during the winter freeze. They are also piscivores that eat native fish and their eggs.

While I realize some anglers may argue "survival of the fittest," I will counter that this is not a natural migration of species. This is completely human caused. We broke it and we need to fix it, at least as much as we can. Once non-native species of plants, animals, fungi, or microbes are introduced, there is no getting rid of them completely; it's like a disease of the ecosystem, which can only be managed.

When we came to the end of the road and parked, I looked at the water in the creek and thought, "This is going to be easy." There are two reasons I came to this conclusion as we strung up our rods. First, the creek next to where we parked looked fairly wide, maybe between ten and fifteen feet, with nice pocket water, pools, and runs. Second, because I am an optimistic fool. As it turned out, this area was brown trout area and we had to hike a few miles into the wilderness before we came to the natural barrier that hopefully would keep the browns out of the Rio Grande restoration area.

The hike up was beautiful. Toner was accustomed to the elevation, and even though I must be careful with my asthmatic lungs and prior near-death experiences with elevation sickness, I did okay. The forest trail was lined in spruce trees and some of the tallest aspens I've seen in a while. Wildflowers sprang from the trailside, and the sound of the rushing creek mixed with birdsong added to the day. Steadily we climbed for about two miles, crossing the creek on V-shaped footbridges every so often until we reached a natural waterfall that was acting as a brown trout barrier . . . we hoped. Now the work began.

In all my years of hiking and fishing, this was the thickest thicket I have ever had to negotiate. All my daydreams about an easy day evaporated like raindrops in the desert. Adventure? Yes! Fun? Not really. Challenging? Yes! That's the word I will use. Challenging. The open little stream had transformed itself into a fast and freezing cold torrent with steep banks, thick brush, and so much blown-down timber that I was having Marine Corps flashbacks of the obstacle course on Parris Island.

At one point I found myself in a pool of fast, freezing cold water, the steep embankment I had descended on one side, another just like it on the opposite bank, and blown-down spruce trees forming a wooden cage around me. There was a nice pool just in front of me, but to reach it, I had to begin breaking off branches so I could make a hole in the blowdown that I could crawl through. I made it, and cast, and caught nothing. The only way out was to climb the hill, which I did, clinging to anything I could get a handhold on. When I made it back to the top of the embankment I had to rest, so I took a photograph of the stretch of the creek I had just fished, and it looked like a tangle of brush with no indication that there is a stream in there . . . somewhere.

Eventually I found a section with a wonderfully wide eddy of water on the edge of a run, and after a few poorly placed bow and arrow casts I managed a good drift and was into a fish. It was a good one, perhaps ten inches long, which on this small creek seemed like a trophy of sorts. I watched in excitement as it darted and danced and fought against my 6X tippet, but I still could not see its color or pattern until that last moment when I brought it to hand, and found myself holding a brown trout.

Buddhists will tell you that all suffering in our lives comes from "expectations." When our expectations are not met, we feel let down, and rather than accept the moment as it is, we resist it. I was having a moment of resistance. Toner had reappeared in the brush next to me and was watching as I lifted the pretty little foreign trout out of the stream and onto the bank where he bent down and unhooked it. "Eat more brown trout!" we said almost in unison as he added it to the stringer of browns he had already caught. This time, Toner's local knowledge and expertise had him catching five trout to my one, and all of them were browns except the sixth, which was our one and only Rio Grande strain cutthroat of the day in a stream that was intended to be a restoration water for these beautiful, magical, evermore rarefied trout. Toner looked at me and said, "It's worse than I thought. Last time I was here the ratio was four to one cutthroats for browns."

The brown trout have obviously taken all the best water and outcompeted the Rios. I felt a twinge of "suffering" when I realized that my expectation of catching the state fish of New Mexico in its native habitat and range was not going to be met, even in a stream that has been designated for their recovery, because humans had once again done something because they could, without ever asking themselves if they should. The Buddhists were right. Once I began to accept the state of affairs and became determined to help change them, my suffering began to vanish. Walking back through the aspen trees, I realized that this is the story of these fish and their relationship to us, but it doesn't have to be the way the story ends. There is hope, with action and determination. We can fix this, at least in part.

⁓

Driving back to Santa Fe, we stopped at the Canyon of the Rio Grande. We walked out onto the large metal bridge that spans its girth and looked down more than a thousand feet to the rushing river below. "It's a wonderful fishery," said Toner, "although it's not easy to access."

"What's in it?" I asked.

"Brown trout," he replied.

I let that sink in. The Rio Grande is no longer a Rio Grande trout water.

As we stood there, I noticed a telephone mounted on the platform overlooking the canyon. Next to it was a sign that read, "Suicide is not the answer. Call the Suicide Help Line." It's true, you know. Giving up is never the answer. Letting go, however, is. I can let go of my prior expectations that these New Mexican waters would be teeming with the state fish of New Mexico and, in doing so, end my suffering. But I do not need to surrender to that reality. I can be determined to do whatever I can to change minds and unite anglers and non-anglers behind the idea of creating a balance. Some waters are no doubt beyond repair. They will remain the new home for our European forced immigrants and transplanted rainbow trout, and a pure-blooded cutthroat may only rarely rise again in those rivers. But we can mitigate what we've done. We can create places where this fish can thrive and grow to its full size and capabilities rather than be marginalized in the tiniest of backwaters. I hope to live long enough to see that day.

After I left Santa Fe, I learned of the results of a couple of electroshock surveys conducted on two Rio Grande trout recovery creeks. In the first survey, not far from where Toner and I had fished, there were 185 brown trout and fewer than 30 Rio Grande cutthroats found in a half-mile stretch of the stream. The second survey found 300 brown trout and 3 Rio Grandes. The scale of the problem is staggering.

There is hope, and I believe there needs to be a sense of urgency and determination to return even just pieces of America to something closer to what it originally was—wild and free. There are places where good things are happening, and I am so enamored with this fish that I want to seek these places out and experience them myself. In the northern part of the Rio Grande cutthroat's range in Colorado, there is a native-only water—ironically, named Treasure Creek—within the watershed surrounding the Conejos. And in New Mexico a concerted effort is being made in the Rio Costilla watershed to restore Rio Grande cutthroat trout from the genetically pure brood stocks being raised at the Seven Springs Hatchery. This particular project is a cooperative effort of Turner Enterprises, the US Forest Service, New Mexico Department of Game and Fish, and TU.

I can envision a time when we achieve the fruits of what Toner Mitchell called "threshold thinking." As he put it, "If we were able to make things turn out so badly for native fish, so quickly, we can also reach that 'threshold' where we turn things around just as quickly." And it makes sense to me that the greatest nation on Earth can learn from past mistakes and adjust so that we end up with the best of both worlds; namely, places where non-natives that do not interbreed with natives will be allowed to persist, and places that contain a purely wild, native fish habitat. We can and should make this dream a reality.

One aspect of this journey that I have loved most is the opportunity to learn about the many homewaters of diverse parts of this beautiful country through the eyes of the people who fish them, know them, and love them. Toner is a perfect example of someone with this level of passion for the place he calls home.

We continued south toward Santa Fe as we chatted about life, writing life, fishing life, and green and red chili peppers. I was watching out for the possibility of spotting a herd of bighorn sheep that Toner said he almost always sees on that stretch of road. (This day turned out to be an exception.) That's when he told me about a time when his dad, Tony, dropped him and his brother off at the top of the Pecos Wilderness near Santa Barbara, and agreed to pick them up at the bottom of the wilderness near Cowles, a distance of thirty-five miles as the crow flies. Toner was twelve and his brother Mike was fourteen, and being young, exuberant "men," they ate all their food by the end of day three of the eight-day journey. For the remainder of the trip, they lived off the land, catching and eating wild trout every day. Quite an adventure for a couple of early teenagers. No wonder he loves this place so dearly! Here's the thing, this was forty-three years ago in the middle of the Pecos Wilderness. I asked Toner, "What kind of trout were you catching?"

He answered, "Mostly . . . browns."

Chapter Nine

Guadalupe Bass

San Marcos River, Texas

When rivers die, as so many have, so too dies an irretrievable part of the soul of each of the thousands of anglers who in their waters found deep, enduring life.

—*Nick Lyons*, Bright Rivers

I love my solitude and fishing alone. Until recently, I had never fished with anyone except for my daughter Megan and my friend Maggie. But then Megan grew up and moved to the United Kingdom and Maggie developed a healthy restlessness and moved to Boston, and suddenly I was *solo mio*, once again. It's okay . . . like I said, I enjoy my solitude in nature. But over the past few years I've begun this amazing adventure of finding my tribe. I have rejected all the darkness of a broken society and damaged world and attracted into my life the absolute best people on Earth. In part, this is what this journey is all about. When we surround ourselves with the things that matter, we discover the people who matter in our lives.

Kevin Hutchison and Kirk Deeter are such people. Kevin is, among other things, a wonderful Texas Hill Country fishing guide, author, photographer, philosopher, philanthropist, world traveler, drift boat comedian, husband, father, and, like me, a divergent. Kirk is, among other things, a wonderful Rocky Mountain fishing guide, editor of *Trout Magazine*, vice president for communications at Trout Unlimited, author, world traveler, husband, father, and, like me, a freethinker. Do you see a pattern here? They are both also my friends. I'm a lucky bastard.

The point here is that life is not a dress rehearsal. This is it. There's no going back, and we can only go forward so far before we run out of runway. And as my runway grows ever shorter, I'm not wasting another damn minute on society's bullshit. I'm determined to surround myself with kind, brave, intelligent people and clean, wild, natural landscapes. I intend to follow Henry David's path and suck out the marrow of every bone that life tosses my way.

Sometimes the voice of doubt whispers in my ear and tells me, "You should be playing along . . . pretending to be a part of the herd." It whispers, "What do you think you're doing?" And now and then I have allowed that voice to slip into my mind, and I ask myself, "Are you wasting time, being a bass bum?" "Is it morally wrong to choose the life of a starving artist?" But then I think about all of those hours, days, and years that I will never get back that I wasted on "normal jobs." When I think about all the time I've wasted in worthless meetings, working on meaningless reports, and listening to megalomaniacal morons pontificating about themselves, I realize that the most responsible thing I can do is to go fishing.

I have learned more from rivers and rising fish than I ever did in college. It seems fitting that all my college diplomas are in bubble wrap in the closet, but my fly rods are in my pickup truck, ready to go. That is a life worth living. That is why I tell that little voice to go to hell. You should too.

———◆———

When we launched Kevin's bright orange drift boat into the San Marcos River, I felt myself unwinding like the current. Everything was moving: the river, the boat, Kevin on the sticks, and Kirk and I casting streamers toward the banks, left and right. This was Kirk's first time going down a river that originated in the Texas Hills and casting a fly rod toward the endemic Guadalupe bass, the state fish of Texas, and my favorite fish on Earth. More than anything, I wanted Kirk to have a wonderful introduction to the place that Kevin and I call home.

We had barely floated a few turns in the river when Kirk hooked into his first Guadalupe bass, and it was a nice one of about a pound and a half. I could not have been more thrilled for my friend, and for me to be there for his first "Guad." Big smiles appeared all around; it was a moment I will always remember. Kirk released his first catch of the day after a quick photo to commemorate the moment. For me, the day was already a success. I was celebrating my fifty-ninth birthday with my friends on a beautiful river, and we were all smiling. Life doesn't get much better than that.

As I've said previously, I am in love with the state fish of Texas. You may ask, why am I so deeply in love with a bass? Well, in part it is because this endemic fish is a bellwether for how we are treating these canyons and hills that I adore. Also, it is a tough fish that never gets much bigger than three pounds but has an attitude like Muhammad Ali. They fight and scrap and leap and dive, and even after you catch them, they stare you down like "you owe them money." (My nod to Robert Rourke.) And if that were not enough, you can bet that you'll receive a face full of stream water whenever you release them, just for good measure. These fish act like Texas fish. They never surrender. They are born fighters. They are tough enough to survive in this often-harsh environment—if we let them.

Kevin knows these waters better than anyone I know, including me. And I've been fishing them for decades, so that might give you an idea of his knowledge and abilities. As we floated down the river, he warned us of each bump and rapid that was coming, and deftly maneuvered the boat from hazard to hazard, all the while calling out likely spots on each bank for lunker largemouth or gritty Guadalupes. He's also hilarious. His logo declares, "We'll Pick Your Buggers for You" and "In the Land of the Blind, the One-Eyed Man is King!" He jokes, "What has nine toes, one good eye, and rules the river?" We all laugh and keep casting. (Kevin lost a toe awhile back, but that's another story.) When I told him that I was going to write about our adventure, he said, "Just remember that 'ass hole' is two words." He jokes about himself with modest self-deprecation, but the truth is, he is one of the kindest people I know.

As happy as I was when Kirk caught his first Guadalupe bass, I was ecstatic as he caught his second, third, fourth . . . well, you get the picture. I think he caught half a dozen Guads and a few non-native yellow-bellied sunfish before I connected with and landed my first and only Guadalupe of the day. When it hit, I felt the usual metaphysical euphoria, except for some reason I swear I could hear the voice of Etta James singing, "At Last!" It had been a long dry spell for this imperfect Texan Buddha, but it was also good casting practice.

Right after I released that pretty Guadalupe bass, a red-tailed hawk flew close overhead and called out. My Marine Corps brother, Dave, had died almost two decades prior. He was a member of the Lakota tribe, and I had been with him as his "guide" during his pipe ceremony, just prior to his first Sundance. That year his chest was pierced with buffalo-bone spikes, and he completed his spiritual journey just before he died. The red-tailed hawk was his spirit animal. I knew this because we were brothers and I was his guide. I looked up to the hawk as I always do and said, "Hello Dave, it's good to see you again." I didn't explain this to my friends, and I'm not sure they even noticed me talking to the hawk. Rivers and raptors hold meaning for me. These Texas Hills are Dave's home and mine, and I don't think even death changes that. A spiritual homeland is our home eternally. Death is just a dimensional change of venue.

The San Marcos isn't really in the Texas Hill Country; it only begins there at its source, San Marcos Springs. The springs flow from the Edwards Aquifer along the Balcones Escarpment and pours pure H_2O out of fissures in the limestone bedrock. In doing so, the springs create a river that winds quick and clean through Texas's Blackland and Coastal Prairies toward the Gulf of Mexico. It's as far east as you're going to find Guadalupe bass, and due to the presence of invasive and non-native smallmouth bass, there is no guarantee that a fish you are holding is genetically pure. There are lessons to be learned here. All too often we are unaware of what we do when humanity seeks to manipulate nature. We are forever running with scissors with no one to warn us of what's coming next.

San Marcos Springs is home to several endemic endangered species including rare fish, amphibians, and aquatic plants that are found nowhere else on Earth. The headwaters of the San Marcos River are considered to be one of the most biologically diverse aquatic ecosystems known in the nation. The US Fish and Wildlife Service and Texas Parks and Wildlife have designated San Marcos Springs and Spring Lake as critical habitat.

It struck me directly in my bioregionalist outdoorsman soul when I noticed that the river has within its waters and along its banks so many invasive species of plants and animals. Non-native nutria, axis deer, and feral pigs negatively impact the riparian habitat, while non-native smallmouth bass interbreed with native Guadalupe bass, threatening entire populations with extirpation and extinction. But what stood out most to me as we floated down the river was the plethora of non-native and invasive plants, including bamboo, giant cane, water hyacinth, ligustrum, Chinaberry, and elephant ears. As anglers, hunters, hikers, or just anyone who loves the outdoors, we need to pay attention to what we are bringing home from the garden store. It matters.

This kind of fishing is active and keeps you moving; that's why I love it. As we drifted with the current, we kept firing cast after cast toward the bank, then we'd strip, strip, strip, then pick up and cast again. At one point we arrived at a long stretch of deep pools, and Kevin suggested we tie on a giant, snaky-looking yellow fly he had created to attract big fish from deep, dark places. Kirk and I began working these sea monsters along the banks, but there were no takers.

We switched back to rubber-legged woolly buggers and then back to white jighead flies, which tend to be irresistible to these bass. We caught most of our fish on white-colored flies, but olive was working too. The big thing with these fish is to get close to the bank and up against anything that looks like it will snag your fly. Then use short strips with infinitesimally brief hesitations, but always keep it moving. Make it look alive! As Kevin said, "These fish are killers, and they don't eat dead things!" Another bit of description I like is, "Fly fishing for trout is like ballet . . . this is a street fight." I guess the Marine warrior in me likes a street fight.

———◆———

There is archaeological evidence that the San Marcos Springs area may be one of the oldest continually human-inhabited sites in North America. The Coahuiltecan people first inhabited this area, followed by the Apache and Comanche. One set of excavations in the area uncovered Paleo Indian artifacts dating back perhaps nineteen thousand years, with confirmed evidence of human activity dating back at least eleven thousand years.

This was also a stop along the Chisholm Trail, the post–Civil War era path used to drive cattle from Texas ranches to Kansas railheads. The trail was established by Native American scout and Oklahoma rancher Black Beaver and his friend Jesse Chisholm. The multilingual and supremely brave Black Beaver was known for his amazing ability as a guide and translator for Union troops both during and after the War Between the States. Jesse Chisholm was an astute businessman who had the good sense to own the property at both ends of the trail that bears his name.

As we drifted downstream, we floated over the ruins of an old cotton gin that had been demolished with dynamite by its owner, and later we drifted past two more cotton gins that are still standing. The cotton gins of Martindale, Texas, were not operated under slave labor but rather by paid labor (albeit low paid) of Mexican American families, who were housed in "kit houses" from the Sears and Roebuck Company. We passed the only remaining kit house from that era, a one-room building with a chimney and no power or indoor plumbing. This area is steeped in history; some cheerful, some tragic, all innately human.

We drifted to a small island in the middle of the river and set up for a shore lunch. I don't care where you've fished or with whom, you are not going to have a better shore lunch than Kevin puts out. Yes, I get it that there is something special about a lunch cooked on a rocky sandbar with the fish you've just caught, but if you are not planning to catch and clean and cook, this is as good as it comes.

Just before laying out the food on the folding table that was complete with tablecloths, napkins, and a tiny salt and pepper shaker, Kevin said, "I'm sorry if you were expecting soggy gas station sandwiches." Then he laid out the barbecue pork ribs, liver pâté with a Texas zing, hummus with crackers, potato salad, orange slices, and fresh-baked blackberry brownies, all made by the man himself. (It made me hungry to write this.)

After lunch Kirk looked at me and said, "I knew I should stop eating but it was just too good!"

I smiled and placed my hand on my extended midsection and said, "I'm there with you brother. I just hope the boat will hold our weight!"

When the boat launched, I kept it to myself that all the good food had made me sleepy. I had the bow seat this time, and we began the quick-shot, strip, strip, another shot, rapid-fire style of casting that this kind of fishing demands, and that I so dearly love. I had not caught a thing on the first half of the trip, but I did enjoy watching my buddy Kirk haul one fish in after another. I finally picked up that Guadalupe bass I mentioned earlier, and then a couple of big, meaty sunfish, all in pre-spawning coloration. I noticed that Kirk seemed to be casting less frequently after lunch, and I wondered if he was just trying to be nice to me or if he was sleepy, too. It was peaceful just drifting down the river, casting methodically, catching occasionally. Even the fish seemed to be a bit drowsier after lunch.

We passed a tree that had clear signs of both beaver and nutria damage on it, and Kevin said there were a lot of beavers in the river but you'd only see them if you were drifting at night. I've never drifted a river at night, but I'd sure like to try it under a blanket of stars and a bright beautiful moon. I've also never seen a beaver on any Hill Country river, even though I know they're supposed to be here.

Kevin and I had hatched a plan prior to the float that I was going to begin speaking of myself in the third person and keep doing it until I got a reaction from Kirk. It was Kevin's job to play along and give Kirk sideways glances like, "Do you see what a weirdo he is?" So I was supposed to say, "Oh, Steve just made a great cast," or "Steve caught a nice fish," or "Steve likes the look of that spot on the river." But the problem was that I just couldn't sell it because Steve *wasn't* catching all the "nice fish," Kirk was. I gave it a try, but it never caught on. After a short while we told Kirk what I was up to, and Kevin smiled, looked at me, and said, "You've got to commit to it if you're gonna sell it!" (Steve knew he was right. Steve didn't commit. Steve regrets that.)

I love fishing. I am addicted to fly fishing and can't imagine doing anything else. But I started out like most kids do in the American South, with a worm on a hook affixed to a simple nylon line, suspended from a cane pole. As I got older, I graduated to a spinning rig with what might now be called "vintage lures." There was the big three of Mepps, Shyster, and the Daredevil spoon with its red-and-white stripes and little devil face on it. I caught a lot of bass and bluegills with those, and we ate more than a few. But now I practice catch and release fishing only.

I use single barbless hooks and keep the fish in the water, releasing them as quickly as possible. The Zen-like pointlessness of it all in the eyes of the uninitiated is, for me, exactly the point. There is absolutely nothing wrong with the legal, ethical harvesting of fish for food; I've been there and done that. But these days I fish for the fishing, not the fish. These days, it's about shared moments and lasting friendships.

The fishing had slowed. I missed a few strikes because I wasn't paying attention. I was too busy enjoying the conversation as we floated down the river. This is the best thing of all, the sharing of the outdoors, the comradery, and those deep, deep conversations that may not happen at a coffee shop but almost always do when you're drinking from a tin cup at a campfire. As Kirk once said, "It ain't about pulling on fish . . . at all. It's about everything else." Amen brother. Amen.

We came to a low metal bridge that showed the telltale signs of flooding, with gobs of woody debris suspended from its underbelly. Kevin paddled the boat to the shoreline just prior to reaching the bridge, asked us to step off and meet him on the other side, unhooked his casting seats so as to lower the profile of the boat, and then deftly did "the limbo" as he slid under the bridge without becoming part of the debris. One gets the sense that he's done this before. Had I been in charge, we'd have become one with the aforementioned woody debris.

Once we were back in the boat Kevin said, "Most people take out at that bridge, but we're going a bit farther downriver, so everything after this is just icing on the cake." And it was nice to have the extra mile or so of drift time and casting. For a long time I kept casting, but I had that feeling you get when it seems that the fish gods have flipped the switch and there was going to be more casting than catching. I didn't care. It was methodically peaceful. Cast, strip, strip, strip, cast. It was perfect, just as it was.

We all grew quiet, just casting and watching the riverbank slide by us or, more correctly, watching us slide by the riverbank. And at one point I noticed Kirk seemed extra quiet, and he wasn't casting as often. I wondered if everything was okay, but I didn't say anything until we were back on land and Kevin was winching his boat back onto the trailer.

I could see Kirk was deep in thought, and I was hoping it was a good thing. In time he told me. He said, "If there were times when I seemed quiet, that's when I was thinking of my best friend from high school; his name was Cy. We both moved to Pennsylvania to swim at Germantown Academy our junior years, me from Wisconsin, he from New Braunfels, Texas. I went to Michigan. He went to the Air Force Academy. He cross-commissioned after graduation and became a Marine Corps helicopter pilot. He suffered from depression, and I did not know it at the time . . . he was tough. But he committed suicide somewhere around here, and that had been a yoke hanging around me for almost thirty years. It was important to fish here . . . and it was important and fateful to do so with a Marine. I feel like a big weight got lifted off my shoulders today. And I think we had a good day because Cy wanted us to. That's Semper Fi from Heaven."

I understood all too well. I had once been that Marine who stayed strong in front of everyone but inside wondered if I could go on. The nightmares became so bad that I did not think I could stand them anymore. I was afraid to sleep, and in the end it was a combination of focusing on my love for my family, hypnotherapy, and fly fishing that saved my life. Fly fishing and nature are tonics that remind us that everything is impermanent, and that in time, joy returns. We need nature; nature doesn't need us.

Unlike the Guadalupe bass of the Llano, Upper Guadalupe, Pedernales, and Blanco Rivers, and parts of the Colorado River, the fish we caught in the San Marcos may have been hybrids, even if they looked like pure "Guads." This is because the non-native and invasive smallmouth bass that Texas Parks and Wildlife once stocked into the San Marcos watershed are still present and therefore able to interbreed with our native Guadalupe bass. Only a fin-snip DNA test can tell for sure. We've created a lot of damage, even with the best of intentions. So I guess I will amend what I said in the last paragraph. Nature does need us, to fix what we've broken, as best we can.

In the end as in the beginning, I was celebrating my fifty-ninth birthday with my friends on a beautiful river, and we were all smiling. Life doesn't get much better than that, and I would not trade a moment. I'm not sure that fishing has all that much to do with catching fish anymore. I think my buddy Kirk is right: "It ain't all about pulling on fish lips; it's about everything else." It seems that if you're really lucky and you set out to cast for natives, you might also connect with your tribe. I know I have, and I can't think of a better birthday gift.

Chapter Ten

Lahontan Cutthroat Trout

Pyramid Lake, Nevada

Poets talk about "spots of time," but it is really the fishermen who experience eternity compressed into a moment. No one can tell what a spot of time is until suddenly the whole world is a fish, and the fish is gone.
—*Norman Mclean*, Weather

PANDEMIC IS ONE OF THOSE WORDS THAT MOST PEOPLE ONLY SEE IN THE title of horror movies and dystopian science fiction novels, but I had been considering its inevitability during many years as a US Marine and disaster preparedness professional. And now it was coming, and I had tickets to fly to Reno via Los Angeles just as things were heating up. Although I had planned this trip for months, I had begun to consider the wisdom of flying anywhere after things spread from China to Korea to Italy and beyond, but I could hear the words of my father ringing in my head saying, "You've got to keep on living, Steve." Yes, I understand the irony of those words when what you are doing might include risking your life, but I've done that before. People risk their lives all the time for something as silly as a job. At least I was doing it for a good reason. I was going fishing.

The plane to Los Angeles was nearly empty, and that gave me a false sense of security, until I arrived at LAX to find a glut of humanity, some wearing surgical masks, some wearing gloves, and some coughing and sneezing, oblivious of everyone around them. The plane to Reno was packed full, and I pulled my Buff up over my mouth, noticing every cough and clearing of the throat around me. Recycled air, carrying who-knows-what, left me wondering if my improvised cotton mask was worthless.

Since my time in the Marines, I've loathed enclosed spaces filled with people. Airports, airplanes, shopping malls, and movie theaters are not in my comfort zone. I need space between me and the masses, so I can take charge of my own destiny if the fecal material ever hits the fan. Today I am a writer and outdoorsman who is so much happier since I left the other life behind me. But once upon a time I was a warrior, and I still know the value of that mindset.

It all seemed surreal. The scene at the airport felt like a flashback clip from *Blade Runner*. My arrival in Reno unfolded like a distorted dream. Slot machines lined the airport passageways, and a tattooed woman hit me up for $20 in exchange for a "scratcher" because she had gambled all her money away. She claimed to need "bus fare." Why does every streetside hustler anywhere in the world always seem to "need bus fare?" Where in the hell are they all going?

While I was waiting to catch the shuttle from the airport to the hotel, I watched as two old gals in wheelchairs were rolled up next to me, chatting back and forth in those gravelly voices that chain smokers accumulate over the years. They were both covered in bling, with oversized bejeweled sunglasses and monstrous multicolored handbags. It was obvious that both women were there to play the odds. Who am I to judge? In my own way, so was I. They would use the cash they had stuffed in those humongous bags, and I would use the Orvis eight-weight rod that I had in the metal tube under my arm. Either way, we had chosen to travel through a potential pandemic so that we could make memories. As I got on the shuttle bus, I noticed a taxi driving by with the words, "rivers wanted" in black letters across the bumper. It would be fitting for me on most trips, but this time I was here to find a lake.

It's worth sharing at this point that I despise casinos, but the hotel and casino packages were the best deals in Reno, so that is where I'd be staying for the next two nights. For me, casinos and clowns are both creepy. It's unnerving to see so many people sitting at slot machines mesmerized by the blaring sounds and flashing lights, pumping money they can ill afford into the slots and pushing the buttons like drug-addicted lab monkeys hoping to catch that one big score. I'm not judging as much as making a judgment, that it doesn't seem healthy or wise to spend your time and money smoking, drinking, and gambling. Then again, I guess casino gamblers could say the same thing about me. After all, I had just spent a good amount of money to travel a long distance and risk my health so I could stand in freezing cold water from sunrise to sunset in the hope of catching a fish that I planned to immediately release. We all have our own way of gambling. Perhaps it is the subtle difference between spending and investing. Perspective is everything.

The First Day

I traveled all this way to meet my friend Cinda Howard and fish for the state fish of Nevada, the Lahontan cutthroat trout. Not all that long ago the Lahontan cutthroat was thought to be extinct. In 1979, fish that turned out to be a genetic match to the original Pyramid Lake strain were discovered in a small stream on Pilot Peak near the Nevada-Utah border. As this was outside their historical range, it was ironically apparent that while the actions of many humans had led to the Lahontan cutthroat's extirpation from its home range, the actions of one human transporting a tiny remnant population far from its original home saved it from extinction. The impact of humanity upon nature both collectively and individually is exponential.

Pyramid Lake is a remnant of a much bigger prehistoric inland body of water that once stretched across the Great Basin of Nevada, California, Idaho, and western Utah. It is a terminal lake, meaning that it is part of a topography that prevents drainage to the oceans, and as such acts as the final basin for water flowing from Lake Tahoe down the Truckee River and into the geologic sink that forms the lake. It is surrounded by mountain ranges including the Virginia Mountains to the west, Pah Rah Range to the south, and the Fox Mountains to the north. And all this is contained within the borders of the Northern Paiute reservation lands. It is a vast and starkly beautiful landscape of mountains, high prairies, and deserts, and it is easy to see why the Paiute people chose to call this home.

We arrived before dawn, and I was struck by the ancient beauty of this massive body of alkaline water. This is the place where anglers wade out to ladders that are set and waiting for them in four feet of water; where part of the challenge is to cast as far as you can so that your fly reaches across the submerged drop-off where these massive trout search for food. We all rigged up quickly, or more accurately, were rigged up by the guides that Cinda had arranged for us. Rob, Ryan, and Chris of Fly Fish Pyramid Lake took good care of us, and if I ever went again, I'd go with them.

You can tell a lot about a person from the company they keep, and Cinda had gathered a wonderful group of fly-fishing friends. I was fortunate to be included in this group of friends, though I was undoubtedly the least talented angler in the lot. There was Chris, who I'd describe as deeply intelligent, compassionate, and well read. He seemed to effortlessly send his line over the horizon as if it were the simplest thing to do. And then there was Adam, who caught more fish than anyone, and who never gave up trying. Patti and Ned were fun to watch because of their wonderful partnership and how they cheered for each other. My friend Cinda's talent as a fly fisher and guide is only surpassed by her kindness, honesty, and courage. I will never forget the kindness she has shown me. I will never cease to seek ways to repay it.

I have traveled to many places around the world but have never been anywhere that was quite like Pyramid Lake. The closest I can recollect was my time at Lake Naivasha in the Rift Valley of Kenya. But Pyramid Lake lacks flamingos, crocodiles, and a volcano, and Lake Naivasha lacks the massive cutthroat trout that fight like striped bass and look like desert sunsets. Still, both places are marked by alkaline shores and the uneven hand of humanity. As I looked toward each vast water, first as a young man in Africa and then later as an older man in Nevada, I wished with all my heart that I could have seen them as they were before the dawn of humanity. Every strip mall was once a forest, meadow, wetland, or desert arroyo.

We began casting before sunrise. There was just enough illumination from the full moon over my shoulder to make out the strike indicator as it bobbed and slipped over the silky chop. And then a sliver of golden-yellow light peeked over the mountains and the wind picked up, blowing brisk and cold into my face, and I began to see the lake come alive with leaping and rolling fish that were likely between four and fourteen pounds but looked more like forty pounds as they leapt like dolphins. One of the guides hollered, "Here they come!" And we all recast our lines in unison, not because we had to, but because it just felt right.

Adam was on the ladder next to me in line, and it seemed almost instantaneous when the fish began leaping and he connected. These are not the small stream cutthroats to which I've grown accustomed. These fish put a serious bend in an eight-weight rod. I stopped fishing for a moment to congratulate Adam for his first Lahontan. We smiled big mutual smiles and then I cast again.

By this time, we were seeing big trout rolling almost up to our ladders. Farther out they continued to leap into the air or porpoise with their massive shoulders glistening in the now sunlit waters. Soon there was another hook-up and then another, and then a fish rolled in front of me, my indicator went under the surface, and I set the hook without thinking . . . just as we always should. Instinct is faster than choice.

I'm not sure that I can adequately express the joy I felt when I held my first Lahontan cutthroat in my hand. These are the moments when you learn things about yourself and others. You learn who your friends are and what you value. To the second point, it was not the size of the fish I was in love with, it was the fish itself. To the first point, I suddenly found Cinda standing beside me with her camera in her hand and a joyful smile on her face. We hugged and celebrated, and I will never forget watching that beautiful wild fish as it swam away. Moments before, Cinda was fishing from her own ladder, which was several positions away from me, and yet she knew what this moment meant to me, and there she was. That, my friends, is kindness. We need so much more of that in this upside-down world. Don't you think?

This electric pandemonium continued up and down our ranks until it stopped, suddenly, like breathing does at the end of life. It's always like that, the end of things. It's always like someone flipped a switch. And whenever this happens, in fishing or in life, I am left with nothing but memories and that feeling you can almost taste. I think it is the feeling of silence. I think it is the feeling of stillness. It's like realizing all at once that the snow has melted in the sunshine and wondering where it went. We cast again, hopeful in unison.

In a way, fly-fishing Pyramid Lake felt like combat. It contained long moments of solitude and peace mixed with brief moments of utter urgency. I'm not sure which of those moments were more meaningful to me—perhaps both. The game goes like this: You cast as far as you can and then squint your eyes into the sunlight until you locate your strike indicator. Suspended below it are two barbless size 14 nymphs. (Yes, twenty-pound fish are eating tiny bugs. It's not so crazy. We eat chocolate drops.) Once your indicator goes under the surface, you set the hook by raising your rod and stripping line at the same time. You "cross their eyes," as one of the guides said. Then you get them on the reel if you can, and if not, you strip the line as fast as you can.

These fish are powerful, and they bear down like a ten-pound striper or a twenty-pound imaginary bluegill . . . take your pick. Once hooked they either run straight at you or run straight away. Either way, you are reacting to the fish's choices and using more finesse than brute force. The fish is stronger than your tippet. You've got to wear it down, not muscle it in.

During one of those long stretches of peacefully watching the little yellow bobber, my mind wandered back in time and forward again. I began to muse about how no matter how much we call it a "strike indicator," it's still just a bobber. I guess it's the difference between saying caviar and fish eggs. I prefer to keep my pinky finger down. After all, I began fishing like so many other sons of the South, with a cane pole and a hook and bobber attached by a length of monofilament to the end of the cane. In a way, it was our version of Tenkara.

Those were magical times for me and my dad, as we pulled everything from bass to bowfin out of a gator hole. Nowadays, I only fish with barbless hooks and a catch and release mentality. Still, to paraphrase John Gierach, we all have a Zebco spincaster and a stringer full of panfish hiding somewhere in our youthful past. I know I do. Don't you?

I was definitely one of the low scorers on the leaderboard that morning, but I was happy with the two fish I had caught and released, and the several

I had hooked and lost. I was still learning, and when you're learning, you need to do it gratefully. Just let it happen. Besides, I had told myself that even if I only caught a single Lahontan on this trip, I'd be thrilled, and I had caught and landed two in the first hour. Things went silent for me after that, although I noticed that Adam, Cinda, and Chris were continuing to catch fish. It was fine.

I was settling into the rhythm of things, casting and drifting, drifting, and casting, and always watching my bobber. (I mean, strike indicator.) It felt right. I felt privileged. I felt happy for each fish anyone caught and released. There was a strange sense of solitude and community in this kind of fishing, like nothing I'd ever experienced before. One of the great unexpected outcomes of setting out on this yearlong journey across America to fly-fish with friends, old and new, in the pursuit of native fish, has been that every place and style of fishing has been different. Through the eyes of the people who live there, I have experienced every native fish and every local fisher's adaptation to that place and time. It has been an adventure in learning.

Having spent most of my life fishing alone, it's been novel and wonderful to experience fishing with others, and Pyramid Lake is the most "others" I've ever fished with, let alone the only time I've ever fished from the top of a stepladder. And while I enjoy fishing with friends, I still find being guided a little awkward. After all, my dad raised me as a single parent, and in doing so, he raised me to be self-sufficient. I've been cooking and cleaning up after myself since I was a kid, so when one of the guides waded up to my ladder and asked, "Do you want cheddar or Monterey-Jack cheese on your burger?" I replied, "Jack, please." But I wanted to say, "Do you need any help with that?"

Our shore lunch was great. The burger tasted like juicy carnivorous nirvana, and the company and scenery were both simply perfect. For a little while, it really helped me forget the looming pandemic. I sat there in my folding chair looking out across that massive ancient lake toward the brightly lit and snowcapped mountains, and watching a horned lark as it watched me. I thought to myself, "I could live with this . . . I hope."

Any teacher knows that the class directly after lunch is a tough one to teach. Kids get sleepy; that's true with big kids too. We had been traveling the day before, and then we were up and on the water before dawn. After lunch we found that a few of our intrepid anglers had fallen asleep in their folding chairs. Cinda took a photo of the boys out cold, one with his unlit cigar perched in his hand, as if he were just about to light it before the sandman arrived. Perhaps he was dreaming of smoking a fine Havana. I don't know.

Back at our ladders we all began to lean into it, casting, allowing the indicator to float as long as we could, adjusting and mending to get the longest drift possible before needing to cast again. Like all fishing, you can't catch fish if your flies aren't in the water. Most of us were fishing a floating line with an indicator and two weighted size 14 to 16 nymphs suspended about seven feet and three feet, respectively, below the surface. They had local names like "Albino Wino" and the "Maholo Midge." A few people were throwing fast-sinking lines with streamers like the "Midnight Cowboy" or "Pyramid Lake Woolly Bugger." I chose to stick to my nymph and bobber rig. It was different from what I was used to, and that made it special.

After lunch I had decided to move from my morning position in the cove to a ladder that was set up near the point, on the opposite end of our casting area. During lunch chitchat I heard a guide mention that around 1:30 p.m. he expected the Lahontan cutthroats to come around that point and into the cove, and since I wasn't asleep, I got myself over there as quickly as I could. It should come as no surprise that the guide was right. Cinda was to my left, closer to the point than me, but I was second in line when her rod doubled over, and she began to fight a big fish. I cheered her on, alternating between glancing at her battle and watching my indicator; that's when it went under, and I set the hook. It was a big one! I looked up and over just long enough to see that Cinda had landed her fish and that rods were bending all along the line. The bite and the fight were on!

I have to admit that I gave up on the idea of prayer a long time ago. (Although I did catch myself once silently offering a prayer that my home air conditioner was not severely broken in the middle of a sweltering Texas summer. It wasn't. Make of that what you will.) I'm happy for anyone who finds the act of prayer comforting, but I've experienced enough things in my life to where I've realized that every kid in every foxhole is praying to live through the battle and yet, some of them won't. Still, I didn't want to lose this fish, and I might have been praying to someone or something. In fact, I might have even been bargaining with the fish, as in, "Just let me bring you to the net and I promise I will let you go quickly, and I will be thankful forever!" Did I mention that I had given up on prayer?

Cinda and one of the guides appeared just behind my ladder, Cinda cheering me on and the guide at the ready with his big net. I tried again and again to wear that fish down, keeping the pressure on, but letting it run when it chose to run. Every now and then Cinda or the guide stopped me from making a tactical error and I would adjust with their expert advice. I was learning fast, but not fast enough. I took my eye off the fish just long enough for it to zig while I zagged, and after a long and protracted battle the line went slack. I watched that Lahontan swim away just as the guide said, "That one was between ten and twelve pounds." Did I mention that I hadn't completely given up on cussing?

After I lost that big fish, I began to wonder what my disappointment said about me. After all, I have always been the angler who could have a perfectly good day of casting while catching nothing. I have often traveled long distances only to feel supremely happy when I caught an eight-inch native fish from some spring-fed headwater that was only four feet wide. I had already caught a couple of four- to five-pound trout that I was thrilled to land and release. Why had I allowed myself to get caught up in this idea of a truly "big" fish now? In a way, I was more disappointed in myself for being upset about losing that ten-pound fish. So I picked my head up, cast my line out, and resumed bobber watching.

People were catching fish all around me, and it didn't take long for me to get back into the moment and manage to miss a few strikes before I hooked into another Lahontan almost as big as the fish I lost earlier. This time I wasn't going to allow myself to get distracted. I could sense that a guide had come up behind me, and I heard the voice of my buddy Cinda cheering me on, but I kept my head in the game, reeling or stripping line as fast as I could when the fish came at me and letting it out when it ran for the center of the lake. I kept my rod tip up and the pressure on, but not so much pressure as to break the tippet. And in a moment that seemed like an eternity, it was in the net and then in my arms as Cinda took a photo.

When I watched that beautiful trout swim away, I heard the guide say, "That one went about nine pounds." Here's the cool thing. I didn't care. I was back to being me again. All I cared about was that this place and that fish were beautiful. Did I mention that I will never give up being grateful?

The Second Day

We arrived at the lake once again before sunrise, but the morning was much colder than the day before. Although I wasn't experiencing it, some of the crew said that there was ice forming inside their guides. I think I felt ice forming inside my bones. It felt different on this second morning, as if the world were shifting somehow. I thought it might just be the weather, and I had heard that whenever the weather is worse the fishing gets better, so I was hopeful.

I waded out to the same ladder from which I had caught my first two fish the day before, then stripped out some line and cast out into the pearly darkness. It took a moment for me to find my indicator floating on the surface of the lake beneath that charcoal-colored sky and ever dimming starlight. We were all silently standing there, just looking out and following our bobbers with our eyes and waiting for the first sign of daybreak or a fish strike, whichever came first. All I could hear was the occasional and distant murmur of the guides conversing somewhere along the shoreline and the lapping of the lake's chop across my legs. It was peaceful, and cold.

I'm grateful that I came to Pyramid Lake and experienced it, this one time. I was fishing with people, including my friend Cinda, who come year after year, but I could tell even on my second day that this would most likely be my one and only trip to Pyramid Lake. If I ever had the chance to fish for Lahontan cutthroat trout again, I wanted it to be on a small mountain stream where the Lahontans are wild, genetically genuine, sustainable, and spawning in nature, not in a hatchery.

Pyramid Lake Lahontan cutthroat trout are all spawned in a hatchery, which means that even though these are native fish in their original homewaters, it is an artificial fishery. If there is any spawning (which is unlikely), it would have to occur in the lower three miles of river due to the water diversion dams along the Truckee River. These dams effectively keep the trout from spawning naturally, as they did when John C. Fremont and Kit Carson ascended the Truckee River in 1844 and named it the "Salmon Trout River" because of the massive Lahontan cutthroat trout they witnessed running upriver to spawn. I definitely want to see the return of those days.

As my friend Brett Prettyman of Trout Unlimited once told me, "There is a big disconnect in the public's understanding that the existence of thirty-pound hatchery-raised Lahontan cutthroat trout in Pyramid Lake does not equate to success in restoring the subspecies to a naturally sustainable and resilient, wild population." Working in tandem with his counterpart at the US Fish and Wildlife Service and various other stakeholders, Trout Unlimited fisheries biologist Jason Barnes works to coordinate genetic rescue, habitat restoration and preservation, and, most of all, to build partnerships with private landowners who control much of the critical habitats including aquatic and riparian zones. Jason told me, "There are somewhere between seventy to seventy-two distinct populations of wild Lahontan cutthroat trout within their historical range. All but one is in trouble from invasive, non-native fish. Non-native rainbow trout cause hybridization, and brook trout simply outcompete the natives for the best habitat."

Prior to my arrival, I had researched the life history of the Lahontan cutthroat trout. Still, once I was on the lake catching these magnificent fish, I noticed an unexpected feeling coming over me. Deep down inside, I couldn't shake the realization that this was an artificial fishery. It felt bittersweet, like hunting kudu that were raised in a zoo. We have African kudu roaming the hills of Texas on game ranches. When I decided to hunt kudu, I flew to Africa and hunted hard for them with Bushman trackers on a massive ranch that had no fences. Elephants, lions, and leopards wandered freely across that landscape, and it took me thirteen days of hard hunting to finally collect my spiral-horned bull. I would not have it any other way. And while fishing Pyramid Lake for these wonderful native fish wasn't easy by a long shot, I could not help but wish that the fish I had caught and released were truly wild and free.

In a way, I think this trip contained many lessons for me. I learned about trout, rivers, watersheds, and lakes. I learned about humans and the healthy and unhealthy choices we make. And I had plenty of quiet time to consider the life lessons that silence can teach. Solitude and silence have much to teach us if we listen.

The morning of the second day melted from dark to light as the sun began to glow over the rim of mountains. The water transformed into broken glass prisms of light, almost blinding, taking away my ability to watch my indicator, even with my best sunglasses affixed firmly to my frozen face. It was glorious. It was the kind of crisp, cold, sunlit daybreak that makes you grateful to be alive. It was the kind of moment that demands you breathe a silent word of gratitude, no matter if you believe in any deity, or not. In that moment, standing there in that cold, cold water and listening to the sound of the windswept lake lapping on the shore, I was supremely happy to be alive . . . fish or no fish.

For a long time, there were no fish. We all stood silently in the morning light, casting and watching as our indicators drifted from left to right, and from deep to shallow water. The rules of the game are simple here. Each ladder is evenly spaced at a distance that seemed steeped in tradition but had no other rationale. You cast within the wedge of water in front of you. During the long periods between strikes you have three options: boredom, meditation, or philosophical meanderings. I chose to alternate between the last two, and only rarely drifted into boredom.

Much of the morning slipped by without a single fish being caught. My groggy morning optimism gave way to a feeling that the day was going to have more fishing and less catching than I had originally hoped. I was okay with that. The fishing had its own charms, and if nobody was catching anything today . . . well, we were all in this together.

Of course, life has a way of slapping you in the face as soon as you get to thinking you've got it all figured out, and the instant that thought came to mind the wind shifted and blew it away. Adam raised his rod tip and was into a fish. I cheered. Then Cinda raised her rod tip and the fight was on, and I cheered for her, too. Since my ladder was between their ladders, I stopped cheering and began focusing a laser beam of attention on my little orange bobber of hope. It never even wobbled. It never even bobbed.

It didn't zig or zag. It just sat there on the water, mocking me as one rod after another connected with a fish and cheers of excitement floated all along the line. By the end of that frenzy everyone in my group had caught at least one fish, except me. I felt like Charlie Brown. I felt like a lunkhead.

Don't get me wrong, I was happy for everyone. But I noticed that when the going got tough, my fishing Buddha-self was a little lacking in inner peace. I mean, I've always believed that when it comes to fishing, size doesn't matter. I despise and reject competitive fishing. To my mind, a day of fishing without catching is still a perfect day. Why then, as the day progressed and my friends caught fish after fish and I did not get so much as a nibble, did I allow myself to lose my sense of joy? Had we all shared a fishless day I would have chalked it up to the vagaries of fishing, but I remained the only fishless person in the group. Why, I asked, was I allowing this fact to leave me feeling unsettled?

Life gives us all so many chances to learn and grow. As an imperfect Texan Buddha, I am always learning, growing, and challenging myself. Sometimes the challenge has been climbing a mountain, or deep diving a coral reef. Sometimes the challenge has been running a marathon or mastering a martial arts kata. And sometimes the challenge was watching a bobber that refused to bob, while all around me there was joyful celebration of bobber after bobber that did bob. And then, as if out of nowhere, I felt at peace again, not because I began catching fish—because I didn't—but because I realized it really didn't matter. Just the day before, I had said to myself, "If I can only catch one fish in the two days, I will feel successful." In fact, I had caught three fish on my first day. I was lucky, and there was nowhere else I'd rather be than right there, standing in that cold water, celebrating with my friends. Life was good.

Every adventure I have ever undertaken has contained many elements that all came together and made the experience memorable. There isn't any reason to boil things down to the "one thing that was best" about a trip. But just to make a point, I want to share that if I were put on the spot and forced to come up with the one thing that made this adventure utterly unique, I'd say it was the comradery.

When I first learned of this unusual place called Pyramid Lake, where anglers stood on stepladders and cast eight-weight lines at ten-pound cutthroat trout, it sounded somewhere between surreal and ridiculous to me. And I wondered if it might cause anglers to become more competitive and combative, which to me misses the whole point. I wondered if a line of anglers all casting in the hopes of a thirty-pound fish might become zombie-like and turn something beautiful into the circus of the casino, casting their lines as if pulling a lever on an old-time slot machine. But that didn't happen. Instead, I saw that what was driving each of us was not greed but passion. Each of us passionately loved and respected the water, landscape, fishing, fish, and, most of all, the comradery. It was an example of exactly what our "civilization" desperately needs. It was a combination of solitude and community. It was supportive, generous, kind, light-hearted, joyful, and, most of all, fun.

At one point in the day when everyone was catching fish except me, Cinda landed a big one, and it was such a wonderful experience for her, and us, that she began singing the refrain to the song, "Who Let the Dogs Out," but had changed it to "Who let the trout out . . . woof, woof!" Soon each of us got the song stuck in our heads, and one by one found ourselves compulsively and repeatedly singing that single lyric as we fished. Realizing what was happening, we all had a good laugh up and down the line and I said, "Thanks Cinda! Now that song is stuck in all of our heads."

I decided to exact my friendly retribution and called out, "Hey Cinda!" She looked over from her ladder and smiled as I began to sing that maddening earworm titled "Baby Shark," but with a slight lyric modification. "Baby trout . . . doot, do doot, do, do, baby trout. . . ." (Tell the truth, it's stuck in your head now, too. You're welcome!) Before long, you could hear almost everyone up and down the line mindlessly muttering the "Baby Trout" song. I had unleashed a monster. I tried to get it out of my own head but only managed to add Monty Python's "Lumberjack Song" to my inner soundtrack. Yes, if I had to choose anything that made this fishing trip special, it wasn't the fishing, it was the friendship. We need so much more of that in this crazy, upside-down world. Nature teaches, heals, and unites.

The night before, I had heard from my wife that our daughter, who lives in England, was feeling ill. Her illness was affecting her to the degree that she was going to call the National Health Service Hotline to speak with a doctor. I must confess that this was lingering on my mind whenever it drifted from meditative to philosophical. At the lunch break I decided to turn on my cell phone, just to check my messages. I found a message that stopped time for me. It read that my daughter had been diagnosed as "Presumptive Positive for COVID-19." I could see in the message that she was assuring her mother and me that she would be fine and was ordered to be in home quarantine. (I would later learn that she was seriously ill, but thankfully, she did recover.)

As you might imagine, fishing wasn't the first thing on my mind that afternoon. Still, I knew what my daughter would say if she were standing there in that moment: "Go fish, Dad!" Did I mention that she is both wise and tough? It's a wonderful thing for a dad when one of his heroes is his daughter. I went fishing. After all, there was nothing I could do for her from seven thousand miles away.

I have learned a great deal from dead prophets and poets. Ram Dass once wrote, "It is important to expect nothing, to take every experience, including the negative ones, as merely steps on the path, and to proceed." It's true, you know. It's as true as anything can be. Life unfolds in fishing and finance. Sometimes you catch fish and sometimes you don't. Sometimes your 401k goes up and sometimes it goes down. The important thing is to proceed, keep learning and living, and be open to the things that a historic pandemic or prehistoric fish can teach us about ourselves and the universe. The important thing is that we keep casting forward, searching for our native selves and those of our tribe. We must learn to accept whatever comes along, without judgment. It's all good. It's all fishing. It's all life. Do you understand?

I stood on my ladder for hours, casting and watching, and yet I caught nothing. But I was at peace with it. I had experienced everything I hoped for and more. There was something magical in that lake. If only we had the courage and the will to re-create the wild, natural, native watershed it once was, it would be so much more magical.

It is the grandeur of our wildscapes and wildlife that made this nation so much more than its pastoral and pacified European counterparts. America once was, and can be again, a nation that prides itself in its natural wonders and treasures. A fish is not a "resource," it is a living being connected to nature as we once were and, in the most important ways, still are. It's time we recover what we have lost in the world and in ourselves. In a very real way, we've become an artificial population, just like the trout of Pyramid Lake. We swim in circles trapped by the barriers of our own choices. And the thing is, we have it within our power to set these fish and ourselves free.

Before the day was through, my friends caught many fish, including a sixteen-pounder and another that went over fourteen. Around five in the afternoon, I decided that I was content with my day of fishing. I peeled off my waders and stowed my gear, and alternated between photographing my friends in their many moments of joy and simply burning the images of this lake and its surroundings into my mind. It was perfect.

A windstorm began to blow in from the south, and in what seemed like an instant, it turned and came even faster from the north. Before long, fifty-mile-per-hour gusts blew dust in our faces, but my fishing-warrior friends kept fishing and catching. I watched as the sun set and the mixture of sun and blowing dust caused the mountains to glow golden in the dying, slanted evening half-light. And toward the end, almost in darkness again, I watched as Chris stood alone and undefeated, like the last soldier on the battlefield, still casting into the wind. Even in that wind it seemed like he could keep casting forward . . . forever. That my friends, is a fisherman.

I doubt that I will ever return to Pyramid Lake. It will take me awhile to process all that I experienced and felt while I was there. I felt moments of both monotony and magic. But if I ever do return, it will be because I find out that we finally undid what we've done. If I ever do return, it will be because those water diversion dams are down and the fish are traveling back up the Truckee River, swimming and spawning, wild and free once more.

If that happens, I might come back. If that happens, I might not even fish. I might just stand there watching and feeling grateful that both the Lahontan cutthroat trout and "We the People" have found our way home. We shouldn't gamble on our future; we need to invest in it, while we still can.

CHAPTER ELEVEN

Guadalupe Bass

Nueces River in the Texas Hill Country

We have not yet encountered any god who is as merciful as a man who flicks a beetle over on its feet.
—ANNIE DILLARD, PILGRIM AT TINKER CREEK

THE WEATHER HAD BEEN BAD FOR A LONG TIME. THUNDERSTORMS WITH lightning and tree-bending wind were the prevailing pattern each day, and if this were not enough to keep me off the water, there was the "stay at home" order due to the pandemic. But nothing lasts forever. I knew that sooner or later the sunshine would return or at least the storms would become a drizzle, and so I hatched a plan to go fishing on the Nueces River with my buddy Preston.

Preston Bean is a Texas Parks and Wildlife fisheries biologist who works at the Heart of the Hills Fisheries Science Center in Mountain Home, Texas. He wrote the ten-year, 2017–2026 plan for the restoration and preservation of the state fish of Texas, the Guadalupe bass. Our mid-pandemic plan was to watch the weather and, on the first decent day, meet up and travel in separate pickup trucks across the western part of the

Texas Hill Country to the Nueces River, where we planned to focus on Guadalupe bass. We led by example and maintained a respectable "social distance" from each other by keeping a casting length of space between us at all times. I suggested that we could replace the traditional handshake with the Vulcan hand greeting from the science fiction series *Star Trek*, but Preston didn't seem quite into the idea. So instead, when we met up, I said, "Hey, you ready to go fishing?" and he said, "Yep." We kept it simple, and I was fine with that. I'm still hoping that we will both "live long and prosper."

The drive to the Nueces River is a long one that winds around some of the highest parts of the Edwards Plateau, across massive ranchlands and vast expanses of oak savanna. It was springtime, and the roadsides were covered in wildflowers. There were blue bluebonnets, yellow coreopsis, red paintbrush, red and yellow firewheel, and scatterings of white fleabane throughout. I love these hills in any season, but my favorite season is always springtime. Summers can be brutally hot, autumn is golden, winter is brisk, but springtime is when the wildflowers show off the most and the songbirds sing out the loudest. Driving to the river can be every bit as nice as being on the river.

When we arrived, the Nueces was running quick and clear—so clear, in fact, it was deceiving. These spring-fed Texas Hill Country rivers can be so translucent that you might step into what appears to be shallow water and suddenly find yourself armpit deep. It was that clear. I could see every darter and crayfish on the bottom. I could see every waving frond of aquatic vegetation. This is the kind of water where you can sight-cast to Guadalupe bass just as if they were bonefish on a Caribbean sand flat. Simply beautiful.

The name of the game was streamer fishing, smack up against the far bank and then stripped back with variations of speed and frequency until about halfway across the river. Preston gave me the prime starting spot with a nice undercut and some tree roots that reached into the river like fingers. I was tossing a store-bought olive woolly bugger with yellow rubber legs and Preston was casting one of his hand-tied diver-fly creations that looked almost too artful to get wet. Preston ties amazing bass bugs and is a spun deer hair wizard. He got his first job tying flies professionally when he was only twelve years old. I, on the other hand, am lucky to tie a decent clinch knot.

Not surprisingly, Preston caught the first fish, a pretty little long-eared sunfish. I saw his rod bend and a splash on the water, but I never got a good look at the fish. At this time of year sunfish are as bright as their name implies. I missed a strike from a nice Guadalupe, and a big one that was cruising up and down a feeding lane managed to ignore us both. Smart fishy. That's how they get big. I made a mental note to come back for him before the day was over.

On the drive over, the clouds and mist had transformed into a light rain, but now the sun was up, and the clear cerulean-blue sky was so pretty it just might break your heart. There was a soft breeze, and the birds were singing. Wildflowers were everywhere, and dragonflies hovered all around us in colors of neon blue, green, and red. I was casting along one section of tumbling river, while Preston cast to another. I cheered him on from afar as he caught fish, one after another, a few more sunfish and then a small Guadalupe in some fast water. Inexplicably, I did not get a bite, even though I was casting toward what should have been perfect holding places. We carried on.

After a few hundred yards of leapfrogging each other, we arrived at where the river wound into an expansive pool that almost looked like a reservoir. I had fished the Nueces before but had never fished this section. This was Preston's homewater, so I followed his lead. At the pool, Preston directed that I work my way around the left bank while he worked the right. He said, "There's usually sunfish near that grove of trees, and bass in the aquatic vegetation in the deeper water to your right."

"Are you giving me that side because you think it's the better side and I haven't caught anything yet?" I asked.

"Yes," he said, and then he turned and walked off into chest-deep water along the base of a canyon's cliff face. I was thinking about what a nice guy he was about the time he caught another bass. As for me, I was casting well and the day was beautiful and I had not yet hooked myself in the ass, so everything was going fine.

I could tell that my buddy was catching a few more fish on that far and deep side. I spooked a big largemouth bass and was glad that a two-foot-long channel catfish ignored my streamer, because to tell the truth, I'm not a big fan of catching catfish. To my mind they fight like slugs, feel like eels, and stab you with those stiletto-like fins, and I always have a tough time getting the hook out of those rubber-lipped mouths. Forgive me, but I like my catfish breaded with hushpuppies and coleslaw, just like God intended.

The vast pool was interesting, but uneventful. I was glad to get back to where the river looked more like a river. We came to a section with a thin central island in the middle, so thin, in fact, that water spilled from one side to the other through the saw grass, depending on the whims of the current. Again, the water was so transparent that it appeared to be knee-deep until you walked in and found yourself submerged up to your chest.

This is a good time to mention that I was wearing my Orvis backpack, which I love because, among its many great design features, it has a small cooler section at the bottom to hold your lunch. Did I mention that it is not waterproof and that I failed to store my lunch in Ziploc bags? I wasn't that hungry anyway, at least not until I saw Preston sit on the rocky shoreline, open his waterproof backpack, and remove his lunch, which was not soaked in river water. Life's funny.

Now I had no food and had just drunk the last of my water, and it was beginning to get hot as the sun rose overhead. It serves me right for not planning and preparing. I had recently come back from my trip to Pyramid Lake, and my fly-fishing gear was still in post-adventure disarray when I tossed a few things in my pack before heading out to meet Preston. No worries. I came to fish, not to eat. Besides, quarantine had become a convenient excuse for eating too often and exercising too rarely. I left my friend in peace and kept fishing.

At one point, as I walked along the bank methodically casting, I looked down to find the stones alive with perhaps a hundred tiny minnows that were flipping on their sides, stranded in the wet spots between the egg-sized river rocks. They were a flash of striped color, and I could not recognize what species they were. Having a fisheries biologist nearby, I bent down and tried to scoop one up in my hand. I told Preston what I was doing. He was still enjoying his lunch about fifty feet away. Every time I'd move a stone to scoop up a minnow, I'd find a bunch more underneath, and they'd flip and flop and wriggle until they were back in the river. In the end I helped release every little minnow from its predicament and did not manage to scoop up a single fish. I laughed and said, "Wow, I can't even catch a stranded minnow today!" We both laughed.

Preston pointed out a pool at a bend in the river and said, "That's a good one there." I asked him what he was catching fish on, and he said, "It's a 'Bennett's Lunch Money' in white . . . sort of like a Zonker with rubber legs." I had been using an olive woolly bugger and then switched to one with some orange and yellow in it, but I got nowhere with either. So I looked into my fly box, pulled out a white Zonker, and tied it on before walking up to the pool.

When I got there I could see it was pretty water, with a nice undercut bank and plenty of tree roots and overhead protection. I cast my furry white streamer into the tail of the pool and received an immediate strike! It was a stunningly beautiful long-eared sunfish. I slipped out the hook, marveled at its amazing colors, and sent it back to the pool. Preston walked up smiling. I think he was relieved that I finally caught something. I looked over and said, "Well, at least I wasn't skunked!" I cast again.

I worked my way up that pool, and about halfway through a nice-sized Guadalupe rose from the depths and seized the rabbit fur fly like it was the last chicken-on-a-stick at Fiesta! It was a brief battle, but he leapt and danced and shook his mighty head as if he was twice his actual size. When I brought him to my hand, I admired his emerald-green and pearly white colors. I set him free while receiving the customary splash in the face that Guadalupe bass love to give you. These fish have attitude! They always seem indignant at being caught. I love that about them. They never surrender.

Preston offered me the next deep pool, but I did not have any deep-sinking flies that could counteract the quick current running through it, and so I offered it back to him. He was using a weighted crawfish pattern in a rusty orange color, and after only a cast or two into the same pool he lifted a pretty Guadalupe bass out of it and smiled. I gave him a cheer and a thumbs-up sign, and then moved on to work some unlikely pocket water that was just above the waterfall that fed the pool. It was a beautiful stretch of river, but I caught nothing. I felt content to just be casting and drifting through each little pocket.

Upriver, I could see Preston had found another bend where modest-sized bass seemed to be stacked up, searching for spawning areas along a downed cedar-elm tree. I was happy for him and stopped for a moment to take a photo of my friend making some beautiful casts across the water. A belted kingfisher flew by, calling out its displeasure over sharing the river, and a purple finch sang melodiously from the treetops. It was a perfect moment, and I felt pleased simply to be alive.

The Nueces River holds pure Guadalupe bass, and they are a self-sustaining population. But although it is geographically in close proximity to the native watersheds of this endemic Texas Hill Country fish, it is not originally part of its native range. When Texas Parks and Wildlife began to realize the error of its ways in planting non-native smallmouth bass in the historical homewaters of the native Guadalupe bass, it had to find a place where a brood population of genetically pure fish could be isolated and drawn upon, and the Sabinal River in the Nueces River watershed fit that requirement nicely. The fish stocked in the 1960s in the Nueces River were intended as an enhancement of this recreational fishery, but ultimately now both places hold a refuge population of Guadalupe bass. The irony of all this is that the solution to the problem of counteracting the negative effects of previous stockings of non-native smallmouth bass was to create a new population of the native bass in a river where it was not previously found. The domino effects of our unexamined actions . . . when will we ever learn?

I had been casting halfheartedly into bits of pocket water while Preston worked the last pool on this section of river before it went shallow and fishless. Once I had exhausted my efforts on those few short sections of possible holding water without results, I decided to sit and simply watch the river pass by. One of the things that can become problematic if we're not careful is we can find ourselves so engrossed in fishing that we forget to see the river.

I try to make it a practice every now and then to purposely stop casting and just pick my head up and look around. Sometimes I will choose to sit on a streamside stone and watch the river and listen to the birds and look up at the clouds as if I were still that boy who once ran out the back door each morning and did not come home until sundown. In truth, I still am that boy, and I am regaining more of him with every passing year.

One of the big advantages to aging is you finally realize that most of what society tells you to value is in actuality a big waste of time and a bunch of crap. My dad tried to teach me that when I was a young man in my thirties trying to earn degrees and work my way up the ladder. I worked hard and I did eventually get to the top, only to find that I had been climbing the wrong ladder. As it turned out, that boy I once was had it all figured out in the first place. Growing up is overrated.

Sometimes I wish I had paid better attention back then, in my early days of manhood. Sometimes I wonder how I could have invested so much of my lifetime on so many things that really didn't matter. Why did I allow myself to work fourteen-hour days and endure endless, meaningless meetings and work myself to exhaustion on reports and spreadsheets that were eventually recycle bin material? You can find a lot of wisdom looking up at the clouds, or out across a river, or down at your feet searching for arrowheads. A man can get to wondering if perhaps long ago some Comanche warrior sat in this exact spot chipping at his one-hundredth piece of flint when it dawned on him, "Damn, I could be fishing!" If that didn't happen, it should have. I was a Marine warrior once, and I can tell you that I'd rather fish than fight.

I was deep in thought when Preston walked up and said, "Hey, that's a good pool over there and the bass are stacked up along that fallen tree. Do you wanna try it?"

I said, "Sure," and wandered over, stripped out some line, and started casting toward the top of a thirty-foot length of undercut bend pool. Almost immediately I got a strike and a hook-up! It was a nice little ten-inch Guadalupe bass. Preston stood on the bank charitably taking a few photos of me landing the fish, and then after I released it, he watched from the bank and we casually chatted as I worked the length of the pool, catching the same size of Guadalupe bass, one after another, along the way. I'm not sure how many I caught, but the bass were forgiving and hungry.

After a while I reeled in, and we started walking back toward our trucks. We stopped along the way to cast into likely spots in a lackadaisical manner. I sometimes fish that way when I know I've already had a full day of fishing, and I'm resisting becoming compulsive about it. Often, the walk back for me isn't about fishing at all; it's about all the things I want to be mindful of before I leave the river. It's about picking my head up and paying attention to the scenery and the sounds of nature all around me. It's about taking time to feel grateful. Catching fish is only a small part of the act of fishing.

When we got back to our trucks, I remembered that I had made a mental note to make another attempt to catch that big Guadalupe bass that had ignored both our offerings earlier in the day. Preston was taking a few final casts to a pool under the bridge, and he ended up getting a hit but missing the hook-up. I saw him reeling in and heading back to the truck, but I wanted to take a couple casts into that run where the big boy was.

After about three casts along the bank, I saw a green and white flash and felt the strike, and before I knew it, I was into a nice-sized Guad that I landed, admired, and released. He was about a pound and a half, which is a good fish anywhere, but he wasn't that bruiser that had previously ignored us both and was obviously ignoring me now. I felt sure that he was there, watching me as I searched for him, laughing as my streamer passed him by.

Fish like that linger in my imagination. I can't help but admire them and appreciate all they must do in order to survive. I reeled in and began walking back toward the truck, still thinking of the big one that got away. I was smiling as I put my gear away. It had been a great day of fishing with a friend on some beautiful water. Just before I drove away, I looked back at the deep run where I knew a big bass was still swimming. It's okay. I was almost glad I didn't get him . . . almost. As I drove away from the river, all I could think of was two little words: "smart fishy!"

CHAPTER TWELVE

Colorado River Cutthroat Trout

Yampa River Watershed—Northern Colorado

Humankind has not woven the web of life. We are but one thread within it. Whatever we do to the web, we do to ourselves. All things are bound together. All things connect.

—*Chief Seattle*

WHEN MY BUDDY KIRK DEETER PICKED ME UP AT THE AIRPORT IN Steamboat Springs, he announced that he'd be grilling steaks for dinner and that he had a cooler filled with cold beer and wine waiting on the back deck. Just as were driving past a small herd of pronghorn on the way to Kirk's house, he asked, "Do you have any food allergies or foods you don't eat?" I answered as I always do, that I don't have any food-related allergies and that the only food I've ever turned down was African bush rat, but that was just because the fur was still on it. He pressed further, "Is there anything you don't like to eat?"

"I'm not wild about Brussels sprouts," I replied. (That's become a pat answer for me, and it's always worked because in my fifty-nine years of being alive no one has ever made Brussels sprouts when I've visited.) We continued through the town of Steamboat Springs and stopped at a wonderful little mom-and-pop Mexican restaurant and had some tacos at a table outside, not far from where the Yampa River runs through town. It was perfect.

When we arrived at Kirk's house, I took a shower and freshened up before walking out to the deck to join him and his wonderful wife Sarah for an evening glass of pre-dinner wine. Kirk looked over to me and said, "Steve . . . how serious were you about Brussels sprouts?"

"Not at all!" I replied, without missing a beat. We sat on the porch sipping our wine and chatting about life and fly fishing while their three-year-old pup Maya circled about hoping for handouts and finally flopped down on her bed in disgust. It was about that time that their son Paul came in from work, greeted me like family, and pulled up a chair. Paul is one of those young men who immediately puts a smile on your face and gives you some hope for the future. He is intelligent, kind, honest, and hardworking, and as a parent, I could immediately see why Kirk and Sarah were so proud of their son. I'm proud of him too.

That night at dinner the steak was amazing, the baked potatoes were perfection, and I had two helpings of the best Brussels sprouts of my life! Thanks Sarah. They were nicely roasted with a crisp bitter-sweet flavor that perfectly complemented Kirk's steak, which was topped with just a dollop of blue cheese. The baked potato with sour cream brought it all together. Potatoes always make me think of Ireland and Idaho, even though I know they are originally from Peru. I guess we humans can't help dragging things we like around the world, no matter if they're spuds or salmonids. Kirk let me softly play one of his guitars a bit as we sipped the after-dinner wine and chatted about past lives and current hopes. It was a meal I will never forget. I guess from now on, when asked that food question I will have to say, "I'm not wild about bush rat." That should be safe enough, I hope.

~◆~

The next morning was wonderfully chilly as Kirk and I drove out to the headwaters of the Yampa River. The previous day we stopped by Steamboat Flyfisher in Steamboat Springs to pick up a few flies and talk fishing with the owner, Johnny Spillane, and manager Wes Fout. We received a few top-secret tips on the various tributaries to the Yampa, and I was sworn to secrecy about their names and locations—a secret I will take with me to the grave, like so many others.

The drive to and through the small, picturesque town of Yampa was a pleasant one, and it wasn't long before we were skirting the edges of the Flat Tops Wilderness where several tributaries tumble out of the high country, ultimately spilling into what becomes the Yampa River. This was originally the homeland of the Ute people, and the word Yampa means "bear" in their language. The Yampa begins in the high country of the Flat Tops Wilderness, meanders toward and through the town of Steamboat Springs, and then heads westward through Dinosaur National Monument. After a journey of about 250 miles, it mingles with the Green River, which itself is a tributary of the Colorado River.

There are important lessons to be learned from the journey of the Yampa's waters. The Bear River becomes the Yampa, the Yampa becomes the Green, the Green becomes part of the Colorado River within the borders of Glen Canyon National Park, and then the Colorado winds its way south into Arizona through the Grand Canyon, which it created. Eventually the Colorado reaches the Mexican border at San Luis, where it is now reduced to a faint memory of the great river it once was . . . a mere shadow of its former self. It once spread out into a vast floodplain that contained the songs of birds and the coughing calls of jaguars as it tumbled into the Gulf of California. There it created a unique brackish ecosystem for fish that are now imperiled because the Colorado no longer reaches the sea.

Designated by UNESCO as a biosphere wetlands of international importance, the Colorado River Delta is now the subject of various schemes to recharge it artificially with water that will be taken from somewhere else, since the water of the Colorado, Green, Yampa, and Bear Rivers ended up everywhere else—across golf courses, casino landscapes, shopping mall fountains, and millions of flushing toilets from Steamboat to San Luis. And this is why we began at the headwaters, where the Yampa isn't even the Yampa yet and the water is pure, clean, cold, and full of rising trout that have no idea where the river is going. Ignorance can be bliss, but it is never salvation.

The Flat Tops Wilderness is vast and beautiful with its namesake flat-topped mountains and mixture of sage- and wildflower-covered high plains and spruce-, lodgepole pine-, and aspen-covered mountainsides. As we drove along the winding dirt road, we crossed larger expanses of fire-damaged forest where new life was already sprouting from the earth. But there were also entire stands of lodgepole pine that were dead and gone, mere skeletons remaining after the ravages of mountain pine bark beetle infestation. I'm not sure if these areas will heal anytime soon.

We parked on a high ridge overlooking the small tributary with mountains looming overhead and the fragrance of sagebrush and wildflowers in the air. We were both hungry and decided this was as good a time as any to have an early lunch, so we feasted on pastrami on rye from the Yampa Sandwich Company, which contained the most amazing spicy coleslaw and dressing I've ever known. (It is making me hungry as I write this, even though I've just had breakfast.)

From our lunchtime vantage point, we could see the river as it twisted and turned along the edges of the spruce forest on the far side, and sagebrush hills along the nearside riverbank. It was good water with rocks and riffles and pockets and pools. It had undercut banks and grassy shoulders that blew hoppers into the air and onto the water. Once adrift, they might as well be gazelles crossing the Zambezi—crocodiles and cutthroats, all gotta eat.

When we reached the water's edge, we both tied on a couple of small hoppers, bright and beautiful in their foam and feather outfits. Kirk, as an act of kindness, went downriver to much more difficult water where he would proceed to outfish me anyway, because he is a better angler on his worst day than I will ever be on my best. That's the truth, not hyperbole.

I began casting into a pool that ran a good twenty feet from top to tail, and almost immediately a twelve-inch trout rose from the depths and inhaled my fly. I was excited because there was every chance that this would be the first Colorado River cutthroat of my life and I did not want to lose it. There was a short tussle, a jump or two, and a soft landing into the grass since the bank was steep and I was working without a net. He was beautiful, but he was a brown trout. Had I caught him in Scotland, Germany, Spain, or Morocco I would have been thrilled, but I caught him in the last bastion waters for native cutthroats of the Yampa River drainage.

I've seen this story play out before as I searched for Rio Grande cutthroat in the mountains of New Mexico and discovered to my dismay that non-native brown trout had moved upriver and simply outcompeted the natives for the best feeding lanes, spawning sites, and overwintering waters. It was a large plunge pool, and I decided to work it a little further in the hope that it might contain a mixed bag of browns and cutthroats. But after a few more drifts, another fish took my hopper, and it confirmed—for me at least—that this pool belonged to the ultimate survivors of the trout world, the European brown.

Brown trout are my buddy Kirk Deeter's favorite fish, and this wonderful fish has led him from Russia to Patagonia to Tasmania. And don't get me wrong, I love them too . . . just not here. I want to find them in their original homewaters, not here, in the homewaters of another fish.

The wind was kicking up a bit just as Kirk appeared at my side like a ninja with a five-weight fly rod in hand. He had caught three fish in the river below, all brown trout.

"Have you fished this before?" I asked.

"Yes," he replied.

"What did you catch?"

"Nothing but cutthroat," he said with a slight sound of disappointment in his voice.

I knew Kirk was trying to get me into the fish I came for, not the ones we were finding. But this is the story of native fish in modern-day America. Native fish are fighting for their last blue ribbons of water on their way up-elevation and into oblivion, all because of the bucket biology of European immigrants, who treated wildlife like luggage and rivers like closets.

That's about the time they showed up, a young man and his pretty young girlfriend, he with a fly rod in hand and her so obviously there for moral support. They were nice enough, but he had parked directly next to us on the road above and followed us to the river.

"Catching anything," he asked?

"A few," we said.

That's when he smiled, waved, then walked upstream and stood directly in the water we were planning to fish. He high-holed us!

We both briefly discussed if we should nicely mention to him the lack of fishing etiquette he had just displayed, but we decided against it and instead fished the last two pools remaining between us and the young interloper. We caught nothing and Kirk walked back to me and said, "I can see the fish stacked up around that bend and there is nothing but brownies in there."

After a moment of consideration, we decided to pack it in and move on to our next objective, which was a reservoir in the area that had been created by a damming of one of the tributaries to the Yampa. It was said by people in the know that this reservoir contained native cutthroats in their pure form, not polluted by the genetics of invasive rainbow trout. And that was about the time that he and she reappeared, smiling, happy, friendly, and fishless.

As it turned out, he was a beginner and fresh out of a tour of duty in the US Air Force. He simply didn't know any better, and I was glad we did not say anything that might have embarrassed him in front of his girlfriend. Instead, Kirk gave him a couple of flies to try out and a few tips on presentation to help him be more successful in the future. We wished them both a good day and made our way back up the steep hill to the notch in the road where we had parked.

It had been a nice morning on a lovely little stream. I didn't catch what I was looking for, but I did catch what was there, and every life story must unfold not as we wish it were, but rather as it is. The story of this river is that at one end we humans have taken so much from it during the course of its long journey that it never makes it to where it was going in the first place. And ironically, at the headwaters we have added so much that doesn't belong in these waters that its native cutthroats are vanishing, like the lodgepole pines. It doesn't make this landscape any less beautiful, but for me it does make it a little less authentic. I have no interest in dancing bears or dolphins that leap through hula hoops. For me, if they are free, so am I.

If I had it to do all over again, I would choose to stay on that tributary of the Yampa and keep working it upstream in hopes of eventually connecting with a native cutthroat that hasn't vanished under the pressure of the more aggressive brownies. I'm curious as to what we would have discovered had we stayed and worked our way up that river, bend by bend.

Once we arrived at the trailhead to the hidden reservoir, we were "all in" as we tied on our bright new hoppers. I had moved on from the morning's peaceful moments on the little river, except for one memory that "stuck" with me. Earlier that morning I managed to hook myself in the finger while fiddling with the fly in the wind, which was when I realized that I had neglected to smash down the barb, a mistake I didn't want to make twice. The little size 16 hook was embedded deep into my flesh, and I had to pull hard to rip it out. It wasn't the end of the world, but it also wasn't pleasant, and I felt for the fish I had just caught and released. Smash those barbs, y'all! We can catch fish without ripping lips.

As we began walking the trail to the reservoir, I could hear the familiar piping whistle of a marmot calling out to whoever was listening that humans were in the area. Kirk did something I could not have accomplished; he hoisted a large belly boat on his shoulders and began the hike in with all that extra weight while I carried nothing more than our fly rods and my chest pack. Having just come from my home at nine hundred feet above sea level and now climbing hills about eight thousand feet in elevation, my asthmatic lowland lungs were having a hard time of it, and the thin air was draining me of my energy and resolve. The guidebook said that the elevation gain was only about ten feet from start to finish, but the beginning and end of every roller-coaster ride is at the same level; it is the rise and fall of things in between that make the ride. Let's just say that I suffered with every uphill climb and found no solace in each descent, which would soon become a climb on the way back to the trailhead.

Eventually we found the reservoir, which was contained within muddy, mosquito-rich embankments and held dark, spooky, windswept waters. I slipped on the flippers and kicked out in the belly boat away from the bugs and into the unknown featureless depths. As I floated alone out there, I was reminded of *Lake Placid*, the 1999 cult horror film where a group of people try to survive the attacks of a giant saltwater crocodile that somehow found its way into a freshwater lake. I kicked out toward deeper waters, thinking of how much each flipper reminded me of a beaver's tail and feeling fairly sure that crocodiles would eat beavers. Nothing swam my way, not a crocodile, beaver, or rising trout. I kept casting, not really sure where to cast . . . kind of like life.

The area around the reservoir was beautiful. It was surrounded by mountains with scatterings of snow still on their highest points, even in July. The dense spruce and aspen forest was said to contain elk, moose, and bears. And a multitude of wildflowers grew in every patch of sunlight that made it through the treetops to the earth. But as I cast aimlessly here and there, and then switched to a streamer and stripped and trolled across the reservoir, I realized once again that I am deeply prejudiced toward moving water. I'll take smaller fish in rushing streams any day over larger fish in big, calm waters. It's the same sensibility that causes me to prefer seashores to sea centers, and cool autumn winds over the stillness of midsummer heat. It's the same *je ne sais quoi* that has me loathing canals and loving rivers. It's why I don't eat veggie dogs on Independence Day or tofu turkey on Thanksgiving. It's not the same. I want the real thing. In both life and art, imitation bores me.

We caught nothing in the reservoir, and after a while we decided to begin the roller-coaster hike back to the trailhead and the car. When we rounded the last bend in the aspen grove, I heard the familiar call of the chubby whistle pig and knew we were back where we started. Poor Kirk hauled that heavy float tube all the way up and down the hills. I would have helped, but the elevation was still getting to me, and it was all I could do to haul myself down that trail. It was a tough trip for me and my lowland lungs to the reservoir and back, but I would not have forgone a bit of it, because we pushed through it together and that's what we do when we are proving to ourselves that we still have some fire in our bellies and some spark in our souls.

We arrived back at Kirk's home to warm showers and a delicious dinner of pulled pork, fresh corn on the cob, and crisp, cold white wine. Throughout the evening we talked and laughed while swapping stories of past adventures and misadventures. As you can see, the food and friendship were at least as important as the fishing—more so, in fact. We may forget the fish, but we will always remember the fishing and friendship.

———

The next morning began with Sarah's green chili quiche and rich Guatemalan coffee out on the deck. We'd strung up the rods and packed the drift boat the night prior, so the only thing we had to do that morning was eat and go fish. I was eager to get out on the water, but not in a hurry for breakfast to end. Life is like that, always a tradeoff between the things we are enjoying and the things we have yet to enjoy. It can be hard to let go, yet easy to grab on. If only I was a Time Lord from *Doctor Who*.

We launched Kirk's drift boat on the Yampa just past first light, and for the most part we seemed to have the river to ourselves. It was late in the season for floating this river, and with the water running low at seven hundred cubic feet per second, Kirk said this would be his last run this year on his favorite river. I felt honored.

The river was smooth and calm at first—"frog water"—which would have less chance of holding fish but still could. I was casting my Orvis glass five-weight and, at least for now, my casting was on target; before long I received a strike and a hook-up to a rainbow trout that Kirk said went about sixteen inches . . . not that I pay attention to these things. All I know is that it felt like my first time riding a bull in the rodeo. I had drawn a big, white Charolais bull that did a straight jump-and-kick pattern out of the chute, and I held on for the entire eight seconds, more out of fear than skill. (Everyone looks brave on a bull, but the people in the stands can't hear the sound of your spurs clicking against the metal chute as your legs involuntarily jitter from adrenaline.) Once the buzzer went off, I realized that I had no idea how to get off the thing, so I pulled my rope, hoped for the best, and somehow landed on my feet like a PRCA pro!

The moral to the story is, don't get too cocky. I left that rodeo thinking I was going to be the next national champion, and then life said, "Hold my beer." I lasted just a few seconds on my next dozen "rides" before being unceremoniously deposited in the mud like the rank amateur I was. Well, after landing that nice rainbow I remember thinking to myself that I was in the zone and ready to haul fish into the boat like Zane Grey. And that is when life taught me another lesson and I missed the next three strikes in a row, all from brown trout, and managed to tangle my line around the end of the rod, the gunnel of the drift boat, my right leg, and almost within the wings of a passing red-winged blackbird.

No worries, we had about nine more miles of river to float. I could redeem myself. There's always a chance of redemption, y'all. No matter what comes our way, we've got to keep casting forward. And that is exactly what I did after untangling my line with all the patience of a Zen master while making fun of myself, as is my practice. I have so much material to work with.

Here in the belly of the Yampa, the river flowed through a vast ranchland area of sagebrush and high-elevation prairie grassland. There were pronghorn and mule deer in the sage and elk, moose, and bears in the mountain forests just beyond the prairie. Yellow warblers skittered among the shoreline brush and blackbirds called out from the cottonwood trees. A short-eared owl flew away silently between tree trunks upon our approach, vanishing in a mass of willows and cottonwoods. A muskrat clambered along the shore, perhaps relieved to have avoided the owl's gaze. Here and there we'd see a merganser with its young in tow, each a tiny replica of the parent. Cattle and horses occasionally appeared along the river, and I was especially struck by three beautiful chestnut-colored horses that were grazing at the water's edge. If fences were present, I did not notice them. Everything felt free, including me.

Kirk remained on the sticks and swore that he was enjoying rowing as much as fishing, and I believed him. Watching him maneuver his drift boat reminded me of seeing a hunter wielding a shotgun that is perfectly fitted to his shoulder and with which he has hunted season after season for a lifetime. The bird hunter's gun and Kirk's boat are both an extension of their human spirit, so much more than a simple tool. Even with the wind kicking up hard, Kirk kept presenting me the best shots at the best water, and I was having the time of my life casting and caring for nothing but the moment. In the end, we forget most of the fish we catch in a blur of color and splash, but we remember the conversations as we drift a river, or walk across a sand flat, or traverse a farmer's field with our trusty shotgun in hand and dog by our side. This, my friends, is what it's all about.

We covered a lot of pretty river miles over the next few hours. I was casting left and right to likely places, but the trout had decided that I needed more practice at inner peace, so just like the imperfect Texan Buddha I am, I practiced. I cast toward every bit of structure, every foam line and undercut bank. I cast into the middle of nowhere when I did not see anywhere in particular to cast. I cast until my shoulder ached and I knew it was time to simply watch the cottonwoods bending in the wind, or the white smoke of a distant grass fire.

It was all peaceful, meaningful, valuable, and timeless. I did not care a lick that I wasn't catching fish. Today, catching fish seemed almost beside the point. I was drifting with one of my best friends down his favorite river in his magnificent boat, and life was sublime.

Just about the time we were getting ready to anchor the boat and enjoy some lunch, Kirk noticed somebody waving at us from a side channel, and it became quickly apparent that they were in trouble. Kirk maneuvered the drift boat over toward the shoreline and anchored, and we both jumped out and crossed the gravel bar toward the shipwrecked couple.

We found a pretty, pale, supremely silent and heavily tattooed girl holding on to one side of an overturned metal canoe, and her skinny, scruffy, not-too-friendly boyfriend half submerged in the current and holding the other side. The canoe was painted in psychedelic colors and was full to the brim with river water, pinned underneath the only fallen tree in the river. I wondered what would ever have possessed him to paddle toward this obvious death trap. Much too young to even have real hippies for parents, these two were playing the part even if they might not have any idea why. I half expected a lava lamp to float out of the debris.

After a great deal of effort, we managed to get the canoe out from under the fallen tree and out of the fast current without anyone drowning, although it got close. Then we all heaved it over on its side and let the water run out of the hull. We made sure that he had two good paddles and life vests and wished them well. He mentioned that he had lost his fishing rod, but I could tell by the look on her face that he had blown it, and fishing wasn't the only area where he wasn't going to get lucky that day. "Thanks man," he said as he nervously indicated that we weren't needed anymore. (I wonder if his stash was in a waterproof baggie.)

Kirk and I walked back to the drift boat and launched downriver to our lunch spot, where we enjoyed a Colorado Kool-Aid (Coors) and more great sandwiches. I never eat pastrami at home, but I liked the sandwich the day prior so much that I opted for another, and I did not regret it a bit. Sometimes certain things just feel right.

When we started back down the river, we ran through a series of rapids, each made a bit trickier for Kirk due to the low water levels, but he weaved us through each one like it was the easiest thing on Earth. I love every bend in a river. I love not knowing what comes next and accepting and adapting to whatever I find. It is a wonderful metaphor for life. Nothing is certain other than entropy. Rivers and galaxies are naturally expanding. The universe grows ever more vast. I'm so glad humanity can't divert the universe; it is still going where it's heading. Outward.

One of the things I wanted to see most on this float was an eagle. For those of you who live in eagle country, you might take such a wish for granted, but I don't and I didn't. We turned a corner and spotted the first bald eagle of the day up in a cottonwood tree on a branch overhanging the water. I stopped fishing. We drifted and I watched, and I watched until the boat came almost even with the bird and then it took flight, and I caught my breath like a teenager finding a thousand-dollar bill in a parking lot. I never want to become so jaded that an eagle doesn't cause me to catch my breath and feel supremely grateful to be alive. We saw four bald eagles during this float. I would have traveled here from Texas just for that and left my fly rod behind. I'm glad I was lucky enough to have both.

You'd be right to wonder, "If your book is about restoring and preserving native fish and their watersheds, why are you floating down a river that is full of non-native rainbow and brown trout with a few mongrel cuttbows?" That's a good question and it has two good answers.

First, this is my buddy's favorite river in Colorado. It is his homewater, and I did not travel all this way just to find fish. I traveled up here to wisely invest time on the water with my friend. This float was important to me because it was important to him, and I would have felt disappointed had we not shared this adventure. This book is about more than fish; it's about people. It's about how we find our tribe and cherish them every day. It's about friendship and pulling together for some common good. It's about living a life worth living.

Second, I believe a writer should never try to create a story as they wish it to be, as much as reveal a story as it is. We should start with a thesis statement and then see where it takes us. And in this case the reality of native trout in these watersheds is one that is all too common in this "Brave New World." They're gone. We caused them to vanish through bucket biology and a flawed "fish and game" ideology whereby the main goal of the state was to establish more and bigger fish to be caught by paying anglers. That story needs to be told and, I believe, it needs to change. We license-paying anglers will either drive or stymie that change. I hope we become the catalyst for better stewardship.

The Colorado River cutthroat trout is the original native trout of the Yampa and Colorado River drainages, but it has been replaced by "wild" brown and rainbow trout whose own original homewaters are in distant lands. This is sort of like the case of "wild" North African aoudad sheep replacing native desert bighorn sheep in the mountains of West Texas. Words in any language all have a subtle context tied to them.

We tend to call creatures brought by humans to places they do not belong "wild" if we like having them there and "feral" if we regret the outcome of our actions. Therefore, many anglers react positively about providing funds to keep stocking foreign "wild" brown and rainbow trout in rivers and lakes, while also lamenting their inability to eliminate "feral hogs" and negate the damage they cause to riparian zones that protect streams from sediment and pollution. It's a complicated and messy business, playing God and trying to outwit nature. And we're in deep now, so there's no going back. It's a "You broke it, now you own it" sort of deal. Nature has been too deeply altered by us to simply be allowed to "do its own thing." We can't un-rub the lamp; the destructive genie is out.

I doubt that ospreys or otters care at all if the fish they're eating is native or non-native, but I do, and I hope you will too. As a boy and now as a post-middle-aged man who is becoming ever more childlike, I love being in nature not for the poundage of meat I can extract from her, but rather from the sense of wonder I can gain from her. There is something wonder-full about how nature all connects and fits together. There is something magical in how one solitary native bee fits one solitary native flower and how another bee seeks out a different flower. There is something bigger than us when we see how perfect it all became, without us. And I am not suggesting that there is no place for the mighty brown trout in our rivers or the aoudad in our desert mountains. . . . I'm just saying, not every place.

When I was a boy I was taught about responsibility and accountability. If I accidentally put a ding in the wall, I was taught how to repair the damage with some putty and paint. It felt good to see the outcome, and I remember my dad being proud of me for "taking the initiative." It is human to make mistakes, and done correctly, we can learn from them, pick ourselves up, brush ourselves off, and move on. Let's do some of that with our waters, lands, and skies. We can't repair it all, but we can heal some of the wounds. All we have to do is care.

I never got a single bite after catching that rainbow trout and missing those three browns in the first minutes of the float. I cast until my arm hurt; although the water all looked good, it just wasn't in the script for this play. Let me tell you, it did not matter a bit. The entire day was wonderful.

We began to round the last bend in the river before the takeout when we saw a massive bird flying heavily over the water and landing on a fallen cottonwood tree. It was the largest golden eagle I have ever seen. It looked like it could eat monkeys or small children. Kirk called to it with a throaty whistle, and it immediately turned its head toward us and called back to him. We just smiled. I have never been happier. Nature, allowed to live naturally, does that for me.

At the pullout I held the boat in place, steady against the current of the Yampa, while Kirk went to get the car and trailer. I was just looking around, taking it all in, feeling grateful, when I looked down into the clear, clean, cold water and noticed a delicately beautiful garter snake twisted along the pebbles at the river's bottom. I love snakes, and as a kid I always felt privileged when I'd see one before it saw me and could simply watch it doing its thing. Snakes, like frogs, turtles, crickets, and fireflies, are all indicative of what is healthy, and what is not, about an ecosystem. Everything is connected to everything else.

I thought about that truism as Kirk, Sarah, Paul, and I sat around the table later that evening, sipping red wine and eating ground elk and green chili burritos. We laughed and talked of great times and hardships overcome, and together we counted our blessings and not our burdens. We were happy and at peace with the world. That's what happens when you find your tribe and value that connection.

Fishing isn't just about fishing, it's about belonging. It's about caring. It's about sharing moments and making memories. Like the creeks, streams, and rivers, we're all connected. And if we allow ourselves to become solitary, selfish, and self-involved, we will lose those natural wellsprings of friendship that replenish us. If that happens to humanity, and we are trending in that direction, then just like the Bear, Yampa, Green, and Colorado Rivers, we will vanish into the bedrock of time and our journey will have meant nothing of consequence. I'd rather flow naturally toward something vaster than my meager lifetime. I'd rather make a positive difference while I'm here. How about you?

CHAPTER THIRTEEN

Greenback Cutthroat Trout

Mount Zirkel Wilderness, Northern Colorado

At one time in the world there were woods that no one owned.

—CORMAC MCCARTHY, CHILD OF GOD

BUFFALO PASS AND THE MOUNT ZIRKEL WILDERNESS STRADDLE THE Continental Divide, that magical geologic line in the stone that decides if a raindrop ends up in the Mississippi River and the Gulf of Mexico or the Pacific Ocean. My buddy Kirk Deeter knew that I was interested in connecting with a greenback cutthroat trout, and he thought he might have found a beautiful place for us to do just that, namely, Jonah Lake in the Mount Zirkel Wilderness of northern Colorado.

If I were to attempt to characterize this day's adventure in a single run-on sentence, I'd say: It was an adventure with great friendships and good food, spectacular scenery and sparkling sunlit waters, long hikes with a shortness of breath, tiny terrestrials connected to fish that looked like living emeralds, and the wild and woolly antics of Kirk's pup Maya. With that said, please allow me to fill in the details. I hope you enjoy them.

I could not have been happier when I heard that Sarah and Maya would be joining us on this expedition. Sarah, Kirk, and I have the best conversations you can imagine, and Maya is simply a joy to be around. Maya is a three-year-old pudelpointer, a breed I had been unfamiliar with before meeting her. According to the American Kennel Club, the pudelpointer originated in Germany by crossing hunting poodles and pointers, and that "a versatile, genetically sound and healthy gun dog emerged from this cross" and "the breed is useful for all kinds of work in the fields, woods and water." The AKC goes on to say that this breed is "a calm, self-controlled, versatile gun dog with a distinct hunting instinct and lacks game or gun shyness," and that "it is friendly, free of shedding, and active." I found Maya to be all these things and more, and for the purpose of this story I will highlight the descriptor, "active!" Maya is one of those pups that are easy to love, easy to value, and easy to forgive.

Kirk's fishing car is a Lexus SUV that is covered in dirt and pine needles on the outside and stuffed full of outdoor gear on the inside. Until now, I had never considered a luxury automobile for the rough work of rocky backroads and muddy boat ramps, but let me tell you, it worked! It got over all the rocks and ridges, dropped and dragged the boat, had cup holders everywhere you'd ever want them, and had tons of space in the back for the cooler, fly rods, gear, and even a rambunctious pudelpointer named Maya.

When we got out of the car we slipped on our packs, pouches, water bottles, water filters, fly rods, and a leash for Maya that seemed like more of an inside joke than something that actually might be considered. (I'm so glad she was free.) Maya took the lead on the trail, which at this point was a closed forest service dirt road. She had no idea where she was going but seemed pretty happy to be going there. I was a bit concerned she might run into a bear or moose, but Sarah mentioned that a porcupine might be a more likely problem.

We were above ten thousand feet in elevation, so having come from the low country of Texas, I and my asthmatic lungs were taking our time as the pup ran ahead inspecting every interesting pile of rocks, blown-down tree, and bright green brushy spot. She was either exploring or looking for birds or both, but every now and then she'd look back at me plodding along as if to say, "Could you please catch up?"

The hike in was about four and a half miles each way from car to lake and lake to car. A ten-mile hike is no big deal for me back home in Texas, but this wasn't Texas. At our highest point in this hike, we were around 10,600 feet in elevation. In contrast, the city of San Antonio is only 650 feet above sea level, and even the highest points in the western Hill Country rise to only slightly above 2,000 feet. It's amazing how much a mere 9,000-foot increase in elevation can reduce your body's ability to function! I'd say that I did okay on the way out to the lake but not so well on the way back . . . but I'm getting ahead of myself (no wonder I feel out of breath).

There are so many things about this day that I will remember for as long as I live. The wonderful friendship, wilderness fishing, and wildflowers were all simply perfect. The scenery was breathtaking (pun intended), with a mixture of high-country meadows, skinny-watered streams, green-willowed marshlands, and stands of spruce, fir, pine, and aspen. Kirk had mentioned that this was a good place to see both Shiras moose and black bears, so I was on the lookout because I wanted to see both.

It was midsummer in the high country, with patches of snow still on the ground, and yet the trailside was covered in wildflowers of every kind and color. In his book titled *Fool's Paradise*, John Gierach wrote a chapter titled "Flowers." In it he considers the use of phenological knowledge to better understand the habits of trout. Phenology, he explains, "is the study of simultaneous natural phenomena like mating, nesting, leafing, blooming, whelping, migrations, insect infestations and such." Like most modern-day American fly anglers, I own every book that John Gierach has ever published, and I read them repeatedly. Still, with all those great stories over the years, I wonder how many readers have paid attention to the importance of that one chapter titled "Flowers."

Everywhere I go around the country and the world, I pay attention to the macro and micro view of that historical landscape. In particular I pay attention to flowers, birds, and trees. They each tell a story of the new watershed and its inhabitants. As I walked mile after mile along this forest service road, I noticed the profusion of wildflowers not only for their beauty but also for the story they told. Plants move not only in the wind, but over time with the changes in conditions. A flowering plant that needs certain temperature ranges to survive will have to move up the mountainside or into protected canyons as conditions get warmer. When they can no longer move, they vanish, along with every creature that was depending on them.

Walking along these high-county trails, I was taken by the colors and shapes of the wildflowers. There were extravagant clusters of the state flower of Colorado, the Colorado columbine. Their blue and white blooms with bright yellow stamens covered the rocky hillsides along with the smaller creamy blue mountain lupine. I thought of the less common variety of columbine that clings to life in some of the cooler canyons just west of my Texas home. I wondered if they would survive the rapid and unnatural changes in climate that are so obviously in progress, obvious to any person who loves the outdoors and chooses to pay attention. In shaded spots I saw the mountain harebell with its slender green stems and bell-shaped blue flowers, each covered in morning dew. And scattered among all these magnificent shades of blue were the yellows of arnica, blanket flower, and golden banner, the pinks of paintbrush and fireweed, and the whites of chickweed, yarrow, and cow parsnip. If this were not enough, each field of flowers was attended to by broad-tailed hummingbirds with their green-feathered backs and pink-feathered throats, butterflies in every color, and some of the over nine hundred species of native bees that depend on these flowers arriving . . . just in time. This stuff matters.

Pay attention each year as you fish, and you will see for yourself that changes are happening way too fast to be natural. Every angler should add naturalist notes to their fishing journal. See for yourself what is happening to the places we love most.

When we reached the Continental Divide at the Wyoming Trail, the forest began to close in and become a bit more foreboding. It's not that it wasn't beautiful, it just gave that feeling that if you met a momma bear or momma moose along the trail you'd have a lot less warning or time to make some potentially important choices. As the trail narrowed, I couldn't help but notice the moose sign everywhere. I started to look down at the flowers less, and up at the next bend in the trail more. It occurred to me that being pounded into the mud like a late-harvest grape might put a damper on my fishing plans.

The lake was worthy of a postcard. A bald eagle flew from the treetops upon our arrival and the sounds of songbirds filled the trees. Flashes of sunlight sparked across the windswept waters while a small stream fed the little lake from above. The lake was shaped like a teardrop, with a small rocky island in the middle, a smaller wet meadow at its top, and a thick forest of spruce trees along the bottom of the imaginary tear.

I tied on a size 16 high-visibility black ant pattern and began to cast it from the small wet meadow, while Kirk began casting from a rocky out-cropping at the top of the teardrop. It didn't take long until we both saw a fish rise . . . and then another, and another, each about forty to sixty feet out from the bank. A bit farther out a bright fish that looked about fourteen inches long leapt clear of the water, arched like an Olympian, and dove back into the depths. I began casting my little three-weight out toward the rising fish, and in short order I received and missed a strike, cast again, and made a hook-up on the second chance.

It was a nice fish that put on a show with a couple of good jumps and a brace of solid runs before I brought him to hand. He was magnificently colored, and although I did not have an instant genetic testing kit in my pocket, this fish looked every bit like a greenback cutthroat trout. It was chunky and firm in my hand, and I took a moment to admire him and make sure Kirk and Sarah saw that I had caught a nice fish, and that is when I realized I was being intently watched by Maya, who was standing next to Sarah, about fifty yards away.

Apparently she saw the struggle with the fish and decided that I needed help and I needed it quickly. She came running toward me at full speed, splashing water along the way like a Labrador that just witnessed a floun-dering duck. Sarah and Kirk called "Maya!" in an attempt to bring her back, but she only glanced over her shoulder as if to say, "I know, I'm getting to him as fast as I can!" I still had the fish in my hand when she arrived, and she was so excited as she tangled her legs in the loops of my line and shook off the water from her coat onto mine. I decided I would try to teach her something about being a fishing dog, so I bent down and said, "Okay girl, you get to sniff the tail and watch as I let him go." She excitedly agreed . . . or so I thought.

I bent down and offered her a quick inspection of the beautiful fish, and she did sniff the tail as if to say, "Yah, it's a fish." (I was relieved that she did not try to eat it.) When I set the fish free, she looked at me as if I were insane and immediately took off at top speed trying to retrieve it for me! I was amazed that she had her nose on its tail for the first twenty feet of shallow water, but as the fish escaped into the deeper lake, Maya decided to take a few victory laps by swimming back and forth across the section of lakefront I was intending to fish. Everyone called out, "Maya!" in hopes of bringing her back to dry land, but she paid us no attention. She seemed to be having too much fun to come out just because some humans were coaxing her to do so. I don't blame her. I envied her youthful freedom. Had the water not been so cold, I might have jumped in with her.

Kirk moved around to the lower east side of the teardrop lake in part to try new water and in part to draw Maya away and keep her from turning my fishing hole into a swimming hole any more than it already was. Sarah wonderfully did her best to keep the pup happy and entertained while we fished. Kirk caught another three greenbacks along that wooded edge. True to form I lost my fly on the only blade of inch-thick grass sticking up from the water, so I began attaching another one exactly like the one I lost when I noticed more trout rising about forty to fifty feet out into the lake.

Did I mention the mosquitoes? As I was attempting to tie on the size 16 ant pattern, I was also dealing with the throng of size 16 mosquitoes that were covering my neck, face, and hands, which, ironically, were also covered in repellent (I think it attracted them). I pulled up my Buff, pulled down my hat, and began casting out to where the fish had been rising and jumping. The rise forms were varied, from head-fin-tail rises to splashes and leaps, all extremely aggressive, although I could not see what was on the water out there.

I cast and let the dry fly drift for only a moment before I received and missed a strike. "Too slow, dumbass," I said to myself and the wind. I missed again on my next cast, then a third time, but rather than scolding myself I took a deep breath, which left me feeling lightheaded due to the thin high-elevation air. I cast again and almost immediately got a hit and a hook-up. I forgot all about the mosquitoes and the lack of oxygen as a beautiful greenback almost identical to my last one twisted and turned until it was landed and in my hands. And that is when I heard the sound of an animal running toward me fast.

Looking over my shoulder I fully expected a medium-sized black bear as I scanned for cubs nearby, but what I saw was a large dog running as fast as she could out of the forest and straight toward me and the fish. Taking no chances this time, I released the trout before she reached me, and she skidded to a halt just briefly as if to say, "Why do you keep letting them go?"

Realizing that the trout was gone, Maya seemed to decide that since she had run all that way to get to me, there was no reason she should be deprived of her victory swim just because I had butter fingers. (I think I heard the mosquitoes laughing in my ear. That's what it sounded like anyway.) In truth, I didn't care. I came in hopes of catching one greenback cutthroat trout, and I had caught two and missed a few others. It was a fine day, and besides, I was starting to really feel the elevation.

I stood up from releasing the second fish and felt my eyes going gray, my vision narrowing, my breathing labored, and a headache forming that made my eyes cross. There was a growing ache in my lungs every time I inhaled, and the ever so slight feeling of nausea overtaking me. I'd been here before; this was the onset of elevation sickness. We packed it in and started back.

The problem with elevation sickness is that the only real cure is to reduce the elevation where you are standing, and that's not possible when you're looking at a four-and-half-mile hike that will fluctuate between 10,600 and 10,000 feet. It seems very hit and miss for me; I have been absolutely fine at high elevation one time, and deathly ill another. In Peru I almost died twice on the Salkantay Trail to Machu Picchu where the trail ran from 13,000 to 15,000 feet. But in Africa I was fine high up on the slopes of Mount Kenya watching forest elephants playing in an icy-cold waterhole. And I was fine in Utah, New Mexico, and Arizona at 10,000 feet. This time I was feeling rough and worn out on the hike back from the lake to the car. I was breathing heavy and deep, feeling drained of energy, and plodding forward with the words, "March or Die," streaming through my foggy head. It wasn't all bad; Sarah walked with me, ever patient with this lowlander, and in between my labored breathing we had some wonderful conversations about life and living in the outdoors. Kirk marched on a bit ahead of us so that he could keep an eye on Maya, who once again was eager to explore whatever was yet to come.

She was so childlike, and it was so refreshing. I don't care a bit that she swam through my fishing water while looking back at me as if to say, "Well, what are you waiting for? Jump in!" If she ever makes it down to Texas, I'm going to take her swimming in the Llano River. I can fish there anytime.

Sarah and I were deep in conversation about the time we rounded a corner and found Maya sitting in front of Kirk at a shady spot in the trail. Kirk was looking down at her and saying, "You are so lucky . . . you are so, so, lucky." That's when he turned toward us and presented a single porcupine quill he had just extracted from her face.

We never heard a yelp or any indication that she had been tagged, and after the quill was out and she listened dutifully to Kirk's instruction that she needed to be more careful where she stuck her nose, she wagged her tail and trotted on ahead, happily sticking her face into every bush and blowdown that might hold a treasure. I have to admire her insistence upon youthful abandon. I think she can teach me a thing or two.

After Maya's run-in with the porcupine, Kirk kept her a little closer and we all walked together. Kirk and I have a knack for enjoying moments together, floating down a river without saying a word or walking down a trail telling stories of our many youthful exploits around the world while simultaneously noting the physical limitations that mileage is placing on us . . . more and more each day. We talked of my times in Europe, Africa, South America, and the Caribbean, and his times that ranged from Russia to New Zealand to the Amazon. We talked about our close calls and most vivid moments of being completely alive, and we talked about the value of "pushing through" hardship and challenge. And most of all, we talked about us both still having "something in the basement," as Rocky Balboa might say. We still have adventures to experience, places to explore, and metaphorical quills to pull out of our ever-smiling faces. As long as we're alive, we are still living life fully. And like Maya, we have not lost our childlike abandon and desire to explore and experience, no matter the cost. There is value in childlike wisdom.

That night over pizza and wine, we talked about the times we've known and the times we hoped lay ahead. We spoke of how much the country and world has changed in a few short years, and how much humanity has remained the same over several millennia. After all, sticks and stone may break my bones, but ICBMs will vaporize a city. We are still the same apes but with car keys, who live the schizophrenic existence of seeking to both kill and save each other with greater efficiency.

And this brings me to an important point my friends: Everything we choose to do in life is habit forming. We can choose to tear things and people down or build them up. Everything in life is a choice. Making no choice is an act of apathy, and apathy is a choice. What does this have to do with fishing and friendship? Everything.

To my mind and sensibilities, native fish in their native waters are a gift in so many ways. They teach us some things and remind us of others . . . if we pay attention. And every angler, hunter, hiker, and outdoor enthusiast can learn so much just by paying attention. It's why I love small-stream fly fishing.

To be successful in connecting with skittish, wild fish in clear, fast water, the angler must pay attention to every detail and nuance. Where are the foam lines and what do they say about feeding channels? Where is there natural cover and where is the water too exposed? What do the trees, birds, and even frogs tell you about the health of the stream? What flowers are blooming or birds singing and what do they tell us about fish migrations or spawning times? Small-stream fishing is one of my greatest mindfulness practices. It is meditation in action.

There was a time when all we had to do to make nature "right" was leave it alone, but that time has passed and will never come back. There is a reason that Aldo Leopold wrote that it is with "fire, axe, and gun" that we manage a forest. In the Anthropocene (age of humanity), there is no place on Earth that has not been touched by the hand of *Homo sapiens* either directly or indirectly. Every place from Pittsburgh to Patagonia has been in some way modified by humanity. Every landscape is a historical landscape, a mix of natural and contrived outcomes. In some ways, that can never be repaired. But there are things we can do to find our "better angels," and I want to do my part. I am trying to do my part now. Join me?

Before the arrival of humans of European descent, Colorado had at least four species of native trout. The yellowfin trout is now thought to be extinct due to the introduction of non-native rainbow trout, which hybridized them out of genetic existence. It's a shame, and unless a remnant population is miraculously found, this large and beautiful fish will never swim the waters surrounding Twin Lakes again. I wish we could bring them back. I sometimes imagine connecting to one of those ten-pound trout with its small black spots scattered along its lower back and rainbow-colored tail. I envision its lemon-yellow body, pectoral, pelvic, and anal fins flashing in the sunlight as I carefully roll the fish over to calm it as I slip out the barbless hook and send it on its way home. But chances are I will never have this chance, and neither will my daughter, or anyone's grandchildren. It's too late, and that makes me sad.

The Colorado River and Rio Grande cutthroats are suffering some of the same issues, plus new ones created by accelerated climate change, but thus far, due to the efforts of various government agencies and private nonprofit organizations such as Trout Unlimited, the Western Native Fish Initiative, and The Nature Conservancy, these fish can still be found. I managed to connect with the Pecos River strain of Rio Grande cutthroat in New Mexico, and I had to travel to Utah to find my first Colorado River cutthroats, but I am so grateful I had the chance to hold these living abstract paintings in my hands, even briefly. I will never forget the joy of watching that first fish of each variety as it swam away, hopefully no worse for wear from our encounter.

Once native to the South Platte Basin, the greenback cutthroat trout is the designated state fish of Colorado. It received this designation in 1994. Prior to that, from 1954 to 1994 the non-native rainbow trout was the "state fish of Colorado." How ironic, but it reflects the widely held ideology of the time that nature was there to be conquered and manipulated as we saw fit, and that the primary goal of state "fish and game" agencies was to create more fishing opportunities for bigger and more exotic fish without regard to the ecological impact on the natives. This specific worldview has led to the loss and reduction of many native fish.

By 1937 the greenback trout was presumed to be extinct. In the 1950s fish thought to be "greenbacks" were located and stocked on both sides of the Continental Divide, even though they were only native on the east side of that geologic line. (We can't even seem to do restoration without screwing it up.) As it turned out, those fish were genetic mongrels and not actual greenback cutthroat trout. In 2013 a remnant population of genetically pure greenback cutthroat trout was found along a few miles of a single stream named Bear Creek. Since then, Colorado Parks and Wildlife and their conservation partners have been working to restore genetically pure greenback cutthroat trout in specific locations within their original range.

I don't know if the beautiful fish that we caught at that high-mountain lake were genetically pure greenbacks or not, but I'd like to think they were, not because I am "checking the box" as I tally up the species I've caught, but because I want to feel some sense of hope for the future of wild America and feral American humanity. Any devil can selfishly tear things down; it takes an act of quasi-divinity to put things right again. Each fish I catch is distinct. I don't treat them mindlessly like stuffing popcorn in my mouth at the movies. I enjoy them in the moment, and after all, the moment and the memories are all we have.

Without a doubt the best part of fishing has been the friendships. As much as I love mountain streams, Texas Hill Country rivers, and the rolling sea off the coast of Cape Cod, it has been the company I have shared in these places that has made all the difference. Angling brings us closer to nature, life's big questions, each other, and our true selves. Angling causes us to pay attention to the nuances of nature and hopefully learn to value it for much more than something as silly as a "trophy." Angling together allows us to see each new place through the eyes of a friend.

Looking back on this adventure, I have so many great memories of Kirk and me floating down the Yampa, dapping in the headwaters, casting into a magnificent high-country lake, and sitting on the deck sipping wine as the sun drifts low over the horizon. In a time where the whole world seems lonely, times like these remind me that we are never alone. Everything and everyone on Earth is connected. We need to remember that, and act accordingly.

Chapter Fourteen

Bear River and Colorado River Cutthroat Trout

East Fork Bear River and Middle Fork Blacks Fork River

*Most people are on the world, not in it—have no conscious sympathy
or relationship to anything about them—undiffused, separate, and
rigidly alone like marbles of polished stone, touching but separate.*

—John Muir

My daughter Megan has been the joy of my life, and being her
father is the most important role I've ever undertaken. Besides unconditional love, the one most memorable gift I ever gave her is the ability to
fly-fish the rivers of our Texas Hill Country homeland. Our times together
on those homewaters were among the best times of my life and, for me,
everything else pales in comparison. That is why I was so happy to discover
that my friends Brett Prettyman and Paul Burnett chose to bring their
sons with them on the day we went searching for Bear River and Colorado
cutthroat trout in the mountains of northwestern Utah. Owen rode with

Brett and me, while Cooper rode with his father in a separate vehicle. The plan was that we would meet up at a turnout along the road that would take us up into the Uinta Mountains. The plan worked out.

Cooper was a polite, soft-spoken kid who wore an Oreo Cookie Buff and who was heartwarmingly close with his dad. Over the course of the day, I would often look over to see them fishing together, making memories, and sharing in the moment. Owen and I hit it off pretty well, and on the way from Salt Lake City to the Uinta Mountains we talked about his pet green snake and geckos and about all the critters I had when I was growing up. He and Brett reminded me of Megan and me when she was that age, and memories of us casting beside each other at our favorite spot on the Guadalupe River flooded through my mind. And then I was reminded of my dad taking me fishing for bluegill in the local lake, and how important those little adventures were, and always will be, to me. Those were some of the best times of my young life, and these are some of the best times of my older life. My connection to nature was passed on to me from my dad, and then from me to my daughter, who in turn passes it on to the children she teaches as a professional outdoor educator. Nature saves generations of us, keeps us grounded and reminds us that, even in troubled times, life is beautiful.

If you think about it (and you should), a love for and connection with the outdoors and nature is one of the greatest gifts we can ever give a child or an adult. The gift of appreciating and gaining a sense of peace from nature that is passed on from generation to generation is so much more valuable than blue eyes, brown skin, or freckles. Those are traits that are involuntarily passed down via the seemingly random lottery of genetic coding. Teaching a kid to love and derive spiritual value from nature is a gift that is intentional and timeless. It is a conscious act of love. Fishing, hunting, hiking, camping, gardening, even beachcombing, when done mindfully and ethically, are all pathways to living a better life. Why wouldn't we pass that on, generation after generation?

This has been a year and a half like no other in my life. I have undertaken an adventure in the writing of this book that has included traveling via airplane or on long road trips in my pickup truck across the country, often meeting people for the first time and going fishing for native fish with them in the homewaters of both the fish and the people. It has been a wonderful journey filled with uncertainty, which is a key ingredient for any adventure. And now I found myself with my new friend Brett and his son Owen, driving up into the magnificent Uinta Mountains in search of wild, native Bear River and Colorado River cutthroat trout. Life can be beautiful if we are willing to make the leap of faith.

The Uinta Mountains are an east–west trending subrange of the Rocky Mountains, whereas most of the Rockies trend in a north–south direction. Elevations of major peaks run from 11,000 feet to 13,528-foot Kings Peak, which also happens to be the highest point in the state of Utah. Between the foothills and tree line are vast forests of lodgepole pine, subalpine fir, Engelmann spruce, Douglas fir, and quaking aspen, with willows lining many of its smaller creeks. The wildlife here is as varied and vast as the landscape. Predators such as black bears, mountain lions, and coyotes abound, while a lone pack of gray wolves has been reported in the Colorado portion of the mountain range. Prey animals include Rocky Mountain elk and bighorn sheep, mountain goats up high, pronghorn down low, and mule deer in the middle. And all of this is fed by several watersheds including the Colorado/Green River watershed and the Bear River watershed. Both contain their own unique native cutthroat trout, and connecting with them was our angling goal for the day. In one day, we hoped to catch and release two of the four required cutthroat subspecies to complete the "Utah Cutthroat Slam."

The Bear River is a big name for a narrow yet beautiful stretch of flowing water. This was the ancestral home of the Northwest Shoshone people, and as we drove and then walked though this land I began to wish for a time machine that could allow me to see it before the arrival of Euro-Americans. The Shoshone people hunted buffalo, elk, deer, and small game; gathered and stored the seeds of wild grasses; and, most poignantly for me, were the native anglers who caught and ate trout from these same waters. I wondered what it was like back then when the fish and the people were all native.

We parked high above the river, which I could hear rushing below and see only intermittently between openings in the wall of pine and spruce trees that surrounded it. We strung up our rods and began the climb down to the river. It was early morning and still had a crisp coolness to the air, and the aspen trees quivered in the morning breeze as we made our way down, down, down into the canyon. We were about eight thousand feet in elevation, and being from the Texas lowlands I am forever aware that down, down, down translates into up, up, up on the return trip. Gravity is one of the only absolute truths I've ever known. All else is simply perception and subjective opinion. I can't change my mind about gravity. It just is.

The first thing we saw upon arrival was the handiwork of humanity. In this case it was ultimately a good thing or, rather, it was a mitigation effort supported by Trout Unlimited to allow farmers with water rights to exercise those rights for irrigation, but to do so in a way that did not result in trout and other aquatic life being spilled out into irrigation ditches to eventually die in the mud. It was a water diversion that was designed to protect the fish while allowing the legally permitted water allotment to proceed to the farms—an elegant solution to a sticky situation. Just beyond the diversion there were several natural pools and a series of pocket water areas. We were all using size 16 stimulators as we began prospecting up and down the river, with Paul and Cooper exploring upriver and Brett, Owen, and me working our way down.

I began working a choice-looking set of plunge pools without result. Brett was watching from downriver, and after a while he expressed his surprise that I had not received a strike. I said that sometimes trout fishing reminds me of snake hunting—you never find them where you think they should be. When I was a young man, I used to dream of being a herpetologist. I would go out into the woods searching for snakes, not to harm, but simply to find, sort of like a birder with a "life list." I would always envision finding a rattler at the base of a cactus or a kingsnake just under a slab of fallen tree bark, or a cottonmouth moccasin resting among a patch of flowering lily pads. Invariably I'd end up finding them asleep in the shade under my truck or crossing the road on the way home. I love irony.

We came to a nice pool just a short way down from the place where we entered the river. Brett said, "Why don't you try that?"

I knew it looked like perfect water and said, "Are you sure you don't want Owen to take it?"

He said, "No . . . Owen lives here and can come back; this is your one shot . . . but thanks for asking." He smiled and I smiled back. I took my shot.

I started at the top of the pool with a series of good downstream drifts, but without results. Again, it seemed impossible that there wouldn't be a nice cutthroat in this most perfect of places. It was mindfulness practice time as I slowly and methodically worked every seam and eddy from top to tail until I was almost out of water to drift down, and that is when I received the strike and missed it. (One and done? I wondered.) I cast again and drifted over the same spot. *Nada!* It mattered not; I knew he was in there, so I took a breather, watched a tiny ground squirrel as it watched me, and listened to the sound of the wind in the aspen trees. Then, I took a deep, Zen-like Texan Buddha cleansing breath and made another soft cast into the foam. Strike, hook-up, excitement, landing . . . brook trout!

He was beautiful, as brookies always are, but I did not travel all the way to Utah to catch brook trout that belongs in West Virginia, Pennsylvania, or even northwestern Iowa. It's not the fish's fault, it's ours. I thanked him and set him free even as I thought the words that should resonate in every western angler's head, "Eat more brookies!"

I moved to the next set of plunge pools and cast toward a foam line below a half-submerged rock and just above a small waterfall. It was a pretty spot, and if I were a trout, I'd want to live there. Lucky for me the trout agreed, and I began receiving and missing aggressive but incomplete strikes from what seemed a smallish fish. It did not matter the size; it was the species that I was after. The Bear River cutthroat was my first stop on the four-fish Utah Slam. Brookies don't count.

After missing those strikes, I decided to take a moment to dry off the fly and give it a little dose of floatant. My fly had lost a little of its "giddy-up," so taking a moment to give it a shake and rest those pools seemed like time well invested. On my next cast I didn't miss, and it was a Bear River cutthroat trout! It was a tiny Bear River cutthroat that I landed, photographed, and joyfully released back to the same pool I took him from. Small or not, he was beautiful, and I loved him.

Just before I connected with my four-inch-long Bear River cutthroat, Owen caught a brookie and released it with the same mixture of happiness and disappointment. It didn't take long before I heard some commotion and excitement where he and Brett were, a bit upriver from me. Owen had been casting under a fallen tree when he hooked into and landed a nice-sized cutthroat. We all cheered, and I could see him holding it as Brett took the photo. I remember thinking that it was the color of autumn sunshine. After it was released and I saw the big smiles on Brett and Owen's faces, I hollered out, "Hey Owen! Your fish was big enough to eat my fish!" His smile was bigger than his fish. It had already been a great day even if nothing else went right, although I hoped it would. We still had Colorado River cutthroats on today's fishing menu.

We fished the East Fork of the Bear River a bit longer, with both Owen and me connecting with a few more brook trout, but no more Bear River cutthroats. I want that to sink in a little bit, my friends. Here we were in the headwaters of the Bear River and, as I have found almost everywhere, native fish were being outcompeted and overwhelmed by non-native transplants. In the cold waters of the West, the damage is being done by the introduction of non-native brown, brook, and rainbow trout. In the cold-water East, it is browns and rainbows that are doing the damage. In the warm waters of the American South, it is the hybridization of transplanted Florida bass with native northern largemouth bass, and introduced invasive smallmouth bass into the waters of the native and endemic Guadalupe bass of the Texas Hill Country. To my mind there is something seriously wrong with so many "state fish" being in danger of extinction and all because of the recklessness of humans. We need to fix this, y'all. It's up to us to make this right.

It had been a nice morning, and we were successful. After all, the goal over the next three days was for me to connect with and document the catch and release of at least one of all four Utah native cutthroat trout from their historical native waters. I had managed to catch and release one Bear River cutthroat, and it was breathtakingly beautiful, even in its minuscule form. Owen's was about three times the size of mine, and just as beautiful—the same painting on a larger canvas. We still had a bit of driving to do to get out of the Bear River watershed, back into Wyoming, and then down into the Green River watershed of northern Utah where we hoped to find some Colorado River cutthroats to round out the day. We were heading to the

East and Middle Forks of the Blacks Fork River, and now it was time for the return trip out of the wide Bear River Canyon, and this time the journey was going up, and up, and up, and up. I made it back okay, with just a few stops along the way to "take in the scenery."

The drive into the Green River watershed was wonderful. The topography grew increasingly elevated and the air even thinner. It was lunchtime, and Brett and Paul had decided together where we'd stop for our feast of amazing deli sandwiches, sea-salt chips, and blood orange–flavored Italian sparkling water. We came to a halt next to a high and marshy-looking meadow with a stream bisecting its willow-filled center and the surrounding aspen trees trembling in the breeze. It was an extremely "moosey"-looking area. There is a story behind that remark, and now is as good a time to tell it as any.

On the way up to the Bear River that morning, we had passed an area in the foothills where Brett told me, "We almost always see moose in here!" It was a vast area that we were passing for some time, and while I appreciated him pointing out the "consolation prizes" of mule deer and sandhill cranes, I could see those in Texas. So I began to kid with Brett, saying, "I'm not seeing any moose on this moose tour." Just a few weeks prior I had been fishing with our mutual friend Kirk Deeter in Colorado, and Kirk told me that we'd have a good chance of seeing moose on our hikes into the high-country lakes we were fishing, but there too, no moose. And a few months ago I was in New Mexico with my buddy Toner Mitchell, and he pointed along the road just north of Santa Fe and said, "We almost always see bighorn sheep along here." Every time one of them told me such tales I'd get my hopes up, and every time all I'd ever see was willow trees and sagebrush. I was beginning to suspect a "snipe hunt." I can't wait until I get them down to Texas and we're driving along, and I say, "I almost always see Chupacabra around here!"

As we arrived at the Blacks Fork River, I noticed something I have not seen before in this country—a shepherd tending to his flock. It was a beautiful sight and it brought to mind one of my favorite Rumi quotes, "Be a lamp, or a lifeboat, or a ladder. Help someone's soul heal. Walk out of your house like a shepherd." I watched as he wandered across the meadow with his flock of sheep, his sheepdog, and only a wooden staff to steady him or to chase off predators. I felt transported to another time when there were far fewer people on the Earth, though humanity was much the same. Then as now, most humans seem to live as sheep. Some are predators, and a rare few are sheepdogs and shepherds. All my life I've had little more than a wooden staff to steady me, but that wood comes from a sturdy tree, so all is well.

I stood on the bridge over the river and looked down into the churning water. It has always amazed me how water moves through time naturally. Every drop we have has always been here as water, snow, hail, ice, vapor, and water again. Life is a circle, not a line. Being a fly fisher causes you to see rivers and streams differently. We see and understand the meaning behind riffles, rapids, pools, eddies, waterfalls, and stretches of pocket water. We learn to pay attention to grasses blowing in the wind and grasshoppers floating downstream. We notice things like swallows dipping and diving over the water or minnows skittering across its surface. We need to notice that bluebonnets bloom as the white bass begin to run, or that birch trees sprout leaves just in time for the hatch. Being an angler or a hunter should heighten our awareness of rivers and creatures and the climate itself. It should, anyway. I notice these things. Do you?

We spread out at first, with Paul and Cooper going upstream on the Middle Fork and Owen and me fishing downstream toward the confluence with the East Fork. Brett already had his Colorado River cutthroat for his second slam, so he decided to chill out and just spend some time guiding Owen, as any good father would. The bond between Owen and his dad was obvious and heartwarming, although it also caused me to long for the days when my daughter was young and still lived in America. At one point I looked over at Brett and said, "Grab every moment, brother. These are some of the best days of your life, and they pass all too quickly."

In time, after not getting any bites, we hiked through a rocky wash to the East Fork and into a real "moosey"-looking forest of aspen and willows. Paul pointed to a wide pool with a long-braided tail and a few nice eddies and said, "I know there is a sixteen-inch cutthroat living in there, Steve.

Go get it and complete your slam." I worked my way downstream and crossed over before beginning the methodical process of casting, drifting, and recasting across the pool from tail to top without result. I never did see that sixteen-inch fish, and if he was in there, he wanted nothing of me.

I looked up and saw that Brett had decided to indulge himself a little and was fishing just upstream, while Owen was trying an eddy not far from his dad. I looked down and saw Paul carefully and lovingly guiding Cooper through some nice pocket water. Truthfully, I was "all in" to the idea of completing the slam in three days, and I wanted to catch at least one Colorado River cutthroat during the one chance I'd get on this trip, but in that moment, all was right with the world. It was about fishing, with friends.

The "Utah Cutthroat Slam" is a joint conservation education and fund-raising project between Trout Unlimited and the Utah Division of Wildlife Resources. It was created as a way to have an angling adventure and support the restoration and conservation of native trout in Utah. I happily paid my $20 to register for this challenge, knowing my money was going to a good cause, no matter the outcome. The challenge is that you must catch, document, and release each of the four Utah cutthroat trout subspecies in their native waters.

Besides the obvious positive outcomes of anglers helping to fund native fish conservation and habitat restoration, this is an absolutely wonderful and enriching experience, if you approach it as such. Programs like the Utah Cutthroat Slam cause the aware angler to think of the planet more realistically, not divided by arbitrary political lines on a map but by watersheds. If you make the most of this experience, you will learn so much about the fish and the places they call home, and that in turn will hopefully help create greater awareness and appreciation for native fish and healthy watersheds. I hope so. After all, we're not really anglers, hunters, hikers, or birders as much as we are participants in nature. We have to get into the fish's head and do as Thomas McGuane once described as going "beyond being a presentationist, reading not only the thought of the trout, but the next thought, which the trout had not yet thought." And being an imperfect but practicing Texan Buddha, I found this journey to be meditative and mindful. Please allow me to explain . . .

Every angler knows that it is all too easy to get into the trap of the "numbers game" and, in doing so, lose sight of why we originally loved fishing. The industry drives the idea of "more fish and bigger fish" as if it is somehow a measure of your virility to chalk up numbers of fish or pounds like the score on a 1970s pinball machine. This makes fishing competitive instead of contemplative. It turns something beautiful into something banal. It turns something that is meaningful into something meaningless. But if you fish these kinds of challenges, the real challenge is to teach yourself once again to be childlike and to value a single fish. Let me tell you, my friend, once you hold that color-splashed native in your hands over the rushing waters of a wild stream that you traveled a long way to get to . . . you value that fish and that moment.

I would like to see every state in the union create a viable and verifiable native fish challenge to raise funds, awareness, and desire for native fish conservation and watershed restoration. I've already reached out to my friends at Texas Parks and Wildlife about the idea. Think about it: the "Texas Native Bass Slam." The only thing it takes to get things going in the right direction in each of our home states is anglers who embrace the idea. I don't know about you, but I'd rather lead than follow. The hind dog in the traces always has the same view.

We worked our way downriver on the East Fork, and all of it looked like amazing water but none of us got so much as a look from a single fish. I ended up in the middle, with Paul and Cooper downstream and Brett and Owen upstream, as we leapfrogged ever so politely around each other. We were always just in sight of each other for safety's sake; after all, the boys were young and the moose, bears, and lions in the area were big. But the real threat started rolling in as a wall of coal-black clouds and a distant rumble, which is comforting when you're sitting on the front porch and unnerving when you're standing in a river waving a stick. Paul walked over toward me and said, "I think that storm is heading this way. . . . Cooper and I are going to walk back toward the Middle Fork so we can be closer to the vehicles in case things get dangerous." I watched as they crossed the river and stepped into the tangle of willows onto what looked like a trail. I reeled in and decided to do the same.

By the time I crossed the river and got to the "trail," I had lost any sight of them or the river. I could still hear the water rushing over the riverbed, but I found myself on a winding and at one time muddy game trail that was moving away from, not toward, the water. Since the mud was dry, I could not see any footprints from Paul or Cooper and no indication that they had come this way. Did I mention that it looked quite "moosey" in there? All along the trail I saw a myriad of moose prints and bear scat that told me that perhaps I needed to come up with a "plan B." I cut through the dense brush toward the sound of running water and away from the rumbling thunder. When I came out on the river again, I recognized the spot where Paul said the sixteen-inch cutthroat lived, and I decided to do what any angler would do when a thunderstorm is coming and you're trying to catch even one fish to make the day complete—I gave it another try, but to no avail.

Back on the Middle Fork, Paul and Cooper stopped at the car until the rumble-clouds seemed to pass. I made the gamble that all was well and began fishing some pocket water, finally picking up and missing a few half-hearted strikes from smallish fish. At least I knew they were in there! I looked upstream and saw a beautiful stretch of water running along some fallen trees, so I decided to take my time getting up there, watching the river, looking for clues as to how best to approach it with an upstream cast over blowdown. I snipped off my stimulator and tied on a size 16 purple haze. Did I mention that I love the color purple? Well, I do. The calm of blue with the fire of red. It's like a wine cuvée of sangiovese, merlot, and petite sirah—who could resist? Hopefully not the trout.

By this time Paul and Cooper had gotten back on the water, and I pointed out the pocket water where I had missed a small fish a few minutes prior. Cooper started to cast a small fly into the stream as I addressed the next pool with all the strategy and focus of a golfer at Augusta. Something just told me, "This spot looks fishy." Clouds were rolling in and this was my only chance to connect with my Colorado cutthroat. It was now or never.

I crept up, kept a low profile, and landed the softest presentation I could manage. I watched the little dry fly breathlessly as it drifted quickly along the most obvious foam line, and then there was a flash of color in the water and a splash on the surface where my fly once floated, and I raised the rod just in time to see my fly come back out of the water and sail over my right shoulder into a bush. Merde! Pas de chance!

Fly fishing teaches many things. One of the greatest gifts it has given me is patience. I am calm and ever so patient when untangling a tangle in a bush or tree, and I am calm and ever so methodical when planning a new approach to an old problem. That never used to be me; fly fishing taught me that sense of "It is what it is . . . and it will be what it will be." It's a lesson that has served me well and made for a happier life. So I unwound the tangle and cast again, this time just a little to the outside of the last attempt, not because I meant to, but because I just did. It was an accident born of my trepidation of catching a tree branch and spooking the fish, but it paid off. A much bigger fish rose to the fly and took it, and I raised the rod just in time to see my little three-weight double over and throb with the power of a beautiful Colorado River cutthroat on the end.

Paul ran over to help me get him into the net and take the required photo to prove I caught it where I said I did. He estimated it at sixteen inches, and with him being a fisheries biologist, I'm inclined to believe him. It's not that I care that much about such things as size and number of fish, but I have to admit, after catching my micro-trout in the Bear River that morning, catching a bigger fish felt nice. I guess I'm still evolving. I set him free and thanked him, as I always do. I will never forget him, whereas I have long since forgotten any of the fish from those days back home when I'm connecting with yet another bass on every third cast.

One fish, in one pool, on one river, in one watershed that drains from one mountain range can become the center of your world. You recall every detail of that fish, from its colors and patterns to the spot in the creek where you both "met." Fishing like this made me feel more connected and less like an accountant with a fly rod tallying up "how many" and "how big." As my buddy Bob White might say if asked, "Fish were caught."

I was thinking about the Zen of all this and simply enjoying the river about the time a massive lightning bolt slammed into the ground some-where that felt like just over my shoulder but was probably a quarter mile away. I looked to find Paul and Cooper quickly heading back toward the cars, and in short order Brett and Owen met us there with the report that they hadn't caught anything and, "That was a close one!" We waited it out for a few minutes until there seemed to be no more lightning and, as you might guess, we went back to fishing. Well, I had my fish, so I left my rod in the car and decided to help Owen try to catch his Colorado cutthroat while Brett got in a little fishing of his own.

It was nice for me to spend a little time trying to help Owen, although I may have annoyed him with my all too frequent reminders to "be careful" as he crossed the river. He looked back at me over his shoulder once or twice as if to say, "Really . . . I've got this!" But guiding someone else's child is a big responsibility, and I didn't want to screw it up by not paying attention and allowing him to get washed downriver, stomped by a moose, or kidnapped by a bigfoot. Any one of these eventualities could ruin an otherwise perfect day of fishing. So I'd rather annoy him by saying again and again, "Be careful."

Owen made a couple of nice casts and drifts into a pool under a spruce tree, and on the third or fourth cast he hooked a nice cutthroat, which almost immediately jumped and threw the hook. A moment later he was casting to a nearby foam line when he caught another smaller fish, and it too shook free. We worked our way up to a beautiful long, deep flat that contained multiple foam lines and nice currents. He cast, hooked, and lost two more fish in there and glanced over his shoulder this time with a look of a tired and hungry kid. *Pas de chance* ("bad luck"). It was okay. Unlike me, Owen will be back here, and he will get his fish another day. He was a trooper and worked hard for every strike. Well done, Owen. Well done!

The drive back out of the mountains and across the high, sagebrush-covered plains was beautiful, with mule deer, pronghorn, and surreal-looking windmills along each side of the long dirt road back to the highway. At one point a family of pronghorn ran directly into our path, and fortunately Brett applied the brakes just as they stepped on the gas. It was a buck, doe, and fawn, and for a second the fawn began to lose its legs from underneath it and was sliding sideways for a single breathless moment when it seemed to move in slow motion, but in reality was traveling at the speed of life. It all worked out, with the antelope making it across the road and into the sage, and we all looked at each other with expressions of relief. You'd be surprised how expressive an ungulate can be when they've just dodged the front bumper of a rental car.

It was a great day. It was the only day of my three days of fishing where we were under pressure to catch two separate varieties of native cutthroat in two separate high-country watersheds. Thanks to the knowledge of Brett and Paul and the hard work of people from both Trout Unlimited and the Utah Division of Wildlife Resources, I had been successful. But the success of this day was much more than simply catching two fish in two distant places and documenting that this was done. The biggest success to me is in the friendships we built together in these wild places, and the legacy we passed on from generation to generation. What made it great was we did this together.

It seems to me that much of the loneliness in this country can be traced back to "virtual living" and the vast and growing distance between us that appears to be causing the extinction of empathy. Instead of "unfriending" each other, we need to befriend each other more often. Relationships are like dry-fly fishing for wary native fish in their native homewaters. You have to pay attention, stay focused, drift without drag, and, above all, care enough to keep casting forward. Fishing and friendships require patience, understanding, and a genuine respect for each other. My dad taught me to be an ethical angler and hunter, and I taught my daughter the same lessons. Is there any greater gift we can give each other? I don't think so. I really don't.

Chapter Fifteen

Bonneville Cutthroat Trout
Wheeler Creek, Utah

Yellowstone Cutthroat Trout
Raft River Mountains, Utah

Maybe your signature as a fly fisherman isn't determined by how big a trout you can catch, but how small a trout you can catch without being disappointed.

—*John Gierach*

THE BONNEVILLE CUTTHROAT TROUT IS THE STATE FISH OF UTAH AND IS native to the streams and rivers of the Bonneville Basin, excluding the Bear River. Geologic and genetic science seem to indicate that although the Bear River and Bonneville cutthroats currently exist in relatively close proximity to each other, the Bear River cutthroat is biologically more akin to the Yellowstone cutthroat trout. This is because a geologic shift once changed the course of the Bear River, which was originally connected to Bear Lake and the Yellowstone and Snake River drainages. It is an example of geology impacting the direction of watersheds in a relatively swift manner, while biological adaptation and evolution occurred over a long, long, long period of time (in human years).

It's important for all anglers, hunters, hikers, and lovers of nature to understand the difference between change caused by nature and changes caused by the darker sides of human nature—namely, ignorance, short-sightedness, greed, and apathy. Even though the course of the Bear River was changed, the water remained cold and clean and in sufficient amounts to sustain wild, native trout, so that over a much longer time they adapted and evolved into their own most perfect form for that environment. But if we take that same river drainage, and instead of moving its direction we begin to raise its temperature, reduce its depth and flow, increase siltation and phosphate-based nutrients from runoff, and add invasive species, we now have a perfect storm of reasons for that fish to decline and eventually disappear. And it's not just the fish that goes; it's the entire original ecosystem of the watershed. The good news is that we are not only the problem, we are also the solution. And the first thing my buddy Brett Prettyman and I did on my second morning is meet with our friend and Trout Unlimited (TU) fisheries biologist Paul Burnett at a fish ladder and water diversion project on the Weber River.

As we pulled into the industrial-looking dirt parking space near the river, I noticed a flock of wild Rio Grande turkeys. It seems that in a bid to increase hunting opportunities and the corresponding license revenue, the Utah Division of Wildlife Resources decided to introduce these wonderful non-native birds into a wildscape where nature never intended them to exist. Apparently the learning curve is steep, and the climb is slow.

I feel certain that the Weber was once a free-flowing and magnificently beautiful stretch of river from its headwaters to its terminus into the Great Salt Lake. But now, a busy highway runs along much of its length and parts of its life-giving water vanishes into the ground along the way, irrigating crops and livestock, and watering lawns and golf courses. It doesn't make it to the Great Salt Lake anymore. It just dies out into the earth and through a myriad of pipes and culverts. It just disappears.

But here where we were standing it still flows at about 750 cubic feet per second, and besides the massive plumes of green algae caused by increased temperatures and nutrients in the water, it's still a healthy trout habitat where native Bonneville cutthroat swim to and from spawning tributaries such as Strawberry Creek. TU and its partners have worked hard to restore habitat and water flow, as well as protect fish and other wildlife from finding themselves flopping in a field somewhere, gasping for water.

On the side of the river where we were parked, I saw the metal fencing and trespass warning signs that had to be erected to keep people from dumping their trash in the river. Just inside the fencing was an elaborate series of concrete passageways that guided fish downstream with most of the water, and then sent the rest of the water to be used somewhere in suburbia or the urban capital city of Utah. This is the reality of things in a world of 7.8 billion humans and a city of over 200,000.

We waded across the cold, clear river and I got a close-up look at the fish passage that allows Bonneville cutthroats to ascend and descend the river safely. I watched the solar-powered scrubbers cleaning the algae off the mesh fish screens, and I saw where TU had to place a metal grate on top of the solar panel because some people seemed to delight in throwing rocks at it, just to see if they could break it (they could). And as I looked back toward the river where we had waded just moments before, I saw a man who looked to be in his late sixties fly fishing just downstream of the dam. I was happy to see him. I'm not sure if he was happy to see us.

After looking at the fish ladder along the Weber River, we drove up to the one that has been installed by TU at the river's confluence with Strawberry Creek, which is a historically important spawning tributary for Bonneville cutthroat. When the highway was built, a hundred-yard-long downward-sloping concrete culvert was built underneath it to allow the creek water to descend into the river. But unfortunately, the water descended at a speed that made it impossible for the trout to ascend and spawn. Under Paul's direction and with the efforts of volunteers, TU installed a metal fish ladder so that Bonneville cutthroats can now swim up the creek and spawn as they always had prior to the construction of the highway. This fix required funding, planning, and labor to complete. It should have been part of the equation when the government built the roadway. You know, "environmental impact mitigation." Thirty years in government has taught me that they won't do it unless we mandate it. Sad but true.

Before we left Strawberry Creek to go fishing, Brett told me a story about when they were building the fish ladder. There is a small, older residential community along the banks of Strawberry Creek, just upstream of the culvert and the highway. While they were working on the construction of the fish ladder, a woman walked down from her house and asked them what they were doing, and they explained. Tears filled her eyes. She said she was emotional because when she was a child she used to love watching the trout swim up the creek each year to spawn, but that she had not seen that beautiful sight since the building of the highway. She thanked them and walked away, tears still streaming from her eyes. I understand. There are so many natural wonders of my childhood that have since vanished because of the actions of humanity, which all too often is called "progress."

It was four years ago from the day that Brett and I hiked into Wheeler Creek Canyon that my father died. His passing left a hole inside me that will never fill. I wanted to share the anniversary of that day with Brett, and honor both our fathers—mine long since gone from this Earth, and his currently in a Salt Lake City medical facility, in poor health.

The places and people we love are as transient as we are, and it is important that we pay attention while we can to those things that matter, and let go of all the many things that don't. When my dad died, I went hiking in his favorite canyon and honored the man who introduced me to nature. I have done this every year since his passing, often choosing to share the day with someone special, like Brett. I told Brett that this fish was dedicated to my dad. I know he understood.

The hike up and into the canyon was along a wide dirt trail that rose high above the creek and contained hikers who could hear the rushing water below, but who would most likely not climb down the steep-sided canyon to see it. The trail was lined in boxelder, maple, aspen, and a smattering of juniper. The trees were different than they are back home, but not that different, and the dryness of the canyon reminded me of my own Texas Hill Country woodlands. Like home, this was rattlesnake country, and we were both being extra careful as to where we placed our hands and feet as we clambered down the rocky canyon side toward the sound of falling waters.

Brett and I get along "famously," as they say in those old British adventure movies. It doesn't take anything for us to devolve into two kids playing hooky and deciding that fishing makes more sense than algebra, which it does. I am fifty-nine years old, and I have never—not once—had to solve for "Y." I have, however, invested my entire life attempting to solve for "Why?"

During the climb down we began to swap spooky rattlesnake stories, as kids are prone to do while playing hooky in the woods. I told of the time when I was about sixteen and swimming in a stock tank on a ranch back home, and as I swam over to the water's edge my buddy Rick pointed from shore and yelled, "Rattler!" Apparently, it had swum up beside me, neither of us knowing that the other was there. I jumped, frightening the snake and earning a lightning-fast bite on the back of my upper-right ankle. It was a good-sized rattler of about four feet in length, and I looked down to find two perfect and profusely bleeding fang marks, along with the little scratches from the other teeth and an ever so slight and localized burning sensation. It was a dry bite, and after realizing that I was going to be okay, my buddy and I went on with our day tending to the livestock.

Brett told me of a time when he was hiking with a friend, and he saw a large rattler curled up in its resting ambush position under a cactus beside the trail. Although he was able to simply walk around it, he was a bit unnerved by its imposing and dangerous-looking demeanor. (I should mention here that I love rattlesnakes and at one time wanted to be a herpetologist and study them as my profession, while my buddy Brett is not a fan.) So the story goes that as he and his friend were hiking along a particularly narrow trail with a steep scree incline on the downward side, he stepped on something that he thought was a snake, which immediately prompted him to jump backward over the edge of the precipice, almost sliding to his death. When he breathlessly made it back up to the trail, his friend said, "What in the hell were you doing?" Brett replied, "I was jumping away from the snake in the trail!" Confused and amused his friend said, "Do you mean that stick?"

Needless to say, by the time we had climbed down to the water, both of us had snakes on the brain and were moving like two guys trying to cross a minefield. Ghost stories around the fire; snake stories along the trail. They both add a little thrill to the experience.

On my last day in Utah, Brett asked me, "What was your favorite of the four fishing experiences?" My answer was immediate: "My favorite fish was the Yellowstone, but my favorite fishing was Wheeler Creek Canyon." The stream was narrow, steep, cold, and fast. It tumbled and churned over stones and gravel with such wild abandon that it seemed amazing that trout could ever live here, and yet it was so beautiful and lush that if I were a trout, I think it would be well worth the effort. Down at the canyon's bottom the vegetation closed in, with maples and boxelder along the canyon's walls, and white-berried dogwoods along the creek's edges. I didn't even care about the threat of venomous reptiles or the steep climb back up to the trail. I was simply happy to be there. It was magical.

Since this was my only shot at a Bonneville and since Brett lives in Utah, he gave me first dibs on catching a fish. We came to a pretty little plunge pool at the base of a narrow waterfall with a long foam and bubble line extending under an overhang of stone. I started by dapping the inside rim of the stone and then progressively casting farther upstream, working the pool methodically from tail to top. When my fly landed in a slick spot on the edge of the bubbles, a fish rose and hit the fly, which caused my arm to rise to set the hook, only the fish was faster than my arm and I was left with a fly in the air and a comical look on my face. Undaunted I cast again, the fish rose, and I missed again. The gig was up. On the first pool the score was trout 1, angler 0. No worries, at least we knew they were here!

The canyon and creek were narrow enough that sometimes we were clinging to dogwoods and trying not to fall in as we skirted along the rocky edge, and other times we simply had to wade through the pool we had just fished. And that's when I came across a seam in the stone that had stream water gushing through it like a firehose, with a small pocket of calmer water along the outer edge. By small, I mean two and a half feet long by a foot wide. It seemed an unlikely spot for anything but the smallest of fish to call home, but I wasn't going to pass up any likely patch of holding water, so I snuck up on the crack in the rock and dapped my fly at the head of the falls. I was adjusting for the short drift just about the time all hell broke loose, and I lifted a good-sized Bonneville cutthroat trout from the same water that seemed too small to hold it!

I was working without a net and hadn't noticed until that moment that Brett hadn't brought his either, so I lifted the flapping fish out of the water with great excitement, bent down to wet my hands before touching him, and watched in horror as my all-important Bonneville cutthroat flipped off the hook onto the steep, narrow embankment and started to flop its way homeward toward the creek. Brett and I both made a dive for the fish like NFL players reaching for the game-winning catch, and lucky for me Brett got to him first, catching the fish in his hat just before it reached the water. It was epic!

Photos were quickly taken and high fives exchanged, and Mr. Fishy was back home in his crack before you could say "belly flop." I now had three of the four fish I needed to complete the Utah Cutthroat Slam, with only the Yellowstone cutthroat remaining. It was Brett's turn.

I hung back as Brett moved his way upstream over waterfalls and rivulets and around sticks and stones until he came to a jumble of boulders that were shaded by dogwoods. "Wow! Come see this . . . it's a Japanese Peace Garden!" he called back to me. I worked my way up and saw a perfectly balanced wide spot in the creek where three separate but equal waterfalls fed a big, broad pool of the prettiest water I could imagine. I stayed back as Brett began casting into the "garden pool."

At first, incredulously, he received not a single rise. The water looked amazing. It wasn't some crack in the rock like I had just fished; it was a picture-perfect pool of clear, cold mountain water with a twenty-foot-long foam line in a creek that is usually four to six feet wide. But no matter what he did, he got no response. He tried the far side of the creek, where he received and missed a half-hearted strike, but it was still bothering us that he didn't illicit a rise anywhere in that big, beautiful plunge pool.

Brett had a fairly meaty fly on his line, and I had a petite purple haze on mine, so I offered him my rod. He took it, made the same perfect cast he had made before to the exact same place, and caught a fish . . . in his hat. Now we both had our Bonneville cutthroats and I had three of the four I needed with one day left in my trip. The pressure was off; we could fish just for the fun of it.

We continued to work our way up the canyon creek, and it continued to be beautiful and seemingly ideal water, but it gave each of us just the one fish we needed and not one fish more. It didn't matter. I was fly-fishing in Eden. I was a lucky man sharing a special day with a dear friend. And when I slipped my only fish of the day back into his watery crack in the Earth I said, "This one's for you, Dad."

The climb back out of the canyon was steep enough that we found our-selves clinging to rocks and hoping they did not come loose, and grabbing on to overhanging tree branches so that at one point it was difficult to tell if we were climbing a cliff or climbing a tree. Once we made it to the trail, I decided to stop for a breather and just take in the mountain scenery.

We walked back along the trail, reliving the day's fishing, happy with the way everything went, and that was about the time I saw Brett stop in his tracks, but not jump off the cliff. In front of us on the trail was the prettiest four-foot-long bull snake that I have ever seen. Brett said, "Pick him up! Let's see some of your herpetology skills in action!"

I smiled. "He looks happy right there where he is," I replied, and we both walked down the trail toward the car and the promise of dinner, feel-ing completely content. In the morning, we'd leave before sunrise for the three-and-a-half-hour drive up into Idaho and back into Utah so that we could fish for the last cutthroat on my menu: the Yellowstone cutthroat.

———

The Raft River Mountains are the only remaining place in Utah to find Yellowstone cutthroat trout. And the thing is, they are stranded there by natural geologic shifts and the unnatural human-caused overuse of limited water resources. The creeks in these mountains used to connect to the Yellowstone drainage, but now they run out of the mountains and under the ground and over the agriculture fields and pastures of two states. I'm glad the streams are still here. I don't want to live in a time when they are gone.

If Wheeler Creek Canyon was my favorite place to fish, the Raft River Mountains were my favorite place to be. I guess this is partly because in some ways it reminded me of home. It felt like home, only different.

The drive from Salt Lake City took us up into Idaho and then back into Utah, and although it could be considered a long drive for a single day of fishing, it felt easy and brief and beautiful. There are a few reasons for this that I can put my finger on, and a bunch of them that I might not yet understand—something to do with a combination of the theory of relativity, quantum mechanics, the possible existence of alternate universes, and the Tao of Winnie-the-Pooh. The things I can identify include wide-open spaces with more birds of prey than I've ever seen, scores of understandably nervous ground squirrels, and a mixture of happy cows and generally content-looking pronghorn. There was also Brett's music, which I will describe as "unique."

As we cruised along a wide, hard-packed dirt road at highway speed, we jammed to the sounds of techno-electronica, one-hit wonders from the 1970s and 1980s, and the Mongolian heavy metal of The Hu Band, to which I have now become addicted. (Absolutely nothing is cooler than Mongolian throat singers and rock music.) A couple of times my buddy asked if the sound level was okay, to which I always responded with a sincere, "Huh?" We only encountered one other vehicle and it was coming from the other direction at warp speed and kicking up rocks, one of which apparently cracked our windshield. Brett said, "Well, sooner or later that's bound to happen on a dirt road like this." I mentioned that I thought it was the music that cracked the windshield, hoping to get a laugh out of Brett, but he just replied, "Huh?"

When we reached the mountains, the music stopped, and the fishing began. It was peaceful, except for the ringing in my ears and the incessant mooing of a grumpy cow. She seemed less than pleased at our arrival, and I was less than pleased to see all the damage she and her sisters had done to the streambanks in some places, but for the most part this place was pristine. It felt like a good place to camp and watch the stars spin overhead like a Van

Gogh painting. It felt more familiar somehow than the moist mountains and canyons of the Uinta and Wasatch Mountains. It felt like home.

The vegetation here was of a drier and hardier sort, not unlike in my Texas Hills where topsoil is thin and only two seasons exist: flood and drought. I felt at home in these hills of juniper and pinyon, with the jackrabbits eerily standing like sentinels in the short prairie grasses, and red-tailed hawks keeping the jackrabbits on their toes. The cattle crossings rumbling beneath our tires and the cattle standing slack jawed and stupid looking in the middle of the road reminded me of home. I liked it here, even if we were a long way from anywhere, and twenty miles from the nearest human being. Perhaps I liked it so much because it was so "out there." I'm not sure.

Johnson Creek is unremarkable as creeks go. It is about six feet wide at its widest parts, and three feet wide in others. Undercut banks and short plunge pools provide shelter for native Yellowstone cutthroat trout that are a lot bigger than you might expect in such a small stream. This was my last stop on the four-fish challenge that is the Utah Cutthroat Slam, and as I strung up my three-weight glass rod I wondered how I'd feel if after coming this far and working this hard I had to go home with only three of the four required fish, or in other words, an incomplete slam.

Think about this, my friends. I had traveled from San Antonio to Salt Lake City, via Houston and Denver, and rode and hiked and climbed up canyon sides and over barbed-wire fences and fished for two wonderfully long days, and in that time I had caught exactly three fish, exactly one of each species I was after, but no more. And the thing is, I was supremely happy with this outcome. As long as I may live, I will never forget those three fish. How often can an angler say something like that, and mean it?

Brett didn't even bring his fly rod; he was "all in" to help me complete the challenge. We walked up to the first stretch of creek and looked at it like it was a billiards table and we had a paycheck resting on the next shot. There was an undercut bank just three feet long and not a whole lot of other likely spots in this stretch. A cow mooed. She was watching me from the bushes with a comical and condescending look on her face. Cows can be mean.

It was a fairly easy plan of dapping while lying low and feeling for the strike, because the fly would have to drift in the blind, screened by grasses and the undercut itself. On the first drift I felt nothing but the breeze on my face and the scornful gaze of the cow. On the second drift the fly seemed to hesitate, and I set the hook into nothingness with the fly going airborne over my shoulder. I said, "I might have just snagged a bit of grass."

Brett said, "No . . . I think that was a fish."

I tried again and this time I felt the tug and raised my rod tip to find a nice-sized Yellowstone cutthroat at the end of my line. I was jubilant!

Brett took the pictures and I set him free, thanking him and wishing him well as is my custom with every fish I catch. We had a short streamside celebration and grabbed some gear from the car so we could hike upstream and see what we could find. I looked over my shoulder for the smug cow, but she was nowhere to be seen.

I know that everyone says the Colorado River cutthroat is the most beautiful of all, but I've never listened to "everyone," when it comes to defining beauty. I make my own decisions about what is beautiful and what is not, and I fell head over heels in love with my first Yellowstone cutthroat. How could I not fall in love with the Yellowstone cutthroat, with its yellow-gold color and parr marks that draw the eye along the fish's body from its finely spotted tail to its ever so slight bloody slash across its throat? I'm not sure why fish need to be so beautiful to survive, but I sure am grateful that they are.

It wasn't long ago that I was beginning to lose all hope for the world and humanity. It's still a dicey proposition, and I'm not sure that we won't destroy ourselves and take this beautiful planet down with us. But once I began choosing my friends based on their passion for nature and the best of human nature and accepting nothing less in my life, I found myself hopeful once more. I now surround myself with the best people on Earth. Life's too short for anything less.

Brett and I had just as much fun walking and talking about life, family, love, and overcoming hardship as we did fishing. Fishing and friendship go together like pizza and wine. They add flavor to the experience and give us the chance to feel a little less alone in the universe. It's true, I will never forget those first four fish that allowed me to complete the Utah Cutthroat Slam. But far more importantly, I will never forget the conversations we shared along the trail and at the water's edge. In times that can seem so dark, good friends carry flashlights.

We walked along the trail, crossing the stream here and there, and I tried every likely spot along the way. Before long I received and missed a strike, then tried again and connected with another pretty, but smaller, Yellowstone cutthroat. I set her free without subjecting her to any smartphone photography, not because she was smaller but because the Slam was complete and now I could just keep the images where I always do, in my mind.

Brett had a plan, and although it was getting warm and I was beginning to feel the effects of the elevation, I wanted to make it far enough upstream to see a bend in the creek that he had described to me before we began fishing. Besides, the scenery was beautiful and the company was great, so we walked and talked and I fished each likely place along the way, at first to no avail.

And then we reached the spot, where indeed there was a run of fast, shallow water and a small waterfall with a hillock of grass on one side and a steep embankment on the other. Small aspen trees surrounded the spot, but the sky was open and clear above, which would make any fish a bit nervous, including the sixteen-inch cutthroat that was living in this tiny bend of the little creek.

For him, a four-foot pool of water was the universe. I almost envied him. Imagine a life without the internet, CNN, FOX, MSNBC, Disney, or any other spin-cycle profit center. Imagine a life where every day you rose to the occasion, lived in the moment, and your food was delivered to you on a floating conveyor belt. I almost felt guilty for trying to catch him. Almost, but not quite.

This was a much more difficult approach. This fish had grown big in these sparse waters by being smart and finding himself a spot in the creek where he could see every approach. He also had a deep undercut and an overhanging slab of stone to hide under if danger was detected. We studied the problem, not solving for "why" but rather for "how." It was decided that I would walk downstream and cross over, then stealthily work my way through the little forest of aspen trees, then get down low and even lie on the ground if need be, and dap the line into the pool, in the blind. This means that while the fish could not see me, I in turn could not see him. I'd have to again feel the take and act on the feeling. Brett stayed high up on the other bank in an attempt to serve as my "eyes." I wasn't catching this fish . . . we were. What did I say about fishing and friendship?

After I moved into position on the other bank, I began working the rod tip through the little aspen saplings and over where I thought the water was falling into the trout's pool. Then I followed the movement of the line while trying to keep just enough slack in the tippet to allow for a drag-free drift. It wasn't easy by a long shot, but then, what of any consequence is easy? After several drifts I felt a hesitation in the line and moved to set the hook, but caught nothing but an aspen sapling. I tried again, but this time when I felt the hesitation there was a sixteen-inch Yellowstone cutthroat trout on the end of the line! As I swung the rod over the saplings, I watched in horror as this beautiful creature flipped off the hook and into a shallow riffle just below the pool. It landed in about three inches of water and, without thinking, all I could hear was that little voice in my head saying, "Fish like a bear!" I dropped my rod and grabbed him in both paws, lifting him just far enough from the water for him to flip from my hands and back into the exact same pool where I had originally found him. I will call this technique a "long-distance to full-contact release with a double spin, triple back flip reentry." For my part I managed to not fall in the stream or drop my fly rod into one of the many cow patties along the bank. Life's funny.

As it turned out I caught the same amount of fish in this last day as I had in the other two days combined—exactly three. In other words, one Bear River, one Colorado River, and one Bonneville cutthroat, and three Yellowstone cutthroats on the final day. But here is the real point of my mentioning the effort it took to catch and release a single fish of each species over three days: It was Zen-like.

Besides the benefits of "native species slams," which include angler education and native fish conservation fund-raising, this program showed me how amazing it is to concentrate on catching a single fish and to experience it fully. I have had several twenty-fish days for bass and ten-fish days for trout, but I can't recall any of those fish now. They all blend into one continuous movie of catch and release. But I can honestly say that for as long as I live, I will never forget my first cutthroat trout from each of these four watersheds. I remember their every detail. There is great value in focusing on a single moment in time, and all that it contains, and feeling profoundly grateful.

At the time of this writing, I am fifty-nine years old—fifty-nine and a half years old, to be more precise. I am at that time in a man's life where things his father said and did make sense to him now, and he sometimes regrets the misunderstandings of his earlier years. It's that time in life where autumn takes on a new meaning and seeing children play is bittersweet. I'm becoming more childlike myself, and I like it.

At fifty-nine I find myself seeing the world in all its beauty and tragedy, and I wish there were some way I could transfer to those around me all that I am learning now, toward the end of my journey. I guess, in a way, that is what I am doing now. Now I know that "modern American life" prompts us to rob ourselves of our lifetimes. We work to pay bills and work to pay taxes. We live the lie of "multitasking," trying to do everything at once, while failing to do anything mindfully. We miss out and when it's over . . . we can never go back. Life isn't a dress rehearsal. There are no "re-dos."

At fifty-nine and a half I can tell you that we are all better off going fishing than sitting in any corporate meeting. And we are all better off mindfully catching and releasing a single fish in a special place than mindlessly catching countless fish anywhere. I will always remember that tiny Bear River cutthroat or the spot in the river where we first met. That, my friends, is living.

We drove downstream to a spot that Brett knew where the creek twisted with the landscape and there was an open place between the mountains and the waters. It was a good place for two friends to enjoy a victory lunch. We feasted on sandwiches and sea-salt potato chips while washing it all down with a wonderful microbrew that was also native to Utah.

It was beautiful except we noticed that some idiots had camped there recently and left a bunch of their trash behind around their fire ring. Brett pulled out a trash bag he keeps for such occasions, and we collected the refuse and placed it in the back of the car. While we did, I wondered if the litterbugs were anglers. I hoped not, even though it really doesn't matter.

Either way, what I see all too often is people using nature, but not loving nature. There is a difference.

People often confuse "using" and "loving." Using is about taking, extracting, and ultimately harming one another. Loving is about giving, exchanging, protecting, and respecting each other. Nature is not a "resource," it is a part of the community that we live within and depend on. I hope that as anglers, hunters, hikers, and lovers of nature, we can lead the way to changing how we see and treat the Earth, and each other.

If you think of a stream or a watershed as being alive (and it is), then you can wrap your head around the idea that how we choose to treat these natural blessings often reflects the way we choose to treat each other. It seems to me that "We the People" are losing the ability to show each other and the Earth the kind of respect, empathy, and kindness that is the hallmark of an evolved people. Have we truly come far from the cave?

Wendell Berry was right when he wrote, "Whether we or our politicians know it or not, Nature is party to all our deals and decisions, and she has more votes, a longer memory, and a sterner sense of justice than we do." If we can't learn these lessons on our own, I feel certain that nature and the Earth will teach us in short order. How we see the world is how we treat the world, and the European traditions of "conquering nature" are coming to their limits with the world's human population at 7.8 billion and counting. We need a new direction. We need new ways of interacting with our environment and each other. We need to become evolved beings.

In his book about the Colorado River titled *River Notes: A Natural and Human History of the Colorado*, Wade Davis speaks to this eloquently. He writes, "There are different ways of interpreting reality, and how people conceive themselves. The Zuni (Native Americans) accepted existence as they found it, the perfect expression of the primordial beings, Sun Father and Moonlight-Giving Mother, the ultimate custodians of life. They live with that knowledge and as a consequence have no interest in changing or improving upon the world that embraced their ancestors. The Mormons (Euro-Americans) by contrast, celebrated an ideology of transformation. The entire purpose of human life was to change the nature of the planet. If the land itself refused to generate rain, the only option was to bring rain to the land, and that meant irrigation on a scale previously unimagined." To me, it should be illegal to murder a river; it certainly seems immoral. If we chose to treat the Earth's watersheds, rivers, streams, and oceans as if we loved them, we would never drain them of their spirits or poison their lifeblood. Would we treat our daughters and sons this way? Some people do. It's a perspective and a choice, like everything else.

As we drove away I looked out the window like I was watching a train pull out of the station with me on it, looking out at someone I had quickly come to care for but knew I'd never see again. I looked at how narrow and fragile this stream was, and I wondered, if I ever did come back, would there be anything left to come back to? I hope so.

We were flying down the dirt road back toward the big city from which we had fled that morning, with Brett's music blasting from the car speakers and ground squirrels running across the road as if they had a death wish. We had the German band Rammstein singing "Du Hast" and sounding like they were invading Poland again, Nitzer Ebb singing "Lightning Man" and sounding like a Swiss mountain opera, and of course The Hu Band and their rendition of "Wolf Totem," which I must admit is one of the coolest pieces of music I've ever heard. I found all this music to be strangely like habanero salsa—both satisfying and a little painful.

About the time the Mongolian throat singers brought the song to a crescendo, we slid to a halt in front of a little western-looking brick building with a white wooden door in the middle and white wood-framed windows to either side of the door. (It looked like a face with a door nose and window eyes.) At the top was a large wooden handpainted sign that read, "Buck's Mercantile & Café." Brett told me they had surprisingly good burgers, but they were closed. Buck's is an example of how rural people can benefit from the preservation of natural areas like the Raft River Mountains. Anglers, hikers, and rock climbers come here to be out in nature and away from people, but even us nature lovers get hungry. To either side of Buck's is nothing but high prairie and the near-distant mountains. But in the middle of it all is a café, a place to rest and find comfort, sort of like that sixteen-inch cutthroat found in that little plunge pool with the undercut bank—or like I found in a friend like Brett.

CHAPTER SIXTEEN

Westslope Cutthroat Trout
Middle Fork Salmon River, Dagger Falls,
River of No Return Wilderness, Idaho

*And maybe that was all that I could expect: the wild clinging to the
edge of the apocalyptic. It didn't seem like enough.*
—*MATTHEW L. MILLER*, FISHING THROUGH THE APOCALYPSE

THE DRIVE INTO DAGGER FALLS AND THE MIDDLE FORK OF THE SALMON
River included twenty-two miles of dirt road and a herd of at least a hundred elk feeding in a vast meadow. The elk were working their way along
the southwest edge of the meadow, while a flock of sandhill cranes moved
like velociraptors as they chased grasshoppers across its middle ground. A
few scattered pronghorns fed near the northern border of the grassy pocket
and the surrounding ponderosa pine forest. Perhaps even more than I love
fish, I'm in love with birds. Those cranes are much like the true *Velociraptor
mongoliensis* that once stalked the high plains of Mongolia, which were
bipedal, feathered carnivores of similar size that also hunted in flocks. The
Jurassic Park movie "raptors" were imaginary amalgamations of two separate

species, one that looked scary and the other that had a scary-sounding name. But no matter if I am watching a flock of Rio Grande turkeys near my Texas home, Osceola turkeys on the edge of the Everglades, or sandhill cranes in the mountain west, I see dinosaurs.

One of my dearest friends, Aileen Lane, and I were following our buddy Matt Miller along the twisting dirt road that ends at the beginning of the Frank Church–River of No Return Wilderness and the Middle Fork of the Salmon River in central Idaho. Matt Miller is the director of science communications for The Nature Conservancy and the author of the book, *Fishing Through the Apocalypse: An Angler's Adventures in the 21st Century*. Aileen is, among other things, an occupational therapist assistant and holistic healer, a professional fly tyer, and the American Museum of Fly Fishing's ambassador to Arizona and Idaho. They are both also my friends. I'm a lucky guy.

The three-and-a-half-hour drive up from Boise seemed effortless because the scenery and the company were both wonderful. The Frank Church–River of No Return Wilderness encompasses 2.3 million acres of rugged and remote mountain forests, meadows, riparian zones, and rivers. The wildlife here includes gray wolves, mountain lions, black bears, coyotes, lynx, elk, bighorn sheep, mountain goats, mule and white-tailed deer, and pronghorn, and it is a critical habitat for the few remaining wolverines in the lower 48 states. It's estimated that less than three hundred wolverines are left in the high elevations of Montana, Idaho, and Washington State, although more live in Canada and Alaska.

The River of No Return Wilderness is good habitat for the threatened grizzly bear, but thus far only transient bears have been seen there, and as is often the case with any large predator, their reintroduction is an emotionally charged and locally controversial topic. Some people are understandably fearful of encountering these predators, and others are concerned about their potential impact on human commercial activities such as cattle and sheep ranching, as well as elk and deer hunting. But fear can be conquered with courage, understanding, and balanced measures that consider all impacts, human and otherwise. I understand and respect local people's concerns, but I ask you, "What good is wilderness without the call of the wild?"

Before striking out for the Salmon River, we planned to do a little small-stream fishing on a tributary that spills into it, just below Dagger Falls. I love small-stream trout fishing, but if you've done it with any frequency you know that at some times and in some places, the going gets tough. This was one of those times and places. Boundary Creek winds its way down the mountain through fields of blown-down pine trees and thickets of willow that could choke a moose. It contains both native redband trout and westslope cutthroat trout, but it was the cutthroat we were after, so we worked our way up-elevation ever so slowly through the brush and blowdown.

Matt took the lead. I knew since this trip was his idea that he wanted us to connect with these fish and was making it his personal mission. I, on the other hand, kept assuring him that no matter what, it was already a successful trip. Yes, in my heart of hearts, of course I wanted to catch and release a few native cutthroat trout, but fishing is about more than fish. Matt is a family man first and foremost and is devoted to his wife and young son, who he had just taken to Yellowstone on a father and son fishing adventure. He is also a skilled professional writer, an angler, hunter, and naturalist, and simply a hell of a nice guy.

We started toward the creek in single file, across a marshy grass-filled floodplain, over an obstacle course of blown-down pine trees that made me have Marine Corps memories, and then into a seemingly impenetrable forest of brushy willow trees. Aileen walked just ahead of me, and I was "tail end Charlie" in our little "fireteam" of adventurous anglers. We hadn't gone far before we discovered another obstacle: holes and chasms in the muddy soil that could swallow you up if you stepped into one, which is exactly what Aileen did. One second, she was walking in front of me and the next, she was nearly gone, up to her neck in a crack in the earth with only her thick black hair sticking up at ground level to give any indication of where she had gone. Luckily, there were no injuries. Aileen is tough, which is good thing, because she also falls down a lot.

After extracting our friend from the soaked soil, we pushed through the willows until Matt called out that he found a nice bend in the stream with a hopeful plunge pool. I guess it's because he knew I had traveled all the way from Texas to be there that he offered me the first shot at what was most likely a "one and done" opportunity to catch a little cutthroat. But I insisted that the old rule of "finders keepers" was in play and offered it back to him. He worked his way downstream to a nice spot on a tiny gravel bar, made a perfect cast, got a nice drift, and an immediate strike . . . and missed it. He gave it a few more tries and then passed it on to Aileen, who stood in the same spot, made an equally beautiful cast, and immediately received another hit from what was most likely the same fish, which she missed.

I guess this is a good time to describe this spot in the creek. It wasn't unlike so many other spots in so many other creeks. It had a small waterfall tumbling over a fallen log and a pile of rocks. It had a plunge pool at the base of those falls with a foam and bubble line that extended through its center. There were thick hillocks of grass and willows on either side.

The reason I love small-stream fishing is because it's a game of strategy. It's like golf without the silly clothes. It's like chess without the long moments of boredom whenever it's not your move. In small-stream fishing, it's always your move. And in a place in the creek like this, you rarely get more than a single chance on a fish before it knows what you're up to and sulks under a rock.

But this fish was different. This fish wanted—even needed—to be caught. So I worked my way up to the same spot, executed a semi-crappy cast, and somehow managed a nice drift that led to a rise, which somehow . . . inexplicably caused the six-inch westslope cutthroat trout to hook itself on the end of my line. Even a blind pig eventually finds a truffle.

We worked that little stream until we grew weary of bushwhacking and decided it was time to get to the main event, the Middle Fork of the Salmon River. I didn't catch any more fish on Boundary Creek, but I did manage to connect with a half-submerged log and an overhanging willow tree that I could almost swear willfully reached out and grabbed my line. I think my buddies caught fish, but we almost never saw each other because the brush was so thick and the casting lanes so thin. We crossed over and climbed the hill toward where we knew the dirt road would be, rather than try to fight our way back through the willows and over the logs again. That was a wise choice as climbing the hill was better than crawling through thickets, Aileen didn't fall, and I was relieved not to undergo anymore flashbacks of the boot camp obstacle course on Parris Island. It was time for some big water!

———

We arrived at the end of the road, which also happens to be the beginning of the River of No Return Wilderness, here on the shores of the Middle Fork of the Salmon River. We could hear the crashing water below long before we saw the river, and there were people milling about with helmets and life vests on, as this was also the launch point for whitewater rafting trips. We geared up and began hiking the narrow trail that took us away from humanity and into the wilderness area.

The trail rises above the river. At times we could only hear the river, and not see it through the trees. Then, on occasion, it would appear several hundred yards below, with a steep incline of soil, scree, blown-down trees, and granite boulders between us and the river. I remember assuming that in time the trail and the river would meet, but then I recalled the dangers of assumption. The trail never did get any closer to the river, and the way down never got any less steep and treacherous. Adventure!

At one point on the trail, we encountered a pretty little mule deer doe. She was walking up the trail and we were walking down, and we all stopped for a moment and just looked at each other as if to say, "One of us is going to have to get off the trail." We spoke to her softly and she wasn't at all afraid. After a moment, she stepped gingerly off the trail and began a slow and reluctant climb up the mountainside. It was a nice moment, but shortly thereafter we came to a spot in the trail where Matt stopped, looked way down to the bottom of the steep incline, and said, "Those pools down there look promising."

I looked down too. I looked all the way down what seemed like about a 70-degree incline of crumbling soil, scree, blowdown, and loose rocks, with a jumble of boulders at the bottom. The river churned and tumbled below, and along the embankment I could see the long runs of good water with seams of foam and eddies all screaming for a good drift of a dry fly.

That's when I turned to Matt and said in a deadpan voice, "You have done this here before . . . right?"

He glanced over and said, "Yes, about five years ago."

I waited a moment for dramatic effect, and then I said, "I only ask because the drop-off where you are indicating we might go down to reach the river looks to me a lot like a place where people come to throw themselves to their death."

He smiled and Aileen laughed. "Well, shall we give it a try?" he replied. And like Bogie on the African Queen, gravity be damned, down we went.

It wasn't bad really. I only slipped a few times and Aileen didn't fall. Before we knew it, we had reached the boulders and Matt was already casting in some nice water while I was still clambering like a lowlander over rocks toward the water. Before I had even made my first cast, Matt was into a fish, and it was so nice to see my otherwise quiet buddy come alive in childlike excitement as he brought in the first Salmon River westslope cutthroat of the day. I was too far off downriver to get a good look at it, but it seemed like a nice-sized fish with beautiful bright colors. We all cheered over the roar of the river, and I was glad I had followed Matt over the edge of the precipice. (Maybe it was more like a 60-degree incline; it seemed less steep once we began catching fish.) Matt hooked another one soon after releasing the first, and it was a nice redband trout. The two varieties seemed to be coexisting in the same pools.

Aileen was working a point just downstream of Matt, and I was in a little cove just downstream of her. We all began to connect with fish pretty quickly, with Aileen picking up a mix of cutthroats and redbands, and me connecting with one nice cutthroat and losing another to a "long-range release." There were a few subalpine fir trees directly behind me that were clinging to life on the crumbling mountainside almost as well as they clung to my fly if my back cast came close enough. I looked over at Aileen, who had similar terrain, and saw that she was smarter than me, as she sent out one arrow-swift roll cast after another. I copied her wisdom as best as I could, and it made all the difference.

After a while the action slowed and then stopped, and that is when Matt looked over and without a hint of irony yelled over the sound of the rushing river, "This might be a good time to climb back up to the trail and hike some more until we find another place to fish."

We gathered our gear and I looked up just before we started the climb. That's when I thought to myself, "Maybe it *is* a 70-degree grade."

The next place seemed steeper yet, but I had gotten used to the idea now and we started down without a pause, Matt sliding once, Aileen sliding into a fallen tree, and me following her purposely to the same resting point. We worked our way down along that dead pine and toward the next, which she clambered over and I clambered onto, and we looked over to see Matt a few yards lower and not far from the river's edge. He was sitting on a rock indicating that this might be a good place to hydrate and get a snack before we started fishing. I stayed put, straddling that big dead tree like on a horse on a trail ride. Aileen sat on a big rock next to the tree, and we all shared a moment of serenity at the river's edge with sips of cool water and bites of sweet dried mango. It was perfect.

This spot was even better than the last spot. Every now and then a line of whitewater rafters would careen by us, paddles digging into the foaming torrents, with multicolored helmets strapped firmly on their noggins. Considering the velocity and ferocity of the river, both seemed to be prudent measures. The tourists looked like tourists and the rafting guides looked like rafting guides, both in demeanor and ability. There was no way to get the two types of humans confused, even though they were all dressed alike and in the same raft. Once they passed us, we were alone again, just the three of us in the wilderness with the river, and it felt magnificent.

Matt began casting to a rock in the river that split the current into two natural foam lines and a slick, smooth run just downstream of the stone. I was next to Matt, reaching out into the second line of foam, and Aileen took up a station just downstream of me on the other side of a jumble of boulders. Matt connected with a nice cutthroat right away and brought it to hand, and over the next few minutes he pulled in another. Then he turned to me and shouted over the sound of the gushing, tumbling, rushing river, "You should try this spot!"

We swapped positions on the riverbank and I began casting, and although I felt like I was hitting my target areas perfectly, I received no response. I was roll casting in a straight line toward each rivulet of foam and current, but to no avail. That's about the time I screwed up a cast and landed it a bit too far inshore, but just as I did, a nice cutthroat latched onto my stimulator like it was a lifeline.

It gave me a nice fight with a couple of good runs where it tried to use the current and a few nice jumps of either determination or desperation. Anyone who says native fish don't fight like the foreigners is speaking either from experiences I haven't had or from delusional groupthink. I've caught browns and rainbows as much as I've caught everything else, and in general they may be different, but no one fish is "better." Besides, if all I wanted was a battle, I'd be fishing in blue ocean water after something that can pull me overboard and drown me at the bottom of the sea. I don't go fly fishing or do anything else in search of exploits of bravado. I come to the mountains for the sheer joy of seeing wild native fish in wilderness. It gives me hope to know that both still exist. In his classic book of essays titled *A Sand Country Almanac*, Aldo Leopold wrote, "To those devoid of imagination, a blank place on the map is a useless waste; to others, the most valuable part." I couldn't agree more.

We were all catching fish, and at one point I hooked a nice cutthroat that was giving me a tussle and I saw Aileen heading toward me with the net. Just about the time I yelled out for her not to bother, and that I'd land it by hand, it shook off the fly and swam away with an obnoxious smirk on its handsome face. I deserved that for being cocky.

I looked over at Aileen just in time to see her fall behind the pile of rocks. It looked like a hard fall, and I started scrambling over toward her when I saw her head pop up smiling and her arm jutting out with a tiny thumbs-up gesture. We both laughed even though we couldn't hear each other's laughter over the noise of the big, rolling Salmon River.

If you're getting the sense that the Salmon River is big water, that's because it is. It travels more than four hundred miles from its headwaters at above nine thousand feet in the Sawtooth Mountains to its confluence with the Snake River. During that journey it loses over seven thousand feet in elevation. The Salmon River has some of the deepest canyons in America and is rugged and remote. Thankfully, the River of No Return Wilderness is still wild country. I want to go back some day and camp there on some moonlit night . . . just to hear the wolves singing.

When the Lewis and Clark Expedition arrived on the Salmon River, they declared it to be too rough to navigate. The Nez Perce Native

Americans considered this river to be sacred, and I believe they were right. Back then it provided them with plentiful salmon, steelhead, and cutthroat, bull, and redband trout, as well as mountain whitefish and other varieties of wildlife, to hunt in a sustainable and respectable manner. They hunted elk and deer alongside wolves, bears, and mountain lions, and all these creatures remained plentiful until the arrival of European Americans. In the 1860s gold was discovered here, and the race was on to have the Union Army transition from Appomattox to Idaho with orders to push the Nez Perce out of their homeland. This military campaign ultimately led to a sad and bloody Nez Perce surrender, as they desperately and valiantly tried to flee to Canada. They never made it. I think it's a shame.

This mighty river is the home spawning pathway for chinook salmon and steelhead, but they have declined greatly and are not going to recover unless we "New Americans" learn to care for them and their rivers, like the Native Americans once did, and I suspect still do. Four dams along the lower Snake River make this miraculous journey nearly impossible for both young salmon swimming to the ocean and adults making their last push upriver to spawn and die in its tributaries. How can we allow this? We put humans on the moon in 1969, and yet more than fifty years later we can't do better than this? I don't want to believe that.

After exhausting my efforts in the one big pool, I noticed a smaller plunge pool in a difficult spot just upriver. I worked my way up through some fast current until my path was stopped by a slab of stone and a rush of river that was too fast to stand in, so I decided to get creative. I leaned my back against the slab, facing away from the pool, and back cast over my shoulder into it, then turned around onto my stomach to manage the drift, which resulted in a quick hook-up and a little redband trout in my hands.

And that's when I looked into the lower pool and saw it from a different angle. At its deepest point, perhaps ten to fifteen feet deep, there was a school of trout hovering just over the bottom, occasionally rising up a foot or two and eating something unseen as it floated by. I told Matt what I was seeing, and he asked, "Do you want to try a nymph on a dropper?" I suggested he go for it as I worked around him and walked up to Aileen, who was sitting on a rock watching us fish. I sat next to her, both of us looking happy and tired as we munched on some more dried mango.

When Matt fishes, his inner child is released. I think that is why Aileen and I fish so well together. We have zero machismo in our fishing. We just want to have fun, and little fish thrill us just as much as big fish do—sometimes even more. We cheer for each other and console each other, and that is what we did for Matt as he worked that pool with his nymph under a bobber . . . I mean "strike indicator," receiving hits and hook-ups. He hooked and lost a fish before he connected with a nice big westslope cutthroat. This fish put on a show with three or four nice leaps from the water before Aileen ran over with the net to help Matt land him. We all cheered. He was a beauty and the biggest fish of the day, which made this the perfect ending to a great adventure.

I don't remember much about the climb back up to the trail other than my shortness of breath and length of gaze. Every now and then I had to look back and burn the memory of this beautiful place into my mind. I wondered if this is what the Nez Perce did when they were told that they had to leave and make way for "progress." I'm sure they felt sorrow, and I did too, because I'm not sure I will ever get to see it again. Still, I could not have asked for a more wonderful time with amazingly kind friends, and in such a magically grand landscape.

When we got back to the cars, I handed Matt a plastic Ziploc bag that contained a book and an ink pen. This was the first chance I had since buying his book that I could ask my friend to write something personal within the pages. He smiled and walked off to write the inscription while leaning on the hood of his Subaru. After a while he handed it back to me and smiled. It was a nice moment.

We followed Matt's car as far as the paved road, and that's when we decided he must have a meatloaf and potatoes in the oven back home because he was down the road and gone! I opened his book and read what he had so kindly written to me, including using the words, "fellow defender of wild places." I smiled and read the entire inscription to Aileen just as we were passing another smaller herd of elk. She smiled too. It had been a wonderful day and we were both supremely happy. Did I mention that Matt is a really nice guy? I think I did.

CHAPTER SEVENTEEN

Bluegill and Other Sunfish
Texas Hill Country

The child in nature is an endangered species, and the health of children and the health of the Earth are inseparable.
                    —*RICHARD LOUV*, LAST CHILD IN THE WOODS

I GUESS I WAS ABOUT FIVE YEARS OLD WHEN MY DAD TAUGHT ME HOW TO fish and shoot, which is about usual for a kid growing up in the American South. Most kids in Texas have harvested their first deer before they get out of middle school. My first rifle was a .22 Mossberg with open sights and a yellowish wooden stock. Dad sat me on his lap and helped me to hold the gun upright as I lined up the sights, controlled my breathing, and "slowly squeezed the trigger." Even at five years old, dad had me hitting the bull's-eye every time.

More often than not, we targeted tin cans, which were more fun than paper targets because they'd jump and spin with every bullet strike. After a while he'd make it more challenging by setting up empty shotgun shells as targets, then as I got better and better, we competed to hit smaller and smaller targets at longer ranges. At one point he folded a dollar bill into a one-by-one-inch square and pinned it to a dead tree fifty yards away. He said, "Hit that dollar bill anywhere, and it's yours." I used the front of the jeep as a rest and took my best shot. When he walked up to the target he started laughing. "Wow!" he said. "You shot Washington right in the nose!" I still have that dollar bill.

My fishing began at a little "for pay" lake that was stocked with bluegills for me and bass for my dad. He fished with his spinning gear, tossing these magical lures that had names like Mepps, Shyster, Daredevil, and Jitterbug. I had a little Zebco closed-face spinning reel and a kid-sized rod with a small brassy hook on the end of the line, and a red-and-white plastic bobber about a foot or two above the hook. The night before, we'd go out into the yard with a flashlight and an empty coffee can looking for earthworms for me to use as bait the next morning. On those days when we didn't have worms for bait, my dad would hand me a little jar of salmon eggs, which looked like candy to a five-year-old and seemed edible enough. The earthworms never seemed edible to me, but the bluegills sure liked them.

When we'd arrive, there was a ritual we adhered to where we'd go to the "bait and tackle" shop and my dad would pay for the day of fishing, then buy me a hot dog with yellow mustard, a soda, and a Dolly Madison fruit pie . . . usually apple. We did it the same way every time, as if any variation would bring "bad Mogambo" to the whole deal. We went to the same spot on the lake every time, too, and Dad would look at me with his serious dad-face and say, "Steve, stay out of the water!"

"Sure Dad," I'd reply.

After I fell in (which I always did), he'd hang my britches on a tree limb to dry in the sun and I'd go on fishing in my Fruit-of-the-Looms, which worked out fine because it was getting hot by then anyway. You can get away with that sort of thing when you're a five-year-old boy, but people seem to frown on fishing in your underwear as you get older. That's a damn shame. Growing up is not all it's cracked up to be. I guess that's why as I get older, I am becoming more childlike. All I seem to want to do these days is play outdoors and eat junk food. It feels good to be back in my second childhood.

For all his casting and spinning and jitterbugging, Dad didn't seem to catch many fish. Sometimes I'd even feel sorry for him. I mean, every now and then he'd hook a bass, but I was hauling in bluegills like it was the easiest thing in the world to do. A hook, a bobber, and a jar full of salmon eggs and I was in business!

Dad always brought a five-gallon bucket for me to fill with lake water so that I could entertain myself by filling the bucket with bluegills. At the end of the day, Dad would look into my bucket and say, "Well, you sure did catch a lot of them!" Then he'd have me "help him" carry the bucket to the water's edge, and together we'd release all the little fish I had captured. Even then, catch and release fishing pleased me. I remember that when we'd first dump the little bluegills back in the pond, some of them would sort of mill around like people at a train station not sure of where to go. In time, they'd find their way home, just like me.

Later in life I moved up from a cane pole or a Zebco to a real spinning rod, and then ultimately a fly rod. I began targeting bigger fish, which I caught less often but, according to the grown-ups, were a lot more satisfying. And I enjoyed catching bass and later traveling around the world fishing and hunting for everything from bonefish to kudu. But I have to admit, none of it thrilled me any more than a bucket full of bluegills or a pile of perforated tin cans.

Bluegills fill my fondest childhood memories because Dad and I often fished ponds and gator holes. (He didn't let me fish gator holes until I was old enough to avoid falling in and feeding the gators.) Later, as I moved up to a fly rod and fished the fast-moving and spring-fed Texas Hill Country streams, I began targeting other sunfish, which all seem to fight outside their weight class and often look like they were painted by Vincent Van Gogh.

In my part of Texas, besides the bluegills in ponds and slow-moving parts of the rivers, we have green, long-eared, red-eared, red-spotted, orange-spotted, and the non-native red-breasted sunfish. We also have warmouth, although I don't encounter them often. Long-eared and green sunfish are the ones I catch most often. Occasionally I catch a Rio Grande cichlid. Although cichlids are not a true sunfish, they are of the same size and disposition. All of them are living works of art that fight with spirit on a three- or four-weight rod. I'm never disappointed to catch one.

In time I became a father, and I introduced my daughter Megan to nature via fly fishing and the short hikes we'd take to get back to the streams. Her first fish on a fly was a bluegill, which she caught in one of the ponds that line the headwaters of the Sabinal River. The fact that it was tiny made no difference to her; she was forever a participant in nature beyond that point. Now she is an outdoor educator and teaches children about the world around them and the powers within them. Life is a circle, not a line.

When we see ourselves as participants in the biome, nature and the best of human nature carry forward and give back a thousand times over. It all comes down to love and respect for self, others, and the Earth. I appreciate and respect the animals and plants that sustain me. Cattle and carrots both want to live forever. I suspect microbes fear my Clorox wipes. Everything wants to live, and yet every living thing dies and returns to the earth. Circles best describe nature, from a bird's nest to raindrops striking the ocean. I'd like my life to be round like that. I'd like my life to be natural.

Across America the hunting, fishing, and outdoor ethic is being lost to the e-generation, who are existing in a virtual world instead of living in an actual one. But this does not have to be, and frankly, if this trend continues, the nature of our nation, world, and humanity will suffer. As there are fewer and fewer hunters and anglers, states are losing a massive amount of funding via decreased tax revenue from licenses, tags, permits, and gear sales. And just as importantly, we are losing a generation of people who learn to love, care for, and respect nature, each other, and themselves.

The point here is threefold. First, we only protect what we come to love, and we only love what we come to know. Second, a growing, rather than decreasing, supply of "nature participants" is needed to ensure the future of our wild spaces and wildlife. Third, introducing children to nature via angling and hunting as well as other less consumptive outdoor interactions, such as nature walks and even organic gardening, is vital to our future and beneficial to the health and well-being of our children.

I heard someone joke recently, "Why should I care about future generations? What have they ever done for me?" Yes, I know this is just a bit of tongue-in-cheek humor intended to make another point through sarcasm, but it brings to mind an ancient Greek proverb that reads, "A society grows great when old men plant trees whose shade they know they will never sit in." Every time we choose to introduce a kid to nature, we are planting a tree of sorts. We are almost always impacting that child's life for the better. I don't remember much about my early childhood, but I recall every detail of my fishing trips with my dad.

In her wonderful book titled *Nature Fix: Why Nature Makes Us Happier, Healthier, and More Creative,* Florence Williams makes a compelling argument about the importance of nature in our lives. She writes, "The dramatic loss of nature-based exploration in our children's lives and our own has happened so fast we've hardly noticed it. We don't experience natural environments enough to realize how restored they make us feel, nor are we aware that studies show they make us healthier, more creative, more empathetic and more apt to engage with the world and with each other. Nature, it turns out, is good for society."

When I think of my time with my dad fishing for bluegill in a pond, or my time with my daughter fly fishing for sunfish in a Texas Hill Country stream, I know that those times rank among the best of our lives together. Time shared in nature builds the kind of trusting and joyful bonds that make life worth living. And I have found that time with kids in nature reminds me about what it is like to experience everything as if it were the first time. It reminds me to slow down, and pay attention, and be grateful.

It seems to me that most American children and adults are suffering from what author Richard Louv has coined "nature-deficit disorder." We all see it, even in ourselves. We spend our time multitasking or sitting in meetings or stranded in traffic, and in the end we are left fatigued, isolated, anxious, and depressed.

Here is the lesson that I learned as a child catching bluegills and watching little green lizards doing pushups. It doesn't have to be this way. All we need to do is go fishing. Once we cast our lines forward and fall into the rhythm of the river, the world comes into color again. We wake up! We feel the sun on our face and the wind in our hair. We hear the birds singing in the trees and the soothing sounds of water tumbling over stones and toward the sea. We notice how amazing a peanut butter and jelly sandwich can taste. Life makes sense again!

Nature is restorative. Connecting with nature is a skill that requires practice, like any other skill. We need to teach our nation's children this survival skill, but first we need to learn (or relearn) it ourselves.

Jen Ripple, editor and chief of *DUN Magazine*, once wrote an article titled "The Overlooked Skillset." In it, she does a wonderful job of outlining a set of skills for introducing anyone of any age to fly fishing. I think they are worth repeating.

1. Choose the right fish—Success supports continued interest. Bluegill and other sunfish are perfect for this task. They are small in size, big in fight, eager to eat, and as colorful as almost any fish alive.
2. Choose the right location—No one is going to have fun if every other back cast ends up tangled in a tree. Choose a location that is easy to access and that doesn't make casting any more challenging than it already is for a beginner. Again, I think bluegills are a perfect target because they live in ponds, lakes, and slow-moving streams that will be less challenging for someone who is trying to learn to fly-fish. They also will try to eat anything that looks buggy that they can fit into their tiny mouths.
3. Choose the right tackle—I suggest a three- or four-weight glass rod that will allow the new angler to slow down and feel the loading of the rod. It will also work wonderfully for bow and arrow casts in tight spaces along creeks, streams, and pond edges. And finally, it allows the new angler to feel the fight in a small fish.
4. Choose the right fly—Consider using terrestrials including hoppers, crickets, beetles, and frogs, as well as poppers, sliders, divers, and streamers. All are simple to fish with and forgiving of a presentation that is . . . less than delicate. Use barbless hooks only, for the safety of the new angler and for proper catch and release fishing.
5. Choose the right day—comfortable temperature, no rain, not windy.
6. Bring the right attitude—a positive, fun, relaxed attitude. It's all about allowing someone to experience fishing and nature in a way that makes them want to do it again and again.
7. Bring a rubber-meshed net—to allow for safe and proper fish handling and to allow the new angler to see and even photograph their fish without causing it undue stress and harm.

As I write this, America is in the middle of a global pandemic, racial and civil unrest, massive unemployment, environmental degradation, ideological fracturing, and a massive vacuum in leadership, but I remain optimistic. You see, I was a child of the 1960s. There was war and crime and riots and the disappearance of insects and birds, which was chronicled in Rachel Carson's *Silent Spring*. In my elementary school we were drilled in the ridiculous practice of hiding under our desks in case of a Soviet nuclear attack. But through it all, my dad and I went fishing. And we survived and thrived, and I grew to love my country with all its faults, and love nature with all my heart.

Nature taught me to be adaptive, resilient, and present in the moment. Nature became my buffer from all the craziness of human misbehavior. Nature saved me as a child, and still does to this day. Now it's my turn to return that favor.

My love affair with nature began as a little boy fishing with his dad, and a bucket full of bluegills that we set free. I will never forget how happy I was with every little fish I caught. And I will never forget how happy I felt every time they swam away, none the worse for the experience.

There's nothing wrong with legally filling a stringer full of bluegills, killing and cleaning them, and eating them for dinner. (In fact, I think it is important to expose children to this process too.) There's nothing wrong with learning to value where your food comes from, whether it is a fish from a pond, the fruit of a tree, vegetables from a garden, or venison from the back-forty.

I have fond memories as a boy collecting wild raspberries, blackberries, and strawberries with the intention of bringing them home, even if I ate as many as I collected. I have legally and ethically killed fish, gamebirds, and big game animals as food for my family. That, my friends, is the real circle of life. But the one thing I have never done is failed to respect the living thing that was feeding me. Someday I will feed a tree or a field of wildflowers, just as I should. After all, I learned long ago that we are a part of nature, not apart from it.

———

Lifetimes pass in a flash. Now I wake up, pack up, and fish alone most days. My first fishing buddy is all grown up and lives across "the pond" in the

United Kingdom. And when I look in the mirror each morning, I see an older man, with a gray beard and tired eyes. But deep inside I am still that little boy with the cane pole. I still run out the door whenever life gets to be a little too much to take and I need some wild time to help calm me down.

Not long ago, I returned to the Sabinal River with my little four-weight glass rod and a desire to feel young again. Life had gotten a bit bumpy, as it is apt to do from time to time, and for me nothing calms my nerves like time outdoors. Nature is my sacred place. Fly fishing is my meditation. Singing birds and rising fish are my best medicine.

I strung up my rod and walked to a clear, wide, lazy pool along the headwaters of the river. Not much has changed since my time as a boy fishing with my dad at that little paylake. I still like to stand in the water as I fish; it seems that getting wet is all part of the fun for me. It was early springtime in the Texas Hill Country, and the bluebonnets and Indian paintbrush were in full bloom, while the Texas mountain laurel flowers were just coming to an end.

I could see a few fish out in the pool and a few spawning redds of bass and bream. I began casually casting, and it didn't take long before I got a follow and a take, so that my little glass rod doubled over and throbbed to the pull of a hefty bluegill. I brought her to my wet hand, slipped out the barbless hook, and gently returned her to the river. At first, she milled about like someone at a train station not sure of where to go. But in a moment, she turned and swam confidently in the right direction, toward the part of the river where she had just come. When I saw her stop over a gravel bed on the other side of the big pool, I knew that she had found her way home . . . just like me. I smiled and then, I cast forward, once again. It's what I do.

CHAPTER EIGHTEEN

Desert Redband Trout

Owyhee Range, Idaho

And his soul seemed to leave him and to go far away, far back, perhaps, to where life was all different and time passed otherwise than time passes now.

—D. H. LAWRENCE

THERE ARE TIMES IN EVERY PERSON'S LIFE, I GUESS, WHEN WE MEET A kindred spirit or two. If we are truly lucky, we meet enough of these rare people to create a small tribe. I've felt this sort of connection a few times in recent life, like sitting down to breakfast and talking about life and art with my buddy Bob White, or drifting down the Yampa River with Kirk Deeter, or walking down a trail in the Raft River Mountains with Brett Prettyman, or casting a line toward an autumn brookie with Dustin Wichterman. These are all people and places I will never forget. My life would be so much less without them.

And there have been so many more such encounters during this amazing journey I have undertaken in the creation of this book. Like standing in a wooden boat in Fletcher's Cove with Chris Wood, or bow and arrow casting toward Pecos strain Rio Grande cutthroats with Toner Mitchell. It's all been a beautiful ride, punctuated with mosquito bites and elevation sickness and an angry yellow jacket that did not enjoy being trapped in my water shoe any more than I enjoyed having it there. And, of course, there were the fish caught and released from creeks and rivers, ponds and lakes, coastlines, and ocean depths, where squid and seals and white sharks played the deadly game of "who eats whom." Each of these moments and memories is everlasting. All are filled with laughter and gratitude and images that bring me smiles. They are like ice cream on a summer day.

Aileen Lane is another kindred spirit. We fish the same. We are both childlike in everything we do, and while we are doing these things together, no one would ever suspect we are both, shall we say, a little past middle-aged. We laugh and even giggle. We get excited over a six-inch trout. We sit and listen to songbirds and watch lizards hunting grasshoppers in the sunlight. We can be happy just because there is a trickle of water that contains a wild, native fish, and a smattering of hope that we might catch and release it. Life is so beautiful when you spend it with like-minded and similar-souled people. It can make a man wonder what the hell he's been doing with the rest of his life.

When I think of all the time I have spent in this finite life, sitting in meetings with academics, politicians, and other blowhards, listening to inflated egos pontificate at length about the grand value of nothing, I become overwhelmed with a mixture of ironic amusement and idiotic regret. After all, I could have been fishing with a kindred spirit. I can't help but think of the words of Nick Lyons in his book *Bright Rivers*, "I have been a juggler, flinging my several lives high and carelessly into the air, never catching them, barely feeling one as it touches my hand." I wish I wrote that.

In the big scheme of things, fly fishing has no importance at all, and neither does anything else, from grilling burgers to brain surgery. After all, in time we all get hungry again, and in the long run the patient eventually dies, even if just from old age. Everything in life is a delaying action. It's all just something to do while our atoms unravel. So if I have a choice, and these days I do, I'd rather go fishing than almost anything else. And for the next two days Aileen and I were planning to chase wild, native redband trout in the desert mountains and foothills of southwestern Idaho. How cool is that?

I often find that the drive to a fishing destination is as enjoyable as the arrival, and it was like that for me as we crossed the high sage-covered plains and meandered toward the Owyhee Range. I immediately fell in love with Boise and the landscape that surrounds it. I loved the high forested mountains to its northeast, and the high desert mountains to its southwest. Perhaps it's my Texan soul that craves wide-open spaces and vast expanses of sky, but whatever it is, this landscape appealed to me in a way that felt like a second home.

For a man who loves rivers, streams, and oceans, it is ironic how much I am drawn to dry places. I love watching the tenacity of life: the wildflowers growing through a crack in the ground, and the trout stream that pours from deep, cold springs and amazingly supports life in the middle of so much parched death. Deserts speak to me. Deserts and other dry places accentuate the life-giving value of clean water. I guess this is why the Devils River in my home state of Texas seems so special to me. It winds through the harsh West Texas desert like a big green snake with scales that look like trees, and there are deer, mountain lions, javelinas, and a myriad of colorful birds that depend on its flowing springs. When the springs run dry and the river vanishes, so does everything else.

Our destination that first morning was Jordan Creek, a tributary of the Owyhee River, itself a tributary of the Snake River. Each little creek that spills down the mountains of the Owyhee Front adds to the river, which adds to another river, which adds to another river, which adds to the ocean and ultimately ends up as clouds, rain, and snow, which fall back into Jordan Creek. These creeks have names like Rattlesnake, Wildcat, Big Antelope, and Battle, and although the water we planned to fish had a less exotic name, it possessed something the others did not; namely, it flows through a ghost town named Silver City and contains pure, wild, native redband trout.

When we arrived at the bottom of the twisting dirt road that rises from the plains and into the mountains, I immediately felt a strangeness deep down inside me. Three young boys came flying down the hill on their knob-tired bikes, and even though I knew they we real and most likely picnicking with their parents nearby, they felt ghostlike. Everything felt that way, as if the town itself was an illusion and might vanish at any moment, taking us with it.

There was a heavy, painful, dark feeling to the place, and the closer we came to Our Lady of Tears Catholic Church and the small wooden school-house that stood just below it, the more intensely the gloom came over me. The church was built in 1868, only a few years after the American Civil War and amid fighting between the settlers of Silver City and the Bannock Tribe. Add to that the bloody feuds between miners of various companies and claims, and you have a town with a history of violent death and suffering.

Even the man who gave his name to the creek we were planning to fish had died along its bank at the hands of Bannock braves. Michael Jordan and twenty-nine fellow prospectors arrived here in 1863, and the town was founded in 1864 after Jordan's death and the birth of the War Eagle Silver Mine. Quartz led to silver, and silver led to gold, and then greed led to killing; like all things human, in time all that was left were the scars. The mountains were left honeycombed with tunnels and tailings, and the town was abandoned, gravestones and all. Gratefully, during the time of this writing, Jordan Creek still runs clear and cold, and is teeming with native redband trout.

We parked on the edge of the ghost town as close to the creek and as far away from the ghosts as we could get. After stringing up our rods, we walked down to the creek where it formed a deep pool before meandering through a tangle of willows. We could see six- to eight-inch-long, fully mature, beautiful redband trout holding in the current. Neither of us could see any bugs in the air or on the water, but we had the feeling that the fish were looking up, and we did not want to disappoint them. Aileen tied on a small caddisfly, and I went to my "go-to" choice whenever I have no idea what to choose: a size 16 Adams. It was a small pool, so we had to take turns. Aileen insisted I go first. Who was I to argue with her? I did.

I worked my way slowly down the embankment toward the upper edge of the pool. I could see them lined up, looking up, sizing up every-thing that passed by, from a floating birch leaf to bits of cottonwood fluff. I made a short cast and got a nice drift in the foam, then a fish rose like an upside-down lightning bolt, and I promptly missed the hook set. "Wow!" we cried out simultaneously. "Did you see the speed of that strike?" I asked. "It was a torpedo!" We both laughed like little kids, and I wondered if I had just blown the pool. But the fish were all still there, lined up and waiting for the parade. These trout were hungry. I cast again.

I ended up getting a series of good drifts at the top and tail of the run, and I received strikes for the first few casts but missed every single one. I could tell that these fish were used to having an instant to choose between rising or ignoring whatever drifted their way. For the most part, they were quick to commit. I don't know how many tries it took before I found myself slack-jawed in amazement that I had actually managed to hook a fish, and I raised it up out of the water and into Aileen's waiting net before it could wiggle free. It was a beautiful little redband trout, and the colors were so vivid that I immediately fell in love with these fish. We were both beside ourselves with joy. There is no other way to describe it. I don't recall being this happy when I caught my first seven-pound bonefish in the Caribbean. I am addicted to small-stream fly fishing for native fish, as they hold a special place in my battered heart. Perhaps it's because we are both hanging on against all odds. I'm not sure.

After a few more misses, the fish began to sulk beneath the rocks along the bottom and under overhanging spruce branches along the far shore. I snuck back up the creek bank and hung out with Aileen until we saw the redbands begin to settle down and swim back out into their feeding lanes. It was her turn.

Like almost all the people I fish with, Aileen is a better angler than I will ever be. She manages to cast with a sort of grace that puts me in mind of wind rippling in the grass of a meadow, as if music is being played that only she can hear. She has a way of making a tiny fly float on a breeze and alight on the water as if it were doing so of its own free will. All this gracefulness would be even more impressive if she weren't frequently tripping over rocks and tree roots and falling down embankments into the stream. My friend is complex. She embraces the paradox of graceful beauty and childlike clumsiness. I, on the other hand, am just clumsy. We spend a lot of time with me asking, "Are you all right?" and then laughing together when she gives me the thumbs-up sign. Aileen took a number of good drifts with her caddis, but they just weren't committing as they did before, so we decided to explore downstream, rest this pool, and return once the trout became hungrier and less wary.

As we walked along the creek looking for likely places to fish, we came to the town cemetery and decided to take a look at the old gravestones, which all faced toward the creek and the mountains, and away from the ghost town. It was a beautiful place to "rest." The top of the graveyard was for the regular townfolk and the bottom was restricted to members of the Masonic Order and their families. Across the top of the hill were many small grave markers that simply read, "Unknown." At first, I thought, "Everything is a tangle of unkempt vegetation," but once I reached the top of the hill and looked down, I realized that it was perfect. These were not "weeds"; they were native wildflowers growing just as they should. I realized that this hill, covered in gravestones dating back to the early 1800s, had reverted back to its natural state, just as it was when the Bannock and the Shoshone hunted and fished along this creek. It was a beautiful place to rest for eternity, or even longer.

We walked down into the lower graveyard where almost every stone contained the square and compass symbol of the Owyhee Lodge of Freemasons, which was established here in 1867. Buildings all over Silver City have this same Masonic symbol on their façade. I was drawn to one particular stone, and quickly saw that it belonged to a soldier, I'm guessing of the California volunteers sent here and elsewhere during the American Civil War by Abraham Lincoln to quell Native American resistance while the rest of the Union Army was busy dealing with the southern resistance. There was so much killing going on in the East that history seems to have passed over all the killing and dying that was happening simultaneously in the West. I looked at the inscription under the Masonic symbol on the gravestone and read, "Here Lies an Honest Man. Oliver Hazard Purdy, Born September 12, 1824, Killed in the Bannock War, June 8, 1878." Next to him were the graves of a husband and wife and their three children, side by side. They all died in 1896, cause unknown. I stood quietly as the creek gurgled past the graves. I thought of my own life as a Marine, and of all the lives that have been lost in wars that never should have taken place. I thought of Oliver Purdy and all the men and women like him, and what their lives might have been. It is my contention that every true warrior wishes for peace.

Aileen and I had both felt the darkness in town—almost an evil feeling near the church—and it was so heavy that we could not wait to get away from it. Down on the creek with the trout, all we felt was peace and joy. Now here among the gravestones overlooking the creek, my friend asked me what I felt. I paused for a long time before I said, "I feel the tragedy and triumph of life." We walked back down to the creek and began taking turns casting into various pools and pockets as we found them, but we found no fish, and I found my mind wandering back to the feeling I had in the graveyard. It felt like sadness. It felt like regret. It felt like lives wasted.

Just before breaking for lunch, we decided to return to the one pool where we had seen the fish and missed so many strikes. We both decided that they preferred Adams flies, so Aileen tied one on instead of the caddis. Almost immediately she drew a strike and a miss, and then another, and then a hook-up! Her fish was bigger and as beautiful as mine. I was so pleased that we had both caught a redband before lunch, and we took turns working that pool of forgiving wild fish, catching a few more until once again they began to hide in the shadows.

Lunch beside the creek was perfect. We agreed that there was no way we wanted to eat anywhere near the ghost town and its creepy lingering fog of past human misery, so we drove down to a pretty spot along the creek where the trees gave some shade and the birds were singing. Our creekside meal consisted of cheese, dried Italian salami, dried fruit, and fresh olives with crusty bread and a chilled white wine. We talked about fishing, family, friendships, and life itself. We talked about the healing spirituality of nature, and how the running water of the creek and the sound of the birds seemed to make everything feel all right again.

After lunch we crossed over the creek and began working downstream through the trees from one likely spot to another. Silver City seemed far away now, and the only sound we heard was the water spilling over rocks and the afternoon breeze blowing through the trees like ocean waves. The water looked perfect here, with lots of nice pockets and pools and a slick run that extended for twenty yards through a grassy bend. The fishing was wonderful, but the catching was nonexistent. After a while we decided to pack it in and hike back up the hill to where we had parked.

Fish were caught earlier in the day, and we had shared a wonderful morning in a beautiful place that few people ever visit. We drove through Silver City for one last look, and as we were about to leave I looked over and saw an old woman and a young girl sitting on the porch of what looked like an abandoned and broken-down house with a Masonic symbol on the top of the front door frame. I waved at them as we drove slowly by, but they both just sat there motionless and emotionless, like dime store mannequins. As we wound our way back down the mountain, I could not get the faces of the old lady and the child out of my mind. I recalled seeing a few stacked rocks and an old board near the old schoolhouse, and a sign that looked like it was written by a child. It read, "Crystals for Sale," but there was nobody there and nothing on the makeshift table. I felt a little chill go down my spine as I thought, "Were they really there, sitting on the porch?" I know, it's a silly thought. I mean, it's not like there really are ghosts in that ghost town . . . right?

If Jordan Creek was an oasis of calm in a landscape filled with the persistent and lingering feelings of human conflict, greed, and suffering, then Homestead Creek Canyon was its antithesis. From the moment I stepped on the trail until the moment I left this little canyon creek, I felt nothing but peace, love, and complete joy. I could tell that people had been happy here. I could tell that nature was happy here. And I can tell you, I was happy here. I have never felt more at peace or more in love with being alive. It felt like home. It felt like a place that needed to be protected and preserved.

Homestead Creek is a narrow, partially intermittent stream that slowly dries up or freezes during the winter months, but runs freely down to the Boise River most of the year. Intermittent streams like this one have been a battleground in the efforts of certain government officials to lessen the protections afforded by the Clean Water Act of 1972. This is a fight we should never surrender to strip miners, real-estate developers, and corporate farming operations, who all too often pollute, drain, bury, and otherwise destroy these critical habitats in the name of "progress." Intermittent streams like Homestead support a lot of life that would vanish without them, and in this case, genetically pure redband trout are part of this living stream's natural ecosystem.

Redband trout and steelhead trout are genetically two variations of the same species, each shaped by its environment and life cycle. If they have access to the ocean and live an anadromous life cycle, migrating to the ocean to feed and grow large and then returning to freshwater tributaries to spawn, then they are considered steelhead. If they do not leave freshwater and are restricted in size by the amount of food and habitat afforded to them, they are designated as redband trout. The two distinct forms of redband trout include the Columbia River redband, which is found in northwestern Montana, Idaho, and Washington, and the Great Basin redband of the high-desert creeks of that region. In Idaho, redband trout have managed to survive from the high alpine streams of the northern portion of the state to the tiny creeks of the Owyhee River watershed, and here, in the dry foothills that drain into the Boise River.

These fish are adaptive, scrappy, and worth respecting no matter where you find them. They are also so much more beautiful than they need to be, with their ample round spots and parr marks that they often retain into adulthood, and their rosy red to brick-red lateral bands. I have chased trout all across this country, and as much as I have loved each and every fish, there are a few that have come closest to my heart, including the desert redband. I love any creature that is a survivor beyond all odds.

The trailhead to Homestead Creek was well kept and narrow. It twisted and turned, rose and fell, up and down the canyon's depths. Although there was bear scat along the trail, I could not imagine bears living in such an open, grassy landscape (though they do). I have no doubt that the dense ribbon of birch, willow, and sumac forest that followed the creek must have provided the food and cover for them to survive and thrive. Wild roses grew head high along the trail's streamside edge, and native grasses, wildflowers, and sage covered the steep hillsides above. Mormon crickets wobbled across the trail like an alien army going somewhere, not too fast.

As spectacular as the sights in this canyon were, the sounds were even better. Windblown grasses waved golden in the hushed tones of organic chimes. Breezy waves blew through treetops that themselves emitted as many varieties of birdsong as I have heard anywhere. And then of course, there was the reassuring sound of running water coursing over stones and around grassy undercuts. If I could, I'd live here for the rest of my life, but it is public land, and I am grateful for that fact. Now, everything wild and native lives here, just as it should.

In time the trail worked its way closer to the water. The vegetation was thick, almost impenetrable, and Aileen said it looked like a different canyon from when she had been there scouting just a few weeks prior. The warmth of early summer had set things free, and now leaves and branches filled all the spaces where only space had been before. We could hear the creek, but not see it. We continued on, down the trail and higher up into the canyon until eventually we found the creek and a small footbridge that held a nice pool just below it, and another downstream from that. Aileen offered me the upper pool, the one we both knew was the better-looking water of the two. Aileen is a wonderful human being, and I am a fortunate man indeed to have such an amazing friend.

She went down to the lower pool with her tiny glass rod named "The Pygmy," and I addressed the upper pool with my three-weight and my favorite reel, a special-edition Trout Unlimited reel by Hatch that was gifted to me by my buddy Kirk Deeter. Before long I heard Aileen call out in excitement, "I saw a redband!" We were both happy that one of us confirmed they were in there, but we were yet to catch one, and we knew from our experiences the day prior at Jordan Creek just how lightning fast and skittish these little desert fish can be.

My pool at the footbridge seemed "perfect." It had a quick current coming out from under the bridge, and then the water tumbled over some rocks creating an oxygen- and food-rich foam line that swirled around an undercut and through an overpass of birch limbs. I set up my bow and arrow cast with as much precision as I could manage, and then sent my trusty size 16 Adams airborne toward its intended destiny with native fish lips! The fly landed perfectly and floated softly along the foam line as I crouched, poised like a cat at a bird feeder. And that is about the time that a fifty-pound standard poodle with a jaunty red bandana around its leash-free neck bounded past me and into this most perfect of fishing spots as I screamed the futile word, "Noooooo!" Muffy had muffed my presentation.

It only took a moment for Muffy's mom to round the corner with a half-smile on her pretty face as she said, "I'm sorry . . . but that is his favorite swimming hole on our morning walk, and we didn't know you were here." Then she asked what I could only call "a Seinfeld question": "Were you fishing?" I reeled in my line, unhooked the fly from the tree limb it ended up in, and shook off the creek water that Muffy had splashed all over me with her triple-flip water entry. Behind the pretty girl was another young woman, who thankfully was holding on to the barber-strap-thick leash of her dog, which I suspect had a name like Cujo, Wolfy, or Death Fang. She was covered in tattoos, in amazing physical condition, with a shaved head, and had the look of a cop who was about to explain the process of a body cavity search. She never cracked a smile, but they were both nice people. I told them that I did not blame Muffy for wanting to swim there; after all, "it was a perfect pool."

I guess it's true that as a writer and philosopher everything is a metaphor, and nothing is as full of allegory and metaphor as fly fishing. Sometimes in life, no matter how well you plan, the universe makes plans too. Sometimes it may be something as unexpected as falling in love . . . or finding a hair in your cheeseburger. Sometimes it can be something life changing like spending a day hiking and fishing with a kindred spirit and just being so damn thankful to be alive that you might burst. And sometimes it's a flying poodle where you least expect a thing like that. Uncertainty is a big part of life's adventure. We moved on.

We worked our way along the trail, and I was grateful not to see Muffy or Death Fang taking a bath in any of the many nice bits of pocket water and the occasional plunge pool we found. I love this kind of fishing. Some of it involves dapping a leader and tippet into a run that is between a network of tree branches and a screening of spiderwebs that seem to have the tensile strength of aircraft aluminum. Occasionally there was enough open space between trees to make a proper cast, but often a bow and arrow cast or roll cast was a much better choice.

What I like about this kind of fishing is that it is tactical, and intimate. You have to pay attention to every aspect of the stream, from hydrology to dendrology. You have to think like a fish. You have to let go of every other bit of nonsense this crazy world tries to tie your mind up with, and simply be in that one place and time, completely. It's Zen, y'all.

There were a lot of "fishy-looking" spots. If you're an angler, you know what I mean. There were lots of places in the creek where you'd look at it and say, "There's got to be a fish in there!" But miles into our exploration, we had only seen exactly one frightened redband trout and a flying poodle. Try as we might, we had caught nothing up to that point. I did have a hummingbird that kept following me and hovering just over my shoulder while I tried to execute the perfect bow and arrow cast between two trees, a clump of wild grass, and a tangle of wild rose. I think he was trying to unnerve me, but who knows, perhaps he was a fly fisher in another life. Still, as much as I love wild birds, he didn't help much. It was like being a pro golfer addressing the game-changing putt and your caddy keeps humming the theme song to *Jeopardy*.

The trail began to rise up the side of the grassy canyon, through the sage and up to a massive lone black locust tree. Next to the tree were the remains of an old homestead, just the stone walls, which had obviously been cut from the surrounding granite. A man who looked to be a little older than me came around the corner, and I recognized him immediately as a fellow bird lover. He had the telltale floppy wide-brimmed hat, wrinkled long-sleeve shirt, and trousers all of the same olive-green tone, and the largest pair of binoculars he could suspend from his skinny neck without toppling over into the dirt. He saw that we were looking at the old stone homestead, and he pointed and said, "Wherever you find these black locust trees you find an old homestead." Then he turned and simply walked away without saying another word. He seemed about as happy to see us as I was to share my fishing spot with a wet dog.

We sat for a while up on the hillside above the creek, snacking on dried mango and drinking ice-cold water. The breeze blew down through the canyon, and it seemed as if every other treetop held a songbird of one variety or another. This was a living place, filled with life and the joy of life. It was a place that felt peaceful and inviting, from the tops of the hills to the bottom of the fast, clean, cold little creek. There was a wild hive of honeybees that oozed out of a crack in the old locust tree, and I began to imagine the lives of the people who once lived in this simple stone cabin. I could see them here in the bountiful springtime, the warm dry summers, and the yellow-gold autumns. I could see them here in the relatively mild winters of the Boise Foothills. And in the end, I envied them and hoped they didn't mind that I was imagining this to be my home.

People always leave their mark on a place, and that mark can be physical, spiritual, or both. We leave the same kind of marks on each other; sometimes we hurt and sometimes we heal. It's a life choice, really. While Silver City felt like sorrow, Homestead Creek felt like joy. Even the birds seemed to feel the difference. Birds are smart that way.

I must admit to having some animist leanings in that I treat every living thing, including the Earth itself, as if it has a soul . . . because it does. I can plant a tree and shoot a deer with the same degree of reverence, respect, and gratitude. When we look at each other and the world that way, life becomes richer and more meaningful. I don't know about you, but as my runway grows shorter, I want to live as rich and meaningful a life as I can manage. And, as much as possible, I want to heal, and not harm, others and the Earth.

By the time we came to a place in the creek where another small tributary spilled into it, we had walked and fished some four and a half miles up the canyon toward the headwaters that lay high above us, at about eight thousand feet in elevation. Aileen and I were having a wonderful day, fish or no fish, and we decided that this would be a turnaround spot. Before heading back down the trail, we noticed that this last place, like the first place, had two pools on either side of a small footbridge. We both saw that the "fishier"-looking water was upstream. Aileen once again offered me the better-looking pool. After making a half-hearted protest, I agreed, and began dapping and flinging my fly into some pretty pocket water. Aileen's pool looked deep and dismal, and I almost felt guilty for agreeing to take the upstream water. Almost . . . but not quite. After all, I had traveled all the way from Texas to be here. About the time I was beginning to be okay with taking the best-looking water, I heard my friend yell, "I caught one!" We both cheered as she netted a six-inch-long redband trout. I was so happy for her. We giggled like little kids who just found Mom's secret stash of chocolate. Now we knew where they were, and hopefully it would soon be her turn to be happy for me!

There was no way to know if we could get any more fish out of this pool. It was deep and dark and slow moving—not at all the kind of place we expected to find trout. But over the next fifteen minutes we took turns working and resting that stretch of stream, and in the end I lost count of how many strikes we missed or how many fish we caught and released. It was perfect.

The walk back was perfect, too. We didn't catch any more fish, but it didn't matter. The air was clear and clean, the birds were singing, the stream was rushing, and everything seemed right in the world. On that day, our whole world was that little canyon creek and those wild, grassy hillsides and our beautiful, kind friendship. Isn't it grand that there is no "bag limit" on happiness?

There is no such thing as forever, y'all. Everything and everyone will eventually come to an end, or at least a transition. The only things we can hold on to for as long as life holds us are the moments and memories we share with others of our tribe. We all need to collect kindred spirits and hang on for dear life, because these times and these people are what make life most dear.

Arriving back at the trailhead was bittersweet, and I turned back and looked at the canyon that I had come to love, just one more time. I knew that except in my memory, I'd most likely never make it back to Homestead Creek. But it had been a magical day, a day I will carry with me always. And just as I was savoring that thought while breaking down my rod and stowing my gear, the grumpy bird-watcher showed up again, a frown on his sunburned, leathery face and a slouch in his shoulders that must have come either from the weight of those humongous binoculars or from all that grumpiness he was carrying within. He looked at us and grunted, "Well . . . did you catch anything?" We told him that we had, and that it was a great day. He grumbled back, "There's nothing in the creek but little fish that aren't worth the trouble." And then he turned and walked away with his head bowed and his shoulders slumped. He was an unhappy question mark of a man.

I wondered how a man who enjoyed searching for little wild birds could not see the value in little native fish. As he walked away, looking back once as if to shake his head in amusement, Aileen and I just smiled. We had found what so many people have sadly lost. All too often as we "grow up" and "grow old," we tend to forget the important truths that every child knows. Too many grown-ups forget that eternity can live in any moment, as long as we live for that moment too. In real life, it's the small things that are the big things. Fishing and friendship, songbirds and laughter, moments shared and memories made—these, my friends, are the things that matter. And that is exactly why my friend and I could not stop smiling. You see, we've never forgotten. We're still children, at heart.

Chapter Nineteen

Redfish

Texas Gulf Coast

It has always been my private conviction that any man who pits his intelligence against a fish and loses has it coming.

—JOHN STEINBECK

THE MORNING AIR WAS COOL AFTER A COUPLE OF DAYS OF STEADY RAIN, and I was grateful. It had been a long hot summer in a series of ever longer and hotter summers that promise to get even longer and hotter if humanity doesn't get its act together. I love Texas but have begun to think that the reason "The Devil Went Down to Georgia" instead of Texas was because even he knew that our summers are too hot . . . just like our fiddle players. Well, you get the idea. I was happy for a cool morning when I stepped out of my truck and greeted my buddy John Karges.

John is a highly respected biologist, naturalist, herpetologist, and writer, and a super nice guy. When we first became friends, John was the associate director of field science for The Nature Conservancy's Texas Chapter. We hit it off immediately with our mutual love of nature, angling, West Texas, and snakes. As a child I dreamed of becoming a herpetologist and traveling the world exploring exotic lands and looking for new species of snakes, especially tree vipers. I loved their bright colors and how they could hang from their prehensile tails like reptilian monkeys. I also had a love of tortoises because they seemed peaceful and ancient and in desperate need of protection from *Homo sapiens* who wish to eat them, turn them into traditional medicines, sell them in the illegal pet trade, or dig up their habitat and replace it with condos. (More than half the 360 species worldwide are currently threatened with extinction.) But my biggest passion as a young man was to become an expert in the most American of reptiles, the rattlesnake. I envisioned myself as the next Laurence Klauber, helping people understand and appreciate rattlers before we extinguish them beneath the tires of our pickups or the ends of our shotguns. I love rattlesnakes. They are uniquely and beautifully designed creatures that evolved in a North America that once had greater mammalian diversity than Africa's Serengeti Plains. Even bison walk around them, not over them, when they sound that warning rattle.

But life happens while we plan, and while John became a biologist, I became a US Marine. Still, we have so much in common in our mutual love for nature that we are never at a loss for topics of conversation. I should also mention that John is an angling fanatic. He is hard core, and once told me, "A single bump on my line can keep me casting into the night for hours, hoping for another bump." I, on the other hand, would have long since been home, showered, and relaxing with a glass of wine. I was determined to hang in there with him today—no matter what we encountered, or how long he wanted to keep casting forward!

The sun was barely rising over the South Texas Brush Country as we drove toward the coast, south of San Antonio. With fifty thousand recorded cases of COVID-19 in San Antonio alone, we were careful and drove in separate vehicles. I missed the wonderful conversations we would have shared during the three-hour drive to our destination, but it allowed me to enjoy the road trip, the sunrise, and the music of Tom Petty and the Heartbreakers. It was a great beginning to a new adventure.

The brush country of South Texas was once a vast grassland and home to bison, collared peccary, mountain lions, ocelots, jaguarundis, and the stunning aplomando falcon, which still exists in limited numbers along the

South Texas coastline and Rio Grande Valley. To my knowledge jaguarundis are long gone and the ocelot is barely hanging on in Texas, now mostly confined to the Laguna Atascosa National Wildlife Refuge. Red wolves, *Canis rufus*, were once plentiful along this coast, but were declared extinct in 1980 and now only exist in captive breeding populations and at a single managed wildlife refuge in North Carolina.

This region has changed from its original grasslands with scattered trees and is now covered with thorny brush-like honey mesquite, acacia, prickly pear cactus, Spanish dagger, and Texas persimmon. These plants are native to the area but have now overrun it due to the human interventions of natural wildfire suppression and overgrazing. It's the same story wherever I've traveled; namely, unrestricted, and excessive consumption. We need to learn how to be more like thoughtful ants than reckless grasshoppers.

As we approached the Texas coast, things flattened out and got ugly. First, we came to the places that used to be coastal prairies but now are endless fields of rice, sorghum, corn, and cotton. Intensive large-scale farming and cattle ranching has changed the landscape, extinguished much of its wildlife, and contributed to the impacts of rainwater runoff into rivers and streams. The runoff, along with its pollutants, ultimately ends up in the region's coastal marshes and the Gulf of Mexico. Coastal development, wastewater discharges, and massive agricultural operations all end up leaching pollutants into the sea. Then, as we came closer to Corpus Christi, we saw the oil refinery smokestacks spewing who knows what into the air, poised to dump known poisons into the waterway if ever there is an accident or act of sabotage. It's just a matter of time. The refineries are all built along the water.

It wasn't always like this, and thankfully there still are wild places along this coastline. Back in the time of the founding of the United States, this was the home of the Karankawa Tribe. The Lipan Apache called the Karankawa people "*Nda kun dadehe*," which is reported to mean "people who walk in the water." They lived, fished, hunted, and gathered all along the Texas coast and into northern Mexico. Unfortunately for them, the Spanish extirpated them in Mexico and the Texan colonists did the same in Texas, so now the only people who walk in the water are anglers.

With all that working against it, this is still a vitally important natural landscape of the remaining coastal savannas, bays, barrier islands, dune communities, and estuaries. Three major estuaries in the region include the Laguna Madre, Nueces, and Aransas. The Texas coast and the scrub country are vital to American bird migration, with the Central and Mississippi Flyways converging. Millions of songbirds count on this area as a resting place before and after crossing the Gulf of Mexico and Yucatan. In fact, about 80 percent of the 332 species of long-distance migrating birds travel through the Texas Coastal Bend.

And the Texas coast is a rich and diverse fishery, luring anglers from across the nation and beyond. As we crossed the bridge to Mustang Island, I was thinking of all the fish we might encounter once John and I managed to toss out our first casts. Sea trout, red and black drum, flounder, snook, tarpon, ladyfish, and even alligator gar all call this area home. According to Texas Parks and Wildlife creel surveys, sixty-three different species of fish have been landed by anglers along the Texas coast. Against all odds this is a rich area for fishing and other outdoor activities. Sadly, we will never return it to the wildlife paradise that the Karankawa people knew, but working together, we can restore much of what has been lost.

———

A brisk seaward breeze struck us in the face when John and I stepped out of our trucks and began stringing up our eight-weight rods. This was a good thing, because it meant that as we walked out onto the flats and turned back toward the salt grass and mangroves, our forward casts would get a little help from Mother Nature. The parking area was at the end of a hardpacked dirt road, where kayakers launched with their spinning reels, while we fly fishers walked out into the water and did our own thing in a hopefully graceful if perhaps somewhat less efficient way. If fishing were just about harvesting fish, I'd be better off using a stick of dynamite instead of bits of fluff and flash on a hook. But for me, fishing is about so much more than catching fish. I can enjoy it in solitude or with a dear friend, but if I do go with another human being, it will be someone like John, who "gets it." I want to share these moments with someone who loves the water as much as the fish, the landscape as much as the water, and the birds in the air as much as the landscape.

We stepped out into the water, which felt cool against my legs as I shuffled my feet farther from the shoreline. I was shuffling because besides all the wonderful gamefish in this area, it also supports a healthy population of stingrays. John wore specialty boots that had thick leg guards all the way up to his knees. It seemed like a wise precaution, and I made a mental note to check out those contraptions as soon as I got back. It was overcast, with the gray-brown, sepia-tone look that I have grown accustomed to along this coast. I've never known it to be without wind and this day was no exception, but as we turned so that the wind was at our backs, we had a good time of it, sending my streamer and his popper toward the waiting coves and shoreline.

This kind of fishing is methodical. You cast and strip, strip, strip, over and over again, until such time as a fish decides what you're offering looks edible. Then you set the hook with a strip-set, not a rod tip rise (you have to get your trout and bass fishing muscle memory to go away for a while). I realized way too late that I had left my casting gloves at home. Don't do that. You might end up with the bloody sliced-up fingers that I had by the end of this day.

We were starting to see baitfish activity, mullet boiling along the edges of mangrove clumps and leaping now and then out in the deeper water. "That's a good sign," John called out over the sounds of wind and water. I nodded in agreement and kept casting. We were searching in the blind, casting toward the shore in a progressive geometric pattern from left to right, then shuffling a few feet farther and casting again. It was meditative and calming, and yet filled with expectation as I wondered if the newest mullet boil was because a big redfish was chasing them, or if it was just something mullet do for fun.

These wetlands are bird rich, and with birds being perhaps one of the only creatures I love more than fish, I sometimes get distracted. A pair of crested caracaras flew overhead. They're striking birds with their black-and-white features and yellow legs, and I always love to watch them flapping those oversized wings. An osprey began to hover over John, watching him intensely for a moment and then soaring over a shallow bay, doing some fishing of its own. Seagulls lined the sandy shore, mostly standing on one leg, just staring at us as if we were the strangest things they had ever witnessed. Seagulls can be judgmental like that, but I ignored them and kept casting.

The thing is, we are all anglers—the birds, John, and me. A pair of great blue herons landed on a point just south of us and began patiently fishing along the shoreline. A great egret walked quickly across the shallows with its wings spread wide, frightening fish with its shadow and then snapping them up whenever they took the bait. The entire salt flat seemed like a swirling deadly dance of things eating and being eaten. Nature is practical, not sentimental.

John said he thought he saw a few redfish splashing along the mangroves and salt grass, probably chasing mullet. I noticed a boil in a small cove that did not seem mullet-like. We each began working toward the place where we saw the most promise. I cast repeatedly into the cove. With one cast, something struck my fly as soon as it hit the salty surface of the cove, but when I went to set the hook there was nothing but water at the other end. That's fishing. Sometimes it all comes together, and sometimes it all comes undone.

It was about that time that I noticed John's rod tip bending, and a bright silver fish leaping into the air. "Ladyfish!" he called out. After a brief tussle he had it in hand and lifted it up for me to see before releasing it to the bay. "They're in this pass . . . come over here and try for one," he said. But I told him that if he caught three, I'd move over but not until then. Well, he caught three in a row, with his last one being the biggest, so I did move over and begin casting into the pass.

Ladyfish really deserve a better name. It makes them sound fragile, delicate, and dainty, and they're not. They are wonderful fighters with acrobatic jumps and headshakes not unlike their cousin, the tarpon. But they are smaller and thinner than their more respected relative, and so they don't seem to get the respect of which they are so worthy. Still, I had always wanted to catch a ladyfish and now was my chance.

I started casting my streamer along the northern edge of the pass where clumps of salt grass grew, and after a few casts I felt a strong tug but somehow missed the hook-up. I cast again and again, working my way across the mouth of the opening until I came to the southern edge, but there were no more tugs, bumps, or bites. That's when I saw a few schools of smallish mullet boiling in the shallow bay in front of me, and so I stepped forward a few feet and cast in the same methodical manner in ever-increasing crescents until I felt another tug, strip-set the hook, and raised the now bent rod tip. Almost immediately the fish broke the surface of the water with a series of beautiful, headshaking acrobatic leaps! It dodged left and right, leapt free of the water, and ran for the bay a few times before I brought the sleek silver predator to hand. It was beautiful, slender, and yes, graceful, like a lady.

Overhead the osprey glared at me as I released the fish, as if wondering why I would do such a thing. I looked up and said, "Well, go get it yourself!" I looked over at John and said, "Well, at least we aren't going to be skunked!" The pressure was off; even though what we'd really come for were redfish, at least now we could say, "Fish were caught."

I looked down and noticed that my fingers were bleeding from the constant stripping of line across naked, salty skin. I looked up and much to my surprise saw a lone male magnificent frigate bird soaring overhead without so much as a single flap of its oversized, scythe-shaped wings. It was unmistakable not only by its wingspan, shape, dark color, and long narrow tail, but also because of its long, dangerous-looking beak with a nasty hook at its tip. It uses that beak to steal fish and other food from seagulls, terns, and even from the surface of the water, though it never lands on the water. I watched as the bird sailed over my head and off into the distance without so much as a "howdy" in my direction. I guess when you have the word "magnificent" in your name, there is no reason to pay attention to a lowly fisherman.

The guidebooks indicate that frigate birds are "casual summer visitors" to the Texas coast, especially preceding or following tropical storms. A hurricane had just struck the coast of Texas and Louisiana a few days prior, and a tropical storm hit South Texas a few weeks back, while Hurricane Sally was on her way toward Alabama. As John and I stood in the shallows casting, there was a long line of tropical storms on their way across the Atlantic from the African coast to the Gulf of Mexico.

I grew up with hurricanes and tropical storms, and there is absolutely no doubt in my mind that they are growing progressively more powerful and frequent. It's ironic that all the best science is showing that human-induced climate change is contributing to rising coastal sea levels, dumping more rainwater with more frequent tropical storms, and yet is also causing the advance of desertification in other areas. I have noticed the changes in bird migrations and wildflower blooms, from the Texas Hill Country to the West Texas desert. The frigate bird is often a weather gauge of sorts along the Texas coast, warning any seaworthy sailor that things might get real nasty, real soon. And those of us anglers who choose to pay attention will notice that nature is also forewarning us of what is yet to come. Again, we are both the problem and the solution.

John had moved out to some deeper water as I worked my way along the mangroves and salt grass, both of us methodically casting and retrieving without a single bite. As we converged back at the truck for some lunch and a bit of hydration, a willet launched itself from the shore, squawking loudly as if to tell every seagull in the pueblo of our return. When on the ground the willet is a drab brownish bird with long legs and a straight-pointed bill, but when alarmed it flashes its bright black-and-white underwings and screams out a rhythmic call, "will-will-willet!" Birds amaze me.

Grackles had congregated at the front of our trucks like velociraptors, leaping up to seize dead insects from the grillwork and then taking them into the shade of the bumpers to eat. We had lunch together. They did not seem to mind.

It was about that time that I looked over at my fishing buddy and to my astonishment saw him eating a banana! "You're eating a banana!" I said incredulously.

He looked up and smiled, saying, "That only holds true on boats . . . we're wading."

I looked at him a little sideways and with a sly grin said, "I don't know, buddy, that banana might be bad mojo!" It's not that I believe in the banana myth; it's just that I don't disbelieve it either.

The clouds had cleared and the sun became hot in the now clear blue sky, so when we waded back into the bay, the cool salty water felt good on my legs. John waded out to where the flats met with deeper water, and I worked my way along the shoreline that was dominated by black mangroves. When I was a kid in Florida, black, white, and red mangroves were an indicator of a healthy estuarine ecosystem, and they grew to a tree size of about ten to fifteen feet tall. Here along the Texas Coastal Bend, with its traditionally frequent winter freezes, black mangroves remain small and shrub-like, and red mangroves are rare and located only in a few isolated areas south of where we were fishing. But with ever-increasing temperatures and fewer freezes, mangroves are moving north. The fact is that plants, like animals, also migrate with changing conditions, albeit more slowly and with the restrictions of soil conditions and geography. And animals follow the plants that they depend on, if possible. If not possible, the plants and the animals simply die out in that region or become extinct as a species. Due to ever-warming waters and decreasing freezes, it is estimated that mangroves may replace coastal prairies within this century, which is bad news for many species, including the endangered whooping crane that winters just north of where I was standing, in the Aransas National Wildlife Refuge.

Everything is attached to everything. When we set the hook on a beautiful redfish, we are also connected to the entire estuary, the rivers that flow into it, the plants that live along and within it, and the climate (not weather) that is impacting all of this. Lose the climate, and you lose it all. Everything is attached to everything.

As I was casting, I kept reminding myself again to shuffle, not step, because stingrays are a real issue here if you don't pay attention. On one shuffle I kicked up a flounder that left a long sand and mud trail from where it was hiding to where it was going. Flounder are one of the "Big Five" Texas coastal gamefish, along with redfish, black drum, snook, and spotted sea trout. I'd love to catch a flounder on a fly rod. They are ambush hunters, burying themselves in the sand and mud bottom while waiting for something edible to swim close to their massive mouths.

Along the bottom were the telltale scooped-out areas of mud and sand that indicate that black drum are in the area. I've not yet caught one of these fish on a fly rod, but I understand that you just hang on for the ride until you can eventually wear them out. It sounds like fun except for my bloody fingers. I didn't see any black drum, but I did see what looked like the massive back and shoulders of a good-sized redfish as it porpoised out of the water over a large school of mullet. I moved in toward the fish and began casting toward every shadow I saw, but to no avail. Not a bite. Not a follow. Nothing but shorebirds and mullet.

I took a break from casting and looked up, as I often do along a river, just so I make sure to take the time to be present and enjoy my surroundings. Off in the near distance was a white ibis probing the mud for crabs, and the egrets were still busy dancing over the shallows, wings extended so as to frighten the minnows into making fatal mistakes. It was a beautiful and deadly display as they flapped their bright white wings and flipped their long white necks with precision and speed toward their quarry. They're better anglers than I am, but then again, I do this for fun and they do it for a living.

It had been a long day of casting and retrieving, and although the fishing was wonderful, neither of us had been particularly lucky in the catching department. John caught a number of ladyfish and I caught one and saw another swim almost up to my legs, then stop, double over, and swim away in the same direction it had come. They are almost eel-like in the way they move. John thought he'd seen a few "redfish-looking" splashes along the shoreline, and I thought I saw the back of a red as it chased mullet in the shallows, but mostly we just exercised our right arms until our biceps were pumped and our backs were screaming at us for relief. I was determined to keep going until John felt we'd done a respectable job of it, but I have to admit I wasn't disappointed when he waded over toward me and yelled out the words, "Barren and sterile!" I could not help my mischievously sarcastic self when I replied in a deadpan serious tone, "I think it was the banana that did us in."

For the record . . . I was kidding. We had tried our best but connected with no redfish or black drum. As we waded back toward our trucks, I recalled a line from a favorite Earnest Hemingway short story, "*Nada por nada por nada.*" That's why it's called "fishing" and not "catching."

I took a last panoramic look around. Not too far away was the busy road and the sound of traffic passing back and forth. In the distance, I could see the massive concrete bridge we would take back to the mainland. The dirt parking lot set up for angler access by the state had an ample supply of plastic dumpsters, but the shoreline was still covered in soda cans, Styrofoam cups, and cigarette butts. Along the way back toward the highway that would carry me to my Texas Hill Country home, I passed endless tacky shops selling T-shirts, boogie boards, and fried shrimp dinners. All this ugly in the middle of all this beauty. I was grateful to get past the refinery smokestacks and back into the scrub country. I was grateful to be watching the sunset over the western horizon as I listened to my buddy John Arthur Martinez singing songs about Utopia, Texas, and the Devil's Backbone. And I was grateful that so much of the Texas Coastal Bend has been protected via federal public lands. But there is so much more to be done, and we who are closest to these waters and wildlife need to take the initiative to restore and protect these delicate, natural treasures.

In my estimation, one of the failings of my home state is that most of the land is private, not publicly protected. We have a wonderful state park system, but as the population grows, they are being loved to death. One of the exceptions to this lack of protected public land is along the Texas Coastal Bend. The Texas Coastal Preserve Program of 1987 was created to promote "cooperation for the preservation and protection of the state's natural coastal resources." The Texas Coastal Preserve System includes South Bay, the US Fish and Wildlife Service's Loma Ecological Preserve, Welder Flats Coastal Preserve, Aransas National Wildlife Refuge, Armand Bayou and Christmas Bay Preserves, and the Brazoria National Wildlife Refuge. Add to that Padre Island National Seashore and I'd say we have a good start, but that is all it is, a start.

As Bob Dylan once sang, "The times they are a-changin'." All across Texas large ranches are being worked by the last generation who will likely want to work that hard for so little return. This is true along the Hill Country rivers and the coastal waterways. The time is right, my friends, for us to beat the developers to the punch. There needs to be someplace for us to go and cast our line without being surrounded by the detritus of civilization. No causeways, buildings, power lines, or refinery smokestacks. Just miles and miles of tailing redfish and, perhaps someday, the sound of red wolves howling as the campfire lingers. I don't know about you, but I don't want an America that is devoid of wild places, and this includes our shorelines, inland waterways, and ever-rarefied grassy marshlands.

I knew we were expecting a couple of days of steady rain after I got home, so this day was the best day John and I could have chosen to make this trip. And it was a good trip. It was an adventure, and like all true adventures it contained uncertainty. I knew that my buddy felt bad that we did not catch any redfish, but I wanted to reassure him that there's no reason for such feelings. After all, I had spent the day fishing with a good friend, and let me tell you, it doesn't get any better than that. And besides . . . we can always come back.

CHAPTER TWENTY

Mixed Feelings—Invasive Brown and Rainbow Trout

Oak Creek, Sedona, Arizona

Gila Trout

East Verde River, Mogollon Rim, Arizona

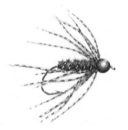

May what I do flow from me like a river, no forcing and no holding back, the way it is with children.

—*RAINER MARIA RILKE*

SOMEHOW, I KNEW ALL THE ROADS I'VE BEEN TRAVELING WOULD EVENTU-ally end up in the red-rock country of Sedona. Not because it is a bastion of native trout, because it isn't. And not because it is an island of untouched wilderness, because it isn't that either. I knew I'd end up here because there is something uniquely spiritual about this place, and although I no longer pray for divine intervention, I still secretly hope for something like that. If I had to describe my relationship with nature in two words, I'd say, "spiritually intimate."

Nature saves me, and that is not hyperbole, it's a simple truth. As a boy I would run into the woods and stay out all day (away from the reach of my abusive mother), not returning until sunset, when dad would be home and I'd feel safe again. I spent my days in farmers' fields trying to get closer to the earth, and in trees trying to get closer to the sky. I built a tree house with salvaged boards and nails that I pilfered from a mason jar on my dad's work-bench. Up there among the branches and leaves I could see a world that was beautiful, meaningful, harmonious, and serene. Whether as an abused child beaten by a parent, or as an adult beaten by the world, nature has always been my spiritual salvation. I guess this journey and these words are intended to be my contribution to healing humanity and the Earth. It's what I can do. It's my way of giving back and paying forward the gifts that nature has given me.

Aileen is someone who quickly became one of my dearest friends. She has the kindest of hearts and an inquisitive mind, and we share a passion for nature that runs the spectrum from childlike to reverent. We both find rivers, red rocks, and rain showers to contain their own kind of spirits and feel that each has the power to imbue us with a feeling of connectedness to something vast. We find joy in the smallest of things. It could be a frog jumping or a bird singing, or a heart-shaped stone. There is no competition in the way we fish. We laugh often and smile at the other's good fortune. I wish the world could be friends as we are.

The first thing we did on the day I arrived in Sedona was take a slow and mindful walk along a beautiful trail beneath Thunder Mountain. Amitabha Stupa and Peace Park contains winding trails that have been specifically constructed to invite each visitor toward "prayer, meditation, and spiritual renewal." Many of the twisted juniper and pinyon trees are adorned with prayer flags, chimes, and temple bells. There are benches scattered here and there, allowing visitors to sit and simply take in the sights and sounds of the wind in the trees, or the calls of western scrub jays as they effortlessly float from branch to branch. All around rise the red-rock spires that seemed to change color and texture as the Earth rotates and the sun stays still. After all, it is not the sun that sets, it is the Earth that moves, like any living thing.

This was once the home of Paleo-Indians who lived here ten thousand years ago, hunting varieties of big game that have also vanished. Later came the Sinagua people, who left behind artifacts of rock art and cliff dwellings as their legacy. Then came the Yavapai, or "People of the Sun," followed by the Apache, who were both rounded up by federal troops and marched to the San Carlos Reservation, with many of them dying along the way. With the arrival of Europeans who reinvented themselves into Americans, a town was established and named "Sedona," for the wife of the first postmaster. It's a nice name and a lovely town, but I must admit I wished this valley had been protected from development and the town located farther downstream, just outside the red rocks. I can imagine how beautiful sunsets were here before the arrival of traffic lights and rooftops. I couldn't help thinking that this area should have been a national preserve.

Oak Creek is a tributary of the Verde River that forms a canyon about twelve miles long, carved out of red-rock sandstone by the actions of the creek's waters and the Earth's Oak Creek fault. Its east rim is higher than its west rim, rising to 7,200 feet above sea level at its highest point, and about a thousand feet less at its lowest. This was originally the realm of native Gila trout, but now has been transformed into a European brown trout fishery. It is tragically ironic that in more ways than one, when Euro-Americans arrived they quickly removed the natives, both people and fish, and replaced them with something that reminded them of the "old country."

It's an old story of human migration, and we have been doing it for as long as we've been migrating. Irish potatoes from Peru and Italian tomatoes from Mexico became "native" in our mixed-up modern minds. But these things are the leftovers of past military conquests. They are the reason that Texas is covered in feral old-world pigs and Oak Creek is full of feral old-world trout. Both tomato sauce on pizza and rainbow trout in Pennsylvania leave me with mixed feelings. I enjoy them, but I know they displaced something else that I will never get to experience. I will never know what the food in Italy or the fishing in Idaho was like . . . before everything got mixed up.

Walking down the creek I felt the scraping, scratching, prickly feeling of briar thorns against my naked legs. Aileen and I had both decided to wet wade in shorts and water shoes because the weather had been warm in the canyon.

So we stepped carefully between the jagged thorns and slippery stones that led down to the creek's edge, as the sound of water spilling over moss-covered rocks soothed the rough edges from our minds. This is the sense of peace and tranquility that small canyon streams always give. The world may be crumbling, but in this place and in this time, everything was beautiful.

When we reached the waterline, it was just below a pedestrian bridge constructed of metal and wood so that hikers might cross over without damaging the sensitive riparian habitat of the creek. We took care to step lightly, not only to avoid the thorns but also to avoid causing harm. Oak Creek was narrow here, a creek in every sense without a chance of being mistaken for a river or even a stream. It was delicate, with bits of pocket water surrounded by dark green vegetation and bright yellow wildflowers. All I could think of was the word "paradise."

Because the creek was so small and the briars so large, I suggested that the only way we could fish this stretch was to take turns walking upstream, pocket by pocket of potential holding water. I love this kind of fishing when I am alone, but even more so when I'm with someone like Aileen. We share well. I love fishing with someone who I find myself hoping for—wanting them to catch the first fish, or the biggest fish, or the prettiest fish—not thinking a bit about myself. And what makes it even more beautiful is that I know that my fishing companion is cheering and hoping the same things for me. The world needs so much more of this kind of loving kindness and friendship. Can you imagine what this planet would be like if we all cared about each other and the Earth in this way? I can only think of one way to describe such a world: "Hopeful."

The water was icy cold against my legs as we worked our way up this narrow stretch of creek, mindfully, carefully, and peacefully casting forward into each small pool, hoping for a tug on our tippets that wasn't an overhanging branch. Occasionally we'd hear the footsteps of hikers crossing the wooden footbridge downstream. They could not see us, and we could not see them, and this added to the wonderful childlike feeling and fantasy of being in a secret spot, where nobody else had ever been.

I had just worked a series of pockets without result and was hanging back as my friend stepped softly upstream, casting from one to another in short, soft loops. That was about the time I looked into the briars and confirmed what I had suspected earlier. Wild blackberries! Bunches of them!

I told Aileen and her face lit up. We both stopped fishing for a moment and began picking and eating the most delicious wild berries we could imagine. And that became a pattern for a while; one of us fished while the other ate berries straight off the vine. It did not matter that we were not catching any fish yet; this was such a perfect place to be alive that in this moment, nothing was lacking. Memories flashed into my mind of picking wild blackberries and raspberries as a boy. I was charged with bringing them home and delivering them to the kitchen table for everyone to eat, but in truth I ate as many as I dropped into the bowl.

We came to a place where two rivulets came together after being split by a large flat stone that was half-submerged in the creek's center. Just below this spot, a moss-covered rock in the middle of the riffles sprouted a beautiful yellow wildflower. "This is the place," my friend said. "This is where we will release Liv." It was perfect.

Liv was a baby girl who never lived long enough to become all that she might have been, and yet she touched a few lives more deeply than many of us will ever manage. And now I hope her story will touch your life, too. You see, little Liv was diagnosed with spinal muscular atrophy shortly after being born. Her parents, Hayley and Bill, are dear to the heart of my friend Aileen. While Liv was battling her condition, Aileen gave her a smooth, heart-shaped piece of rose quartz that symbolized love and protection. But while we can give people all the love we can, we can't protect each other forever from life's ending, and Liv died just a week after her sixth month of life. That heart-shaped rose quartz was placed with the baby during cremation, and it survived the experience, ultimately ending up in the urn with her ashes. Love lives on.

Liv's mother Hayley gave Aileen a small vial of the child's ashes to be released into nature at the time and place of her choosing. This place and this time seemed right to her, and so I captured the images of my friend releasing Liv's ashes into this beautiful life-giving water. They flowed with the currents around the moss-covered stone that held the bright yellow flower. They vanished downstream, as we all do, when our time comes to cross over. Aileen looked up with tears streaming down her cheeks, and we smiled, and I said, "I think it's still your turn to fish those nice pools up there." I picked a few more wild berries as I watched my friend fish. There were no more tears on that day, only smiles.

We came to a place where the creek grew wider and deeper, with several large pools and a moderate to slow current. Here the creek was wide enough to be mistaken for a stream, but not for long. Aileen reached the first pool and called back, "Steve! There are some big trout in here!"

"Go get 'em!" I replied. I saw her lay out a perfect roll cast across the water, and I decided to wait and watch from downstream, to avoid spooking the fish. After a while, I decided that they didn't want what she was tossing, so I slipped behind her and waded carefully upstream to the next wide, flat, trout-filled pool.

I was beginning to suspect that these old brown trout were wise to the angling game. Aileen and I were both being stealthy in our approach, but nothing we threw at them seemed to interest or even spook them. They'd just look at a passing dry fly as if to say, "You're kidding me . . . right?" We tried jigging micro-streamers, drifting grasshoppers, and swinging wet flies. We sang to them, pleaded with them, and called out to the "trout gods" for guidance, but every time we did, these fish exhibited all the apathy of a man getting a wedding invitation from an ex-girlfriend. They just couldn't get excited about it.

Aileen was determined to make those trout eat something, and I admired her passionate persistence but did not emulate it. Instead, I waded upstream to a place where the water began to look like a creek again, casting to likely deep pools without good fortune, and finally positioning myself at the base of a fast-moving foam line where the tiny creek pretended to be a stream. All around me were acorn woodpeckers that flashed their bright black-and-white wings as they screamed out their crazy call that sounded like *waka waka wakaaa!* They flew back and forth across the treetops as if they had somewhere important to go and were running late. Upon arrival at the opposite side of the creek, they seemed to have a change of heart, flying wildly back to where they came, screaming all the way.

I looked into my fly box with a questioning gaze, which sounds better than to say that I was dumbfounded. I'm not sure why I was looking so hard, because whenever I am stuck, I always go to the same choice—a size 16 Adams with a high-visibility parachute to compensate for my ever-aging eyes. I looked downstream toward my determined but fishless friend and sent a silent wish that she'd catch one. I was happy that she had not fallen into the water, as is her common practice. I am forever saying, "Be careful . . ." as she wades. Aileen was watching the woodpeckers too, and in the middle of all the commotion we just looked at each other and smiled.

I cast to the bottom of the foam line and began working my way upstream, watching the drift of the fly and extending it as long as I could manage until reaching a place where a birch tree had fallen across the water. Eventually, there was nothing left but about twenty feet of fast-rushing water that seemed too fast to hold anything. I had almost surrendered when I noticed a small patch of smooth water within the white, foaming torrent. It was a long shot, but I remembered the words of "The Great One," Wayne Gretzky, when he said, "You miss 100 percent of the shots you don't take." So I took the shot.

Like so many of the most wonderful or terrifying moments of our lives, this one played out in slow motion. I cast and watched the line unfold toward the target, landing miraculously at the perfect place in the pool. I watched in amazement as a twelve-inch brown trout rose and engulfed the little Adams like it was his last chance for a meal. I set the hook and pulled him out of the current into a long flat of shallow water. Aileen saw him jump and hollered out, "You got one!" I did not have a net and saw her coming toward me with hers, but she was a long way downstream from me and I just had a funny feeling as I said, "I hope I don't lose him!"

Isn't it amusing how a guy like me will drive to an airport, fly to another state, drive and hike and wade to a spot in a stream, only to catch and release a fish? And I guess my face looked comical as I stood there with my mouth open, my line slack and drifting toward Aileen, watching that beautiful brown trout swim right back to the same little slick of water where I found him just a moment ago. At first, I bowed my head toward the earth, then looked up through the treetops toward the heavens, and then over to Aileen, who was smiling at me, kindly.

"You caught one," she said. "I saw it jump . . . so it counts." Everything counts, I thought. The moment was just as perfect now as it would have been had I let the fish go a moment later. I was happy for him. He was free and clueless that this was not his home. There was no way for him to know that he belonged in Scotland or Germany. For him, the universe was a small patch of water in a lovely canyon creek near Sedona, Arizona. Who was I to tell him any different?

Aileen returned to her pool filled with snarky fish, while I began to wade up through the place where the creek narrows and gushes between the rocks and over the fish I had just lost. The current was fast here and the rocky bottom uneven and slick. I reached for a pocket of water just upstream in a tight spot between two birch trees but couldn't quite reach the top of the pool. So I stepped forward into the next likely casting place with the idea of sending a short bow and arrow cast into the pocket, but the creek had other ideas. I quickly found myself submerged up to my neck, with the ribs of my left side being abruptly introduced to the aforementioned rocky bottom. It was more of a splash and dull thud than a hard fall, and I was able to regain my footing and stand up just as Aileen waded up behind me. She looked at me standing there like a wet puppy dripping in creek water, smiled, and said, "Be careful!" Well played, my friend . . . *touché*!

———

Like Oak Creek, the East Verde River is a tributary of the Verde River that begins high up along the Mogollon Rim and flows through portions of the Mazatzal Wilderness. Also, like Oak Creek, this was once the homewaters of native Gila trout, and now Arizona Game and Fish is taking some actions to restore the East Verde as a Gila trout fishery, though not as a pure, spawning population. During chats with my friend Zach Beard, who is a fisheries biologist with Arizona Game and Fish, he shared with me that the intent in the East Verde is to conduct an experiment to see if native Gila trout can be utilized as a "put-and-take fishery" for anglers. The upper reaches of the river still contain wild, non-native, and evasive rainbow trout that have the potential of polluting the genetics of the Gilas being stocked into the East Verde. The hope is that by creating "put-and-take" fisheries of native trout for anglers, we may be able to increase the desire of anglers to save and expand the range of native trout that humans have pushed to the edge of extirpation or extinction.

I think it's sad that it takes so much effort to get anglers to recognize the mistakes of the past and prioritize repairing the damage we've caused. Everything is connected to everything. Native fish act as a bellwether to what is happening to the whole watershed, region, state, nation, hemisphere, and planet. Here is my hope: "Every angler is a naturalist." If we genuinely love the great outdoors, we need to actually *love* it.

So many people seem to mix up love with use. When you love someone, you don't use them, you participate in their lives. You are on their team and they are on yours. If you love someone, you protect them and help them grow healthy and free. Love is always a key and never a cage. Love is unconditional, not transactional.

I love wild, native trout, even if I will never be able to catch them. I love wilderness, even if I will never step foot within its borders. It's time we begin changing the way we love people and things. It isn't a "natural resource," it's a natural part of our homeland. We are a part of this community, not apart from it. Think about it—every angler, hunter, hiker, paddler, climber, and scuba diver needs to become a naturalist.

The drive from Sedona to the East Verde is a beautiful one and well worth the trip even if all you were going to do is drive up, have a picnic by the river, and drive back. You begin in the red-rock country around Oak Creek and slowly dip into the edges of the Sonoran Desert, then rise up the escarpment through the pinyon pines and junipers until finally reaching the high country where ponderosa pines and spruce dominate the flora. This area is known as a "floristic and faunal boundary," containing habitats with characteristics of both the Rocky Mountains of the western United States and the Sierra Madre Occidental of northern Mexico.

The Mogollon Rim rises up on its backbone of Kaibab limestone and Coconino sandstone to an elevation of eight thousand feet above sea level. It is home to deer, elk, bighorn sheep, coyotes, black bears, and, at its southeastern edges, some of the last Mexican wolves. The Mogollon Rim, and the mountains arching southwest of it, contain unique ecosystems called

Madrean Sky Islands. Due to the elevation of these mountaintops and the receding landscape surrounding them, they preserve the last remnants of the pine-oak woodlands that are part of the Sierra Madre Occidental to the south—home to El Tigre, the North American jaguar. I, for one, love the idea of having someplace within our national border where Mexican wolves and jaguars can still live and thrive.

On the way to the river, we slowed for a young bull elk as it crossed the road and walked into the brush on the other side. The ponderosa pines were stately and stunning as they rose up toward the sun, and the aspen, Arizona sycamore, and birch trees softened the scene as we drove down the dirt road that led to the river. That is where we met up with my friend Cinda Howard, who had driven three hours in the dark from her home in the White Mountains so that we could all fish together. I was happy to see her, and just as happy to have my two friends finally meet for the first time.

We strung up our rods and walked to the river, which looks more like a stream. Aileen and I tied on the olive-colored tungsten-weighted micro-streamers that she had tied for us. I'm not sure what Cinda tied on, but I knew it was going to work for her. There was another angler already fishing right next to the parking turnout, so we walked upstream to give him some space and privacy. In time we came to a nice stretch of water with lots of quick currents around rocks and massive tufts of grass, and a series of plunge pools, each three or four feet deep. It looked perfect, so we split up and began leapfrogging upriver in a slow, methodical, and relaxed manner. *Relaxed* is the optimal word.

Whenever I am in nature, I can feel myself healing. Add a clean, rushing stream and the sounds of songbirds and I'm in heaven. This, my friends, was heaven. The entire area is forested with vast stands of ponderosa pines, Engelman spruce, and Douglas fir in the higher places, and sycamore, maple, birch, and willow along the creek banks. Some of the sycamore trees were as large as I've ever seen, and it occurred to me that two people hugging the same tree on opposite sides might not be able to touch fingers. I loved the multicolored, peeling-paper bark in shades of gray, green, brown, and white. Just as impressive were the massive green leaves with silver-white underbellies fluttering in the breeze. Do you notice these things when you're fishing? I do. I make sure that I do.

It didn't take long for Cinda to catch the first Gila, and we all cheered! Fishing and friendship are such a perfect match. Shortly thereafter we came to a bend in the stream with some fast water spilling over and around large, rounded stones and huge clumps of dark green grass. I began casting downstream, allowing my fly to tumble freely in the current, and as it swung out of the foam line, I'd retrieve it in short, stop-and-go strips. Cinda was downstream, and before long she was into another Gila, which she brought to the net with a big smile on her face. I looked upstream and saw Aileen casting up and across a fast current, and almost instantly she too had caught a Gila and brought it to hand. We all cheered; the fish were beautiful, golden-yellow, spotted works of natural art. Now it was my turn.

I was feeling good about the place I was casting. It just felt fishy, so I persisted. After feeling the joy of one of my dearest friends on Earth as she lifted her first Gila trout out of the water, I noticed that my fishing buddies were getting worried about me. I was fine. I was having fun no matter if I caught a fish or not. So I kept casting and swinging that micro-streamer in ever increasing arcs until I felt a mighty pull, set the hook, and found myself attached to a beautiful Gila trout. I didn't bring my net on this trip, a mistake I will not repeat. Once again, as soon as I got the fish close and before Aileen could reach me with her net, I said, "I hope I don't lose him!" In that moment, he was gone.

Suddenly, I flashed back to every time as a boy that I failed to catch a football because I allowed an instant of doubt to enter my head. Why had I done that now, twice? I knew that mistakes are fine if we learn from them, so I reeled in, moved upstream, and cast forward once again. Losing a fish is a good lesson in impermanence.

Life often flips off the hook. Nothing lasts forever, and all we can do is enjoy whatever comes our way. And I was having a great time. The fishing was magnificent. Cinda caught several fish and Aileen caught her first Gila ever. It was a perfect day, no matter if I caught one or not. I said as much to both of my friends, but I don't know that they believed me.

In time we came to the last pool before we were planning to turn around and walk back, fishing casually along the way. Aileen and Cinda insisted I take that pool, and I happily accepted their generosity. Aileen walked up to me and whispered in my ear, "You are going to catch one here and I am going to net it for you!" I did not want to let either of them down. So I cast and swung my streamer into the current in a perfect-looking spot along a perfect-looking current and immediately received a perfectly good rise and take, and I somehow managed to set the hook . . . perfectly.

Both my friends came running to my side, and Aileen was as good as her word as she netted my fish. Cinda grabbed her camera and filmed the landing and release while Aileen cheered, "Aww, that was so beautiful!" My friends were happy for me, and I was happy for them and so grateful that we had shared this day together. This is what fishing is all about. It's the whole experience, from the drive up, walk in, cast out, and release, to the sounds of bluebirds in the air as you sit on a rock untangling a wind knot. There is so much more to angling than catching fish. I'd still do it with nothing at the end of my line but a feeling of hopefulness and gratitude.

On the walk back we came to a place where a flock of tiny painted redstarts were flitting in the air over the stream, catching mayflies in mid-flight. They were magnificent, with their black-and-white wing and tail feathers and bright red breasts and bellies, as they darted from branch to branch and launched into a dance among the glistening, sunlit mayflies. I have seen so many amazing and beautiful things in nature in all my years and all my travels. Still, I can say without a doubt that I have never seen anything more beautiful than those little birds dancing in the wind, and the smiles on my friends' faces when I finally caught a fish.

I could feel the crushed rock crunching beneath the soles of my boots as we walked the red-tinged trail toward Bell Rock. I could see the bright blue flashes of wing and feather as western scrub jays flew from pinyon to juniper and back. These brilliant birds had become meaningful on this journey, as they seemed to follow us everywhere, and somehow they felt a bit timeless to me, as if they had some ability to slip between alternate realities. As if they were Native American shamans in non-human form. The birds and this place felt spiritual. The red-rock country of Arizona feels like home, even though I've never been here before, that I can recall.

Sedona and Oak Creek are spiritually centered places. They have a reputation as places where people gather to seek enlightenment, solace, and healing. Like any place in capitalistic America, people have found ways to monetize this desire for healing, and the town itself is replete with signs offering various forms of alternative healing—for a price. But this commercialized pseudo-spirituality does not negate the fact that this place feels special. The buildings, roadways, and street signs advertising everything from psychic readings to aura photos are distractions, like a church rummage sale or the boring speeches at college graduations. They have little to do with the importance of the moment, but they do not make the place in time and in life any less valuable.

If you look away from the markers of humanity and out toward the red-rock desert, you will feel the spirituality of this native landscape. It is here if you are open to it. And once you feel it, you will never forget that feeling of wholeness. You always leave a little of yourself behind among those rocks, or perhaps that is where you find a part of yourself that was lost. I know I did.

I have traveled much of the world, from Europe to Africa, South America, and back and forth across North America. There are few places that have felt like home to me as soon as I found them, once again. I say "once again" because I was left with a feeling in each place—something more than déjà vu—something like remembrance. I felt that way in the Abruzzo Mountains of Italy, while paddling down the Loxahatchee River in Florida, in a canyon in Idaho, in my beloved Texas Hill Country, and here in the red-rock, twisted-tree landscape surrounding a busy little tourist town. Go figure.

A vortex is described as a "swirling center of energy that is conducive to healing, meditation, and self-exploration." Believers find all of Sedona to be a vortex but have designated several areas as especially powerful centers of "healthy energy," and one of these is Bell Rock. I am neither a believer nor a disbeliever, which is my point of view for any article of faith. But I can say this: I felt different here. I felt at peace, centered, and complete. Perhaps it was all a self-fulfilling prophecy, but whatever it was, this place moved me. It is part of why I came here in the first place. To find out.

Still, I don't think it was a vortex of energy or an act of divine intervention that caused me to feel so alive and complete here, although I cannot discount either. I feel that it was "Nature" with a capital "N" that led me to feel healed, whole, and at peace. It was nature and the best in human nature that was saving me from spiraling down into the dark morass of modern society. Nature teaches, centers, and heals—if we are open to it.

The path meandered upward toward the base of Bell Rock, and in time we began to climb, coming ever closer to a ledge where we planned to sit and simply absorb the rock's energy. It was warm, and my asthmatic lungs were feeling even this brief climb. I was reminded once again of the fragility of the body, and the power of the soul.

I do believe in the "ghost in the machine." We are not simply a mass of minerals and water, helplessly reacting to a stimulus with a response. We are something more, something timeless, or at least some of us are. I have nothing to back up any of this—no science and no scripture. It is simply how I feel.

When we reached our destination, we sat and looked out across the desert, around the rocks, my mind swirling like a vortex, not down, but up. Below we could see a girl dancing joyfully, not caring a bit about being seen or who saw her. She seemed so happy that I wondered if she was under the influence of a psychedelic mushroom. How sad that I thought that. How wonderful it would be if we'd all stop worrying about what other people think and simply enjoy life.

In time we noticed that she had stopped dancing and calmly sat crosslegged facing the setting sun. She seemed peaceful, joyful, calm, hopeful, and lovely. "Why is that so unusual?" I asked myself. It doesn't matter if it's songbirds dancing in the sunlight or a young woman dancing in the sunset, we should all just dance, and not give a damn what the world thinks.

Here is something I hope you will remember my friends. Nature doesn't need us; we need nature. It has been scientifically confirmed that meaningful time in nature can create healing and health in humans. The Japanese have known this for some time and are now using *shinrin-yoku* ("forest bathing") to counter the deleterious effects of their now westernized, industrial/ information age, high-speed capitalistic society. The South Koreans have been learning the same hard lesson, and we Americans need to realize that while some stress is healthy, chronic stress is deadly, first to your spirit and then to your body.

Immersion in nature has been clinically proven to heal people, both physiologically and psychologically. Nature therapy involves being mindfully present in the moment, with intention, and without judging. For me, "river therapy" is the best medicine. Others have discovered its benefits with the creation of such programs as Project Healing Waters, Casting for Recovery, and Reel Recovery. Nature and loving friendships are healing.

Studies by the Cleveland Clinic show that nature therapy reduces harmful cortisol levels; has positive healthful impacts on blood pressure, blood sugar regulation, sleep disorders, anxiety, and depression; and gives an overall feeling of well-being. Sometimes, it's not the weight on the scale that matters as much as the weight of the world. Nature teaches us balance, and how to have a healthy perspective on life and living.

As we sat on Bell Rock, simultaneously looking out and in, I felt peaceful, calm, comforted, complete, and at home. These winding desert trails contain many wonders. They contain flashing blue scrub jays and singing brown sparrows. They contain intricately patterned snakes and lizards and multicolored dragonflies. And they contain twisted juniper, pinyon, and rare bristlecone pines that can live for thousands of years. But even the ancient bristlecones will eventually return to the earth, just as I will. Only the earth remains.

I could feel the crushed rock crunching beneath the soles of my boots as we walked the red-tinged trail away from Bell Rock. My visit had come to an end, but I knew that part of me will remain on that rock ledge for as long as I live. I could feel my spirit blowing freely across the desert toward the Mogollon Rim. I had experienced a spiritually intimate moment, not unlike I had while climbing in the mountains of Italy, walking in a canyon in Idaho, or paddling down a river along the edge of the Everglades.

We need wild places. Shopping mall water fountains are no replacement for natural waterfalls and riffles. We need wild creatures. Apartment poodles and windowsill kittens are no replacement for wolves and jaguars. We need native trees and plants. Golf courses and greenhouses are no replacement for meadows and forests. We need nature, and right now nature needs only one thing from us: "Respect" with a capital "R."

There is magic in the descending song of the canyon wren, the rise of a Gila trout, or the cough of a jaguar in the starlit Arizona night. Wildness feeds my feral soul. Wilderness gives me hope. And loving friendships cause the light to shine in my weary eyes. I am so grateful for all that rivers and canyons have given me. These words within these pages are my best attempt to give something back.

CHAPTER TWENTY-ONE

Just One More Cast—Brook Trout

Headwaters of the Potomac, West Virginia

Never doubt that a small group of thoughtful, committed, citizens can change the world. Indeed, it is the only thing that ever has.

—*MARGARET MEAD*

THIS JOURNEY BEGAN WITH ME STANDING IN A JON BOAT ON THE DIRTIER end of the Potomac River with my friend and Trout Unlimited president Chris Wood. We were casting rope flies into the murky water just before it drifts past the Lincoln Memorial, Capitol Building, and White House. We spoke of our mutual love for the "Nation's River," and how in many ways its health reflects our nation's health, or lack thereof. Now the journey of thousands of miles and hundreds of casts concludes on the cleaner end of the same mighty river. This time I was with my friend and Trout Unlimited biologist Dustin Wichterman. Dustin is a son of these wonderful West Virginia mountains and another passionate advocate for this place, its people, and its wild landscapes. At either end of the Potomac, I could not possibly be in better company.

To say that Dustin loves West Virginia is about as much an understatement as me saying I love pizza. I've already made it clear to my cardiologist that if he ever tells me I need to cut pizza out of my diet, then he might as well tell me, "I'm sorry but your diagnosis is terminal." That's how Dustin feels about these ancient mountains and the culture and creatures that live here. If he were forced to leave, I think he'd expire. And his love of the native brook trout is so complete that he named his beautiful daughter Brooklynn Vale (Brook Valley). That's true love, y'all, for an old landscape and a young girl, both filled with the questions of life.

The drive to Seneca Creek was winding, foggy, and splattered with the multicolored images of autumn. Long ago the original forest of this region was converted into paper and boards, but it is healing, slowly. The unaware might never know that this forest is but a shadow of its former self. The hand of man is evident everywhere I've ever been. And everywhere I've ever been, nature tries to regain some of what was taken. It's tragically beautiful.

Forests are like people. If you think about it, and you should, there are people in your past who would not recognize the "you" that you've become. Like the forest, we are all changed by our choices, the choices of other people, and the vagaries of life. Yet like the forest, we can become something lesser or something better, depending once again on our choices. Choices make all the difference—in forests, rivers, landscapes, and lifetimes.

These second-growth forests are still diverse and beautiful, even with the impact of humanity, both Native American and Euro-American. The first Europeans settled here in 1746, and prior to this various Native American tribes traveled, traded, and tormented each other along the "Great Indian Warpath" that followed the Potomac from its headwaters to the Chesapeake Bay. Tuscarora, Seneca, and Algonquian-speaking tribes moved across this landscape and along these waters long before the first Englishman arrived. Both "tribes" impacted the land. It's what we do.

The geology of these ancient mountains is a mix of metamorphic granite, gneiss, and basalt, along with the sandstone, shale, and limestone sedimentary rocks that tell the stories of volcanic beginnings and an ancient shallow sea. And this geology matters as much as the biology of the watersheds and their ability to sustain healthy forests, streams, creeks, and, ultimately, native brook trout. The limestone in some areas works to counter the effects of acid rain, which can create conditions that are potentially lethal to trout. And sadly, the geology of West Virginia, western Kentucky, and southeast Ohio has led to the massively destructive extraction of large deposits of bituminous coal across these once pristine mountains. I have been told that "Coal" owns West Virginia. It's no wonder that bituminous coal is the state rock.

Seneca Creek is simply lovely. That morning, I could have chosen either to take my blood pressure medicine or just stand in the spilling waters of Seneca Creek, with the same healthful results. I chose both. By the end of the day, I suspected the rhythm of my pulse matched that of the stream. Nature heals.

We strung up our rods, tying on a weighted nymph of Dustin's inclination, and then he took a few quick exploratory casts right next to the grassy flat where he had parked the truck. I watched as red and yellow leaves tumbled to the earth with every breeze. I listened as the birds and the stream sang, each song different, like wind chimes of polished glass, bells of brass, or hollow lengths of suspended bamboo. I could feel myself breathing, my heart beating, my mind unwinding—life should always be lived like this.

On his third cast he hooked a twelve-inch rainbow trout that was as beautiful as any invasive species could be. It's not the fish's fault that its ancestors were forcefully transported and dumped from New England to New Zealand, Patagonia to Pennsylvania, South Africa to South Dakota. In fact, I'm glad he caught a rainbow trout; it too tells the tale of this place, and our place within it. With the brightly colored trout released, we moved along the trail into brook trout territory.

The walk upstream through the mixed forest of eastern hemlock, red pine, mountain ash, red maple, red and white oak, and rhododendron was as beautiful as the creek's rushing, cold waters. Dustin pointed out a deep pool that had quite a few nice-sized brookies hanging at the bottom and near an overhanging exposed root. I hadn't adjusted yet to the light and waters, so some of my casts were under his direction because I could not make out the location of the fish he was so clearly seeing. This is normal for me. In Africa it took me a couple of days to start spotting kudu in the distant thorn bush, and it always takes my eyes and mind a bit of adjustment time when seeking bonefish on my first day back on a sand or turtle grass flat.

After a while, each trout began to clearly show itself to me, hiding in plain sight. Still, no matter what I did, they ignored my offerings. In a dozen or so casts, I managed to get one follow and rejection. I also caught the aforementioned tree root and blew the pool. We moved on.

The hydrological profile of this creek contains everything you'd want in a trout water. There are many small waterfalls and, at the base of each, pools that contain fish from head to flat to tail. There are rapids and riffles that pump oxygen into the cold water and carry food to the waiting mouths of hungry fish. There are patches of pocket water and eddies that circle and swirl beneath ancient stone outcrops. The trees provide shade, and the sedimentary geology provides an alkaline element to offset the impacts of acid rain. And if this were not enough there are caddisflies and mayflies, grasshoppers and crickets, tiny frogs and tadpoles, silkworms falling from the treetops, and damselflies suspended from the tips of grass. Clean oxygenated water, shelter, and food. This is how a mountain creek, stream, or river should be maintained.

It was still my turn, according to Dustin, even though I had botched up the first pool. We came to a long, shallow pool with a small but wide waterfall at its head and another at its tail, and Dustin spotted a nice brookie holding in the current just above the second falls. I love this kind of fishing because it forces me to take it slow, pay attention, and thoughtfully plan my approach. I made my first few casts from the relative safety of distance from the right bank. But my first cast was too cautious, and the nymph drifted too far from his feeding lane. The second cast was closer, and I saw him turn, follow, and then turn away as the current carried the fly quickly toward the end of the pool. The third cast got a follow all the way to the end, but not a take. I decided to take a short pause and let him rest for a moment while I repositioned myself ever so carefully into the center of the creek. Then I made my cast, watched the weighted nymph tumble along the bottom past the brookie, which followed and plucked my fly from the current just as I raised my rod tip. He flashed and danced in the sparkling sunlight and soon rested in my cold, wet hand, just below the water's surface. He was stunning, and I was thrilled.

The first brook trout of my life was the color of autumn leaves and as precious to me as any bonefish or bluefish I'd ever caught. You see, my friends, it was important to me to catch my first brookie in its native waters, not in a Colorado stream or a reservoir in Wyoming. If this doesn't make sense to you, then you probably won't understand why I traveled to Africa to kill my kudu when they are running freely across many a "hunting ranch" in my native state of Texas. For me, it's the difference between going to Paris and going to Disney's Epcot Center. I want the real deal.

If there is anything that I like more than catching a fish, it's letting it go. Dustin took a few wonderful photos of the release as I sent that beautiful brook trout back to the waters where he was found. I watched as he swam away back to the exact spot in the river where we first saw him, shimmering in the dappled sunlight. It was a captivatingly beautiful moment that I will never forget.

Dustin took the next run, and in short order he caught a nice brookie. We worked our way upstream, taking turns, catching and missing fish along the way. Walking up a shallow riffle we noticed a trout steadily rising and picking something off the surface. Neither of us could see anything floating on the water, but as we searched a caddisfly landed on my arm as if to say, "It's us, dummy." I tied on an elk hair caddis and began carefully casting upstream, drifting it over the water where the brookie was rising. He hit my fly and I missed the hook-up, and after a few more tries it became obvious that he was done with me.

At one point we came to an amazing waterfall that gushed through the rocks just left of center. At its base was a pool that must have been ten feet deep and twenty feet across in every direction. We could see some nice brook trout taking something off the surface at the tail of the pool, and so we both worked different parts of the same pool. Dustin began casting a small streamer into the foam below the falls and immediately brought up a nice brookie. I was casting my caddis dry fly to the rising trout at the tail of the pool but didn't get more than a look and turning rejection. I snipped off the dry, switched to a streamer, and began working the deep far side of the pool, which soon led to a hook-up with a pretty little female brookie.

It seemed we had done what we could in this lovely spot in the stream, and so we worked our way around the falls and found a place on the massive stones beside the next set of riffles to have our lunch break. It consisted in part of sandwiches made by "two little old ladies who run a local sandwich shop," who Dustin said wouldn't forgive him if he got his lunch from anywhere else. The sandwiches were wonderful, on many levels.

Even a simple sandwich can be made more special by the care of someone who makes them, and the appreciation of someone who accepts them. In this case we enjoyed them next to the prettiest mountain stream anyone could ever wish for, with multicolored autumn leaves still clinging to the trees, and others fluttering in every breeze and floating along the currents, over rock and root, and onward toward the sea. And then there was the conversation that was shared in between each bite of these simple sandwiches, lovingly made. Life is beautiful when we pay attention.

I have spent most of my life hiking and hunting and fishing alone. When I was a boy, I sometimes had my dad beside me, casting our lines into stagnant gator holes and flowing streams. Then I became a man, and I sometimes had my daughter beside me, casting our lines into Texas Hill Country rivers as herds of deer watched from the shore. But then my dad grew old and passed away, and my daughter grew up and moved away, and once again I walked and fished alone. I got used to it, sort of. I came to love my solitude, and I've always known that I'd rather be alone than in the wrong company. But then something truly life-changing began to happen. Once I set out to cast for and connect with the native gamefish of this beautiful country, I began to find my tribe. I've met the best friends of my lifetime while writing this book, traveling the nation, and seeking out native fish and new waters. I have been able to write of these magnificent wild, native fish and the places they call home through the eyes of the people who call those waters their "homewaters." It has been a great adventure, and I am forever grateful.

And so we sat there on those massive stones as the creek tumbled and trickled over smaller ones, and we spoke of our love for our homewaters and homelands, and a handful of people. I spoke of my grown daughter Megan, who has become an outdoor and environmental educator in Britain, and he spoke of his young daughter Brooklynn Vale, who was learning to fly-fish and had already caught brook trout that were bigger and brighter than any I have known. I laughed as he proudly told the story of Brooklynn when he asked her if she wanted 4X or 5X tippet tied on her leader, and how she thought about it for a moment, put her hands on her hips, and confidently declared, "I want 6X!" (She assumed the higher number made it better.) It was a moment to remember, two fathers from different generations sharing our tales of fatherhood and our love of nature.

By the time Dustin reaches my age, I will be long gone. But as long as I live, I will remember the day we spent together at Seneca Creek catching brook trout and setting them free. These are the things and times that matter. This, my friends, is what life is all about. Anything less is a waste of life, and a waste of life is a "mortal sin." After all, it's not a dress rehearsal. This is it.

Fly fishing teaches us to pay attention, not to what "may happen" or what "did happen," but rather to what is happening in the moment. That's an important lesson in any lifetime. I have sometimes referred to myself as an "Imperfect Texan Buddha," and "imperfect" is the operative word. But there is much that the East can teach the West, and one of those things is mindfulness. Fly fishing done right is a mindful, present, accepting, grace-ful, and grateful practice. The old axiom is that if we are feeling depressed, we are living in the past; and if we are feeling anxious, we are living in the future; but the only place we can truly be alive, is now, in the present. Every fish I've ever missed was because I forgot that lesson. Rising trout are wonderful teachers.

As the day grew longer, we began to work our way back downstream, casting here and there in places where we had seen fish, but not caught fish, on the way upstream. We picked up a few, but mostly we were heading back, and in time you realize that the best thing you can do is snip off your fly and enjoy the walk in the woods. That's another thing about fly fishing: I travel thousands of air and road miles and walk hundreds of foot miles just to catch fish that I immediately release. That's about as Zen a lesson as any imperfect Buddha can learn. Everything is impermanent. We can hold onto nothing. Once we accept the letting go, we come to love, not loathe, that sweet release. Fly fishing and love are both about freedom. Love lets go.

———

Dustin is as close to this land and these watersheds as anyone I've ever met. His life and the life of his family intertwine with the streams filled with trout, and the seams filled with coal. I've been told by people who know that the power of Big Coal rules this landscape, and that no politician can be elected here unless they say two magic words: coal and jobs. Every drug dealer knows that if you want to be in the money, you have to sell the idea that you can't live without the drug, and once you're in the money, you'd better buy off the people who might otherwise tell your victims the truth, so that the dependency never ends. Marketing always sells either fear or greed. Big Coal does both. Someone needs to make sure these good people and this beautiful land are not left for dead. There are other options and new economies to be created. But as Buckminster Fuller once wrote, "People never leave a sinking ship until they see the lights of another ship approaching." We need a new ship before the entire ocean is dead.

I've made the best friends of my life while fishing. When you fish together, you figure out a whole lot more than just about where the fish are and how to catch them. There are a bunch of reasons why I couldn't be a guide, one being that I lack the skill and knowledge as a fly fisher, and I know it. I will always consider myself a lifelong novice. But the other reason is because I think life's too short to waste time on the water with assholes. I fish with friends, or alone. Dustin and I became instant friends, and with friends the conversations and the silences all hold meaning and value.

While we sat in his truck bouncing over the rutted dirt roads through the forest and down the mountain, Dustin told me a tale of his West Virginian roots. His story rings true like the lyrics to a John Prine song. As he told it, I could almost hear the sound of a guitar, fiddle, dobro, and mandolin playing in the distance. It's an American story, and one we can write differently, if we choose.

Bob Blankenship was Dustin's grandpa and an important man in his life. After the war Grandpa Bob came home and found work in the only way that he thought he could in southern West Virginia; he began working the dragline for a coal company. A dragline is a crane with a bucket "the size of a house" that is used to strip-mine mountains into rubble and valleys into deep pits. Like his neighbors, Bob was told he was lucky to have a job and that coal was the lifeblood of West Virginia. But it never set well with him, and after repeatedly warning his company of the dangers of the operation, Bob walked off the job with nowhere to go. That's raw courage, y'all.

The mining accident that Grandpa Bob warned of happened a few days after he walked off the job, but nobody was killed. The mining runoff that Grandpa Bob worried about did leach into the watershed and kill off the streams, but nobody cared. Bob reached out to the governor's office and the state regulators but received no reply. Soon after, Dustin's grandpa was jobless and blacklisted. That's when Grandpa Bob became an environmental activist. Irony.

Dustin was only thirteen when his dad died, and so he was raised by his single mother, Betty Lou, and in part by his paternal grandfather, Eugene Smith. Eugene taught Dustin how to fish on the North Fork of the Cherry River, a waterway that is still fishable but suffering from the effects of acidification caused by the sulfur dioxide that is expelled from coal-fired power plants. Once it is released from the smokestacks, it joins with water vapor in the atmosphere and falls into the Earth's waterways as acid rain. Everything in nature is a circle and a cycle. The water is supposed to be in this circle; the sulfur dioxide isn't. Nature isn't prepared for our stupidity, and apparently, neither are we.

As we drove along the forest road, I watched the tree line hoping to see a black bear, but to no avail. I love seeing bears in the wild, whenever I am inside a truck or on the other side of the canyon. I mentioned to Dustin that my dad had raised me as a single parent, that I had lost him a few years back, and that my memories of him and me fishing together are the best memories I have. And we spoke of Dustin and his daughter Brooklynn Vale, and me and my daughter Megan, and how fishing with them became our best newest memories. The acts of fishing, hunting, and just being in nature brings people together, and helps people hold themselves together. We need more of this, not less. We need to bring people closer to the earth, not further away.

There was one more family story Dustin told that I think needs retelling. It is his own story of getting out of college with a degree in biology and a graduate degree in fisheries biology and being hired by a company that provided "environmental consulting." I guess human nature moves in circles and cycles, too, because in short order he found himself like his grandfather, between a bituminous coal rock and a hard place. He was being pressured to provide a favorable environmental report for a proposed mining operation that he knew would negatively impact the watershed of Hominy Creek and its tributaries, like Brushy Meadow Creek where Dustin's family used to fish. He resisted and refused and ultimately left the job without falling to industry pressure, but his successor did, and the permit was granted, and the coal was extracted, and the waste ran into the watershed, and all the fish died, along with the creek and every creature that depended on it for existence. All that so someone could leave the light on in the hallway while nobody is in there.

Dustin looked at me and said, "In 1976 my mom caught a sixteen-inch brook trout in Brushy Meadow Creek. I've heard of no fish being caught nor electro-fished there since the 1990s. Coal mining wiped Brushy Meadow off the map and is currently killing the rest of the Hominy Creek watershed as well." Brushy Meadow Creek is dead and everything around it is dying. No one will ever fish there again with their child.

It's not all bad. In fact, there is a lot of good, and we who love to fish, hunt, and hike need to see to it that the good overcomes the bad. I still remember the movies of my youth where the sheriff stood up to the marauding outlaws and ultimately defeated them with the help of the people in the community. We need more of that. And today that comes in the form of organizations like Trout Unlimited, The Nature Conservancy, and, more importantly, regular people who love the outdoors simply saying, "Enough is enough."

But there are two sides to every story, and while I don't give a damn about the fate of the barons of extractive industries who feed off the desperation and addiction of the working man and woman, I do care about the people of these lovely mountains that extend from southwest Pennsylvania through West Virginia, Virginia, Kentucky, eastern Tennessee, and North Carolina. We can't write these good folks off any more than we should the ones trapped in canyons of concrete.

If we realize that the legacy of extracting and burning fossil fuels is death, we need to find innovative ways to bring new life to these beautiful places and people. America is up to the challenge. We can revive the clean, cold Appalachian homewaters of native brookies and the livelihoods of the good folks who live beside them. And we are doing exactly that, in some places. West Virginians and Americans everywhere are fighting the good fight and winning a few battles. It's time to win the war.

When we arrived back at the spot in the road across from an elementary school where I'd parked my truck, we parted ways the way two true friends do, not with a handshake but rather with a brotherly embrace. Dustin flashed that easy smile he seems to carry like an outlaw packs a six-shooter, and we both agreed to do it again, either here in his lovely West Virginia mountains or far to the west in my beloved Texas Hill Country.

As I drove away, I could hear John Prine singing in my head about "Paradise." Driving with my window down, I could smell the freshness of an Appalachian autumn day coming to an end. I was ready to go home, but not really ready to leave. I could feel that some of who I am would always be standing ankle deep in the clean, cold waters of Seneca Creek.

As the miles fell behind me, I thought of how this journey began with me standing in a jon boat on the dirty end of the Potomac with my friend Chris Wood, casting rope flies into the river, not far upstream of the Lincoln Memorial, Capitol Building, and White House. I thought of how the people in those big stone buildings have been failing the river that brings them all the water they're drinking. And then I thought of how it all concluded here in what is now the healing and healthier headwaters of the Potomac, where organizations and people who love nature and the best of human nature are working side by side to save this place and its people.

After I returned to Texas, Dustin wrote to me about his work in the waters of his West Virginia homeland. He wrote, "Across TU's focal watersheds of the Potomac and Greenbrier headwaters in West Virginia, TU and partners have documented increases in fish size and abundance. Though data sets are still infantile in nature, being less than five years post project, they show that these streams are on a good trajectory toward recovery. TU has seen fish numbers quadruple in some project waters thus far, and the fishing reports following up the work, though anecdotal, show some incredibly happy anglers. Multiple seventy-plus-fish days have been documented by anglers fishing these publicly accessible restored reaches."

We can do this . . . we must. It's not about saving a "resource" or "fishery." It's all about saving our home, and our own souls.

As long as I live, I will never forget the sight of my first brook trout as he gracefully held his place in the current. I will never forget the way he looked in my hand, the color of autumn leaves. I will never forget as he swam away, back to his place in the creek, back to his place in time, back home. As long as I live, I hope I never forget that this is what being alive is all about, and that there is no greater joy than being a father and hearing your little girl say, "Dad, I want to go fishing." This, my friends, is a life worth living. After all, in the end, it's not about how much we took, but rather, how much we gave away.

Choosing to Change the Fate of Humanity . . . and the Earth
Moving from the Anthropocene (Age of Humanity) to the Naturaecene (Age of Nature)

We are not going to be able to operate our Spaceship Earth successfully nor for much longer unless we see it as a whole spaceship and our fate as common. It has to be everybody or nobody.
—R. BUCKMINSTER FULLER

WHEN I BEGAN MY LIFE AS AN ANGLER, I WAS A SMALL BOY CASTING A hook and bobber toward a diminutive bluegill. I suspect back then, as I stood next to my father, I was trying to become a man. Now I find myself casting a tiny hook with an even smaller bobber toward massive Lahontan cutthroat trout. I know now, as I stand alone in the ice-cold water, that I am trying to become a boy again. I think I'm growing younger. I like how it feels.

When I began this journey across the American watersheds and shorelines, I had no idea where it might lead me or who I might meet along the way. I had no specific destination or outcome in mind. It's not as important to fully understand where you are going as it is to know what you are choosing to leave behind . . . and why. I knew what I was leaving behind, and I had no desire to regain it.

Sometimes the wisest and bravest action we can take is to let go and walk away. I have not looked back, except to learn. I have not looked forward, except to remind myself of the power of entropy and the passing of time. I am living sunrise to sunrise while embracing the space in between. I have found the illusion of certainty to be laughable, and have made the reality of uncertainty my dear friend. It has been a true adventure, and I am grateful for every moment—even the difficult ones.

It would have been easy to lose all hope and simply allow the insanity of the Anthropocene to unfold as it may, but I'm just not ready to do so . . . yet. This is a beautiful world and worth fighting for, so I fight on with words and ideas, hoping to make some small positive impact. Instead of losing hope and feeling alone in the world, I chose to set out to find hope and connect with members of my tribe. And by seeking out my kindred spirits who love both nature and the best of human nature, I have found some of the most beautiful humans on Earth. I have found some of the best friends of my lifetime. I have found reasons for hope in these all too often seemingly hopeless times. And I want you to know, my friends, these times are not hopeless. The hope resides in each of us.

My buddy Kirk Deeter once said, "Fishing is about a lot more than pulling on fish lips." Amen brother . . . amen! I will expand on that by saying hiking is about more than covering a distance, hunting is about more than making a kill, gardening is about more than making a salad, and life is about more than making a living. All of these things are about connection to each other and the Earth.

When I was halfway through this great adventure, the COVID-19 pandemic arrived in North America, and at the time of this writing it had led to the death of hundreds of thousands of Americans and widespread economic turmoil. But during the initial twelve-week period of the pandemic, we witnessed massive, albeit temporary, changes in the nature of society and the nature of the environment. We witnessed cleaner water and clearer air. We witnessed lower crime rates and higher rates of human cooperation and caring. We witnessed the Earth breathing a sigh of relief. It was palpable. It was observable from space. It was short lived. Have we learned nothing? We have been given a gift. Let's open it. Let's pay attention. Let's learn something new and act on that learning.

The ancient indigenous peoples of North American were flawed humans, just like my Euro-American ancestors. But all indications seem to support that they understood something vital that we have forgotten; namely, that we are all a part of nature, not apart from it. They understood that we must respect the Earth and every living thing if we and the planet are to be sustained. They seem to have understood better than us the importance of balancing individual liberty with collective responsibility to the tribe. We are losing sight of this great truth, and we need to pay attention before it's too late. I hope it is not already too late.

A tribe is defined as "a group of people of the same race, language, culture, or interests." May I offer the following suggestions? I recommend that we adopt this creed:

- Our Race is "Human."
- Our Language is Respect.
- Our Culture is one of Kindness and Courage; Individual Liberty balanced with Collective Responsibility; Individual and Collective Resilience, Resourcefulness, and Resolve; and an Optimistic "Victor" (not victim) Mentality.
- Our Common Interest is to live in such a manner as to promote the Health of Nature and the Best of Human Nature and to reject anything less.

This is not the world we have; it is the one we must create if there is to be any hope for humanity and much of this planet.

What if we choose to stop fouling our own nest? What if we choose to change the way we do business, so that service becomes more valuable than things (monetize doing good services for the Earth and each other)? What if we choose to put the brakes on this extractive, disposable, consumption-driven worldview (refuse, reuse, recycle), before we crash? What if we choose to promote the creation of fewer humans on Earth, and improve opportunities for sustainable, enjoyable, meaningful living for the smaller world population? What if we choose to begin learning from our past and acting responsibly together? Can you imagine how wonderful this world could become if we simply started listening, learning, and solving challenges . . . together?

Yesterday I stepped into my favorite little stretch of my Texas Hill Country homewaters. Even though it is summer in Texas, which can be a bit grim, I was there early enough to avoid the heat, and it was glorious. The cave swallows were dipping and diving overhead, tiny frogs exploded across the shoreline like amphibious landmines, and a white-tailed deer stood in the river browsing on the bright green leaves of overhanging limbs. The water was cool and refreshing as I wet waded downriver toward the first pool, and a massive swirling hatch of tiny mayflies filled the air. I could not see any on the water and nothing seemed to be feeding on the surface, but they were pretty to watch, and so I did.

I had planned to christen my new three-weight Orvis Superfine glass rod that I had recently purchased to match the five-weight that I've been fishing with for years. I love glass rods. I have a four-weight Echo glass that I use for small trout streams with even smaller native trout, but I wanted something a bit lighter, shorter, and green rather than yellow for those times that I want to be stealthy. I tied on a size 10 woolly bugger with a little flash in the tail, sent it sailing toward the first pool, and received an immediate strike! It was a nice-sized Guadalupe bass that I failed to set the hook on and lost in short order. I wasn't used to how soft the little rod was, but I was learning. On the next cast I caught and landed the tiniest sunfish I've ever seen. I love irony.

As I look down this river and see the march of civilization encroaching upon its shores and draining its lifeblood, I know that we have come to the most important time in the history of humanity. In the past, nature impacted and controlled the destiny of humans. Now humans impact and control the destiny of nature. We have created the Anthropocene (age of humanity), and it has allowed us to increase in numbers way beyond the carrying capacity of the Earth. We have addicted ourselves to extraction and growth like a horde of mosquitoes or a mass of cancer cells.

But this is not a story of gloom, but rather a story of light. We can do better. Working together, we can become the light and hope of the world, rather than its parasite. Mother Nature is teaching us a lesson, and I hope we pay attention before the end of our term. Together, let's move from the Anthropocene to the Naturaecene (Age of Nature).

If we listen to and follow the lessons nature teaches, and if we choose to bring out the best in ourselves and others, we can change direction and avoid the precipice we are all running toward. It's not a zero-sum game.

We can think win/win. A healthy natural world is required for a healthy human world. Nature heals like no other medicine. It is our last, best hope.

I think I'm growing younger, and I like how it feels. As a boy I knew that every day was an adventure, and as an older man, I am reminded of this. As a boy my entire lifetime was contained in a moment, and as an older man, this is self-evident. As a boy I had no interest in the bickering of so-called grown-ups, and now, this is increasingly true. Life is beautiful and brief.

These stories that I have written are intended as a gift. There is hope, and that hope resides in how we choose to see the world and our actions. If every angler, hunter, and hiker became a naturalist, we'd make better choices and create a better world. Whenever we are lost, we must remember that our compass is all around us. Nature is our guide. Everything is connected to everything. We are One.

ACKNOWLEDGMENTS

ONE OF THE GREAT JOYS OF THIS ADVENTURE HAS BEEN SHARING IT WITH some of the best people on Earth. I want to thank Bob and Lisa White, Ted and Donna Williams, Chris and Betsy Wood, Kirk and Sarah Deeter, Kevin Hutchison, Cinda Howard, Charles Cantella, Toner Mitchell, Preston Bean, Brett Prettyman, Paul Burnett, Matthew Miller, Dustin Wichterman, John Karges, Maggie Serva, and Aileen Lane for their friendship, guidance, and support. I am also grateful to my lifelong friends, Janice "Lil Red" Bowden Hardaway, Margarita Quihuis, and Pam Uschuk, for their unending support and kindness. Without each of these wonderful people, this work, and my life, would be so much the lesser.

I am deeply grateful to my editor and friend, Gene Brissie of Lyons Press, for taking the time to read my story and then for choosing to bring it from the original manuscript to the completed literary work you now hold. And I appreciate the guidance and support of my production editor, Kristen Mellitt, my copy editor, Ann Seifert, as well as Max Phelps, Emily Cable, and Maura Cahill at Lyons Press. They have made this long journey so much more pleasurable and meaningful with their professionalism, knowledge, and heartfelt dedication.

Most of all, I am grateful to my wife and best friend of thirty-eight years, Alice, our amazing daughter Megan, and her wonderful partner Nick, who together form our tight little family that we refer to as "The Regiment." And although I love my entire Regiment, I would be remiss not to single out my wife Alice, who has proofread and given constructive input to every word of everything I have ever written and published, including this acknowledgment. With a lifetime of dear family, friends, and fishing, I am a fortunate man indeed.

Selected Bibliography

Ackerman, Diane. *The Human Age: The World Shaped by Us*. New York: W.W. Norton & Company, 2014.

Ackerman, Jennifer. *The Genius of Birds*. New York: Penguin, 2017.

Ausubel, Kenny. *Dreaming the Future: Reimagining Civilization in the Age of Nature*. Chelsea Green Publishing, 2012.

Behnke, Robert J. *About Trout: The Best of Robert Behnke from Trout Magazine*. Guilford, CT: Lyons Press, 2007.

Carson, Rachel. *Silent Spring*. New York: Houghton Mifflin Harcourt, 1962.

Davis, Wade. *River Notes: A Natural and Human History of the Colorado*. Washington, DC: Island Press, 2013.

Haggerty, Michelle, and Meuth, Mary Pearl. *Texas Master Naturalist*. College Station: Texas A&M University Press, 2015.

Harari, Yuval Noah. *Sapiens: A Brief History of Humankind*. New York: Harper, 2015.

Kolbert, Elizabeth. *The Sixth Extinction: An Unnatural History*. New York: Picador, 2014.

Leopold, Aldo. *A Sand County Almanac: And Sketches Here and There*. New York: Oxford University Press, 1949.

Louv, Richard. *The Last Child in the Woods: Saving Our Children from Nature-Deficit Disorder*. Chapel Hill, NC: Algonquin, 2008.

Lyons, Nick. *Bright Rivers*. New York: Skyhorse Publishing, 2014.

Miller, Matthew. *Fishing Through the Apocalypse: An Angler's Adventures in the 21st Century*. Guilford, CT: Lyons Press, 2019.

Monbiot, George. *Feral: Rewilding the Land, the Sea, and Human Life*. Chicago: University of Chicago Press, 2014.

Nash, Roderick F. *Wilderness and the American Mind*. 5th ed. New Haven, CT: Yale University Press, 2014.

Ripple, Jen. "The Overcooked Skillet," *DUN* magazine, 2019.

US Global Change Research Program. *The Climate Report: The National Climate Assessment—Impacts, Risks, and Adaptations in the United States*. Brooklyn, NY: Melville House, 2019.

Weisman, Alan. *The World Without Us*. New York: Picador, 2007.

Whitlock, Dave. *Trout and Their Food: A Complete Guide for Fly Fishers*. New York: Skyhorse Publishing, 2014

Williams, Florence. *The Nature Fix: Why Nature Makes Us Happier, Healthier, and More Creative*. New York: W.W. Norton & Company, 2017.

Praise for *Casting Onward*

"Simply, a book about fish species to be forever cherished from a writer to be revered. *Casting Onward* deserves a prominent place on every angler's bookshelf."

—Gerry Bethge, deputy editor, *Field & Stream* and *Outdoor Life*

"Steve is a naturalist, conservationist, and an activist, but most importantly has a deep understanding of the human soul. He understands that in the end, changing hearts and minds is the only way to save America's native fish."

—Ross Purnell, publisher/editor, *Fly Fisherman* magazine

"*The River Why* by David James Duncan so profoundly influenced me that I named a beloved dog after the protagonist, Gus. *A Fly-Fisherman's Blue Ridge*, by Chris Camuto and *Holy Ghost Creek* by Frank Weissbarth, are two of the finest fishing books I have ever read—mostly because they are not really about fishing. *Casting Onward* sits in the pantheon of these books. It is a book about fishing, but on a much more important level, it is about us, our relationship with one another, and our relationship with the lands and waters that sustain the planet."

—Chris Wood, president/CEO, Trout Unlimited

"In an era of social media 'influencers' and pan-flashed digital commentary on fly fishing, it's easy for anglers to lose context . . . even hope. Thank God Steve Ramirez is willing and able to give us some real, hard-earned, and eloquent words on *why* we all care to flyfish in the first place. His prose is sharp, honest, and deeply meaningful. *Casting Onward* reinforces the spirit and soul of angling, and it underscores the importance of community, place, and species in ways that has seldom been touched with such respect and eloquence."

—Kirk Deeter, editor-in-chief, Trout Unlimited/*Trout* magazine

"I wish there were more anglers, writers, and Americans like Steve Ramirez. He understands what most don't—that fish are wildlife, too. And he understands that our remnant native fish—genetically undefiled by aliens flung confetti-like around the waterscape in the age of ecological illiteracy—are national treasures. This book contains some of the finest angling writing I've seen. But it's not just for anglers. It's for all who delight in wild things, wild land, and wild water."

—Ted Williams, national chair, Native Fish Coalition

"For Steve Ramirez, the presence or absence of native fish is a metric by which to measure the wholeness of a landscape. After reading this book, your presence or absence in the fight for wild waters and wild fish may well be the metric by which you evaluate your own connection to the natural world."

—T. Edward Nickens, author of *The Last Wild Road: Adventure and Essays from a Sporting Life*

"This is a book about many important things—friendships, love, humor, and the joys of living—and fishing too! Cast your fly into the circle of life—connect with nature, live in the moment, change the future. I couldn't close the cover until I finished it."

—Randall Kaufmann, author of *Bonefishing: Fly Fishing the Flats for Bonefish, Permit, Tarpon, and Trevally*

"Fish on! And heart hooked too! Set the drag to play Steve Ramirez's words for a while. Enjoy the long runs with nature nurturers knee-deep in western trout streams and strapped into the fighting chair over the ocean's abysmal deep. With rod and reel connecting us to places wild and within city limits across the country, we see how Ramirez's adventures with fellow fisher people bring us closer to making this world a better place—fish by fish. No slot to heed other than your soul's span. Heart is in the creel with *Casting Onward*. Enjoy!"

—J. Drew Lanham, author of *The Home Place: Memoirs of a Colored Man's Love Affair with Nature*

"Steve Ramirez is a man with a mission. He challenges us to be our best selves and recognize we are all in the same boat, whether fish, birds, wolves, or humans. Our defense against the storm surge of destructive human activities that will drown us is to recognize we are one. Beautifully crafted, *Casting Onward* teaches us this lesson."

—Lillian Stokes, coauthor, *Stokes Field Guide to the Birds of North America*

"Steve Ramirez is an author of rare talent, whose prose reads like poetry. In *Casting Onward*, the follow-up volume to his widely acclaimed *Casting Forward*, Ramirez travels the country, fly rod in hand, in search of America's native gamefish in both fresh water and salt, from cutthroat trout in the West to striped bass and bluefish in the East, and much more. Along the way, he reminds us—in his signature lyrical, evocative style—that fishing is about much more than fish."

—Bill Bowers, writer, editor, and angler

"You open this book expecting to connect with fish, but what you don't expect is even better. Steve offers readers an authentic experience with every character in every chapter. You feel everything but idle when you spend time with these pages."

—Kris Millgate, author of *My Place Among Fish* and *My Place Among Men*

"With *Casting Onward*, Steve Ramirez has crafted a beautiful meditation on the natural world and our relationship to it. Though Steve describes the various perils of neglecting either, he is, like all anglers, an optimist. By the time you reach the end of this splendid, heartfelt book, you'll be one, too."

—Monte Burke, author of *Lords of the Fly* and *Saban*

"Faced with a pandemic and a world gone mad, Steve Ramirez follows the time-honored tradition of taking to the wild. But his is no voice crying alone in the wilderness. Ramirez knows if we're ever to get out of our current mess, we need each other. This is a lyrical, funny, and frequently moving account of what matters in a life well lived: friendship and fishing and wild places among them."

—Matthew L. Miller, author of *Fishing Through the Apocalypse*

"*Casting Onward* is nothing if not a conversation—with native fish, with nature, and with the people who love and fight for both. Steve Ramirez asks numerous important questions in that conversation, but more importantly he has the unique—and increasingly rare—gift of listening wholeheartedly to the answers. Pull up a chair, it's a conversation you don't want to miss."

—Jason Rolfe, editor of *The Flyfish Journal*

"Ramirez is your knowledgeable cross-country guide who cracks a joke or two while he introduces you to a place, makes you love it, and (now that you love it) advises you on how to care for it. An evocative, big-hearted book, highly recommended."

—Tim Cahill, author of *Jaguars Ripped My Flesh*